32ND PUBLICATION DESIGN ANNUAL

ROCKPORT PUBLISHERS, INC., GLOUCESTER, MASSACHUSETTS
DISTRIBUTED BY NORTH LIGHT BOOKS, CINCINNATI, OHIO

ACKNOWLEDGEMENTS

The Gala

The Society wishes to thank The New York Times Company Foundation for its generosity to the New York Public Library, which has enabled the Society of Publication Designers to hold its annual awards Gala in this very special place.

The Sponsors

The Society thanks its corporate sponsors for their continuing support:

American Express Publishing
Apple Computers, Inc.
Condé Nast Publications, Inc.
Dow Jones & Company, Inc.
Hachette Filipacchi Magazines, Inc.
Hearst Magazines
Meredith Corporation
The New York Times
Newsweek
Spectragraphics, Inc.
Wenner Media
Time Inc.
U.S. News & World Report
Westvaco Corporation
World Color

Special Thanks

Condé Nast Publications
Gala Brochure Color Separations: Wenner Media
Gala Brochure Illustration & Photography: Geof Kern
Competition Photography: Antonin Kratochvil
Call for Entries Design & Gala Brochure: David Armario
Gala Slide Presentation: Show & Tell Anagraphics

The Society of Publication Designers, Inc.

60 East 42nd Street, Suite 721
New York, NY 10165
Telephone: (212) 983-8585
Fax: (212) 983-6042
Email: SPDNYC@aol.com
Web site: HTTP://www.SPD.ORG

The SPD 32nd Design Annual

Jacket and book designed by Design Park, Inc.
Jacket illustration & photography by Geof Kern

Copyright © 1997
The Society of Publication Designers, Inc.

First published in the United States of America by:
Rockport Publishers, Inc.
146 Granite Street
Rockport, Massachusetts 01966-1299
Telephone: (508) 546-9590
Fax: (508) 546-7141

Distributed to the book trade and art trade in the U.S. and Canada by:
North Light, an imprint of F & W Publications
1507 Dana Avenue
Cincinnati, OH 45207
Telephone: (800) 289-0963

Other Distribution by:
Rockport Publishers, Inc.
Rockport, Massachusetts 01966-1299

ISBN 1-56496-387-X

10 9 8 7 6 5 4 3 2 1

Manufactured in China

In the three decades the SPD has mounted this exhibition, hundreds of the most talented art directors have donated their time and trained eyes to curate this unique show. The selection of the winning pieces in this volume is an exhausting process. Each of the thirty judges spends two days immersed in pop print culture, viewing and judging thousands of entries.

What is assembled becomes a touchstone, one that shows not only how we designed, through the images and stylistic treatments, but also what we as a society were doing and thinking. The design community and the Society continues to benefit from this generosity with the impressive group who have judged this year.

The Society is growing and moving forward, and includes new categories for the competition. This year we initiated a classification for catalogs—reflecting the increased use of editorial design talent and techniques for these volumes. The resulting pieces included in the show are impressive. Our online and interactive categories are maturing and in this their second year, are yielding an impressive body of editorial design delivered on CDs or the World Wide Web.

To encourage the next generation of publication designers the Society holds an international student competition named in honor of B.W. Honeycutt, former art director of Details Magazine. In this volume you will see the best student work selected this year.

This year we have included the winners of the tenth annual Spots illustration competition in this annual. These are those small but powerful gems of art that grace countless department and story pages in publications. Their small stature tends to get them overlooked by other competitions but here you will find over a hundred beautiful and compelling spot illustrations.

The inclusion of design, illustration, photography, print, online and student publication work makes this volume a complete overview of the state of editorial design today.

ROBERT ALTEMUS
PRESIDENT, THE SOCIETY OF PUBLICATION DESIGNERS

THE 32ND ANNUAL DESIGN COMPETITION

SHELDON BRYAN, ART DIRECTOR OF VIBE ONLINE
NANCY CUTLER, ART DIRECTOR-NEW MEDIA
JANET WAEGEL, ONLINE AND INTERACTIVE CHAIR, PARTNER-ALTEMUS & WAEGEL DESIGN
ANDREW WANLISS-ORLEBAR, INTERFACE DIRECTOR OF TOTAL NEW YORK

JILL ARMUS, ART DIRECTOR, SAVEUR
ANTONIN KRATOCHVIL, PHOTOGRAPHER
JOLENE CUYLER, ART DIRECTOR- THE NEW YORK TIMES MAGAZINE
SUSAN CASEY, CREATIVE DIRECTOR-OUTSIDE
DENNIS FREEDMAN, CREATIVE DIRECTOR-W
INA SALTZ, GROUP CHAIRPERSON & SPOTS COMPETITION CHAIR

PORTRAIT PHOTOGRAPHY BY CHRISTIAN WITKIN

Established in 1965, the Society of publication Designers was formed to acknowledge the role of the art director/designer in the creation and development of the printed page. The art director as journalist brings a visual representation to the editorial mission to clarify and enhance the written word. This graphic design skill, developed and specialized, presents endless challenges in the current technological advancements of the publishing industry.

The Society provides for its members a monthly Speaker's Luncheon, a Speaker's Evening series, a monthly newsletter GRIDS, the publication design annual, the Design Exhibition held annually and the annual SPOTS Competition and Exhibition for illustrators. It also actively participates in related activities that bring together members of the numerous design communities in the New York area.

In 1996/97, SPD mounted a major design conference in Monterey, California, named Mag2000, and a mini conference in NYC exploring the role of the designer in the expanding technological world of the internet and online publications, Zine2000.

"The annual SPD Competition and Judging acknowledges the skill and style of the publication designer, who takes information and turns it into communication.**"**

BRIDE WHELAN
DIRECTOR, THE SOCIETY OF PUBLICATION DESIGNERS

GEORGE PITTS, PHOTO EDITOR-VIBE
LUCY BARTHOLOMAY, ART DIRECTOR-THE BOSTON GLOBE MAGAZINE
ROBERT NEWMAN, GROUP CHAIRPERSON, ART DIRECTOR-NEW YORK
ERIC PIKE, ART DIRECTOR-MARTHA STEWART LIVING
MARK DANZIG, ART DIRECTOR-J.CREW
EDMUND GUY, ILLUSTRATOR

TOM BENTKOWSKI, GROUP CHAIRPERSON, DESIGN DIRECTOR-LIFE
MICHAEL GROSSMAN, DESIGN DIRECTOR-MEIGHER COMMUNICATIONS
MARGERY GOLDBERG, PHOTO EDITOR-NEW YORK
DAVID PLUNKERT, ILLUSTRATOR
MARGOT FRANKEL, ART DIRECTOR-TOWN & COUNTRY
DAVID HARRIS, ART DIRECTOR-VANITY FAIR

KENT HUNTER, PRINCIPAL-FRANKFURT BALKIND PARTNERS
PHYLLIS RICHMOND COX, ART DIRECTOR-BRIDES
JANE PALACEK, ART DIRECTOR-HEALTH
LLOYD ZIFF, GROUP CHAIRPERSON, PRINCIPAL-LLOYD ZIFF DESIGN
PAMELA BERRY, ART DIRECTOR-TRAVEL & LEISURE
CHRISTIAN WITKIN, PHOTOGRAPHER

STEPHEN DOYLE, PRINCIPAL-DOYLE PARTNERS
JOANNE HOFFMAN, ART DIRECTOR-MACWORLD
DEBORAH NEEDLEMAN, PHOTO EDITOR-HOUSE & GARDEN
BRIAN CRONIN, ILLUSTRATOR
DIANA LAGUARDIA, ART DIRECTOR-HOUSE & GARDEN
STEPHEN COATES, ART DIRECTOR-EYE

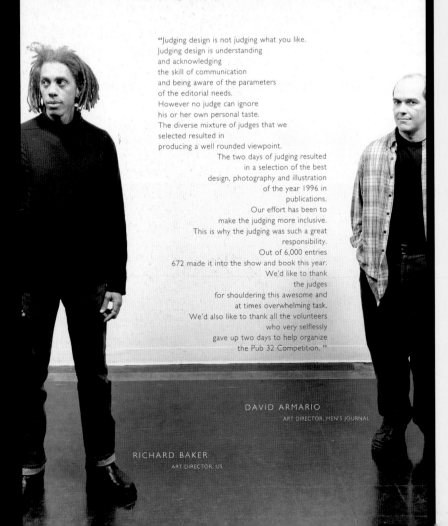

"Judging design is not judging what you like.
Judging design is understanding
and acknowledging
the skill of communication
and being aware of the parameters
of the editorial needs.
However no judge can ignore
his or her own personal taste.
The diverse mixture of judges that we
selected resulted in
producing a well rounded viewpoint.
The two days of judging resulted
in a selection of the best
design, photography and illustration
of the year 1996 in
publications.
Our effort has been to
make the judging more inclusive.
This is why the judging was such a great
responsibility.
Out of 6,000 entries
672 made it into the show and book this year.
We'd like to thank
the judges
for shouldering this awesome and
at times overwhelming task.
We'd also like to thank all the volunteers
who very selflessly
gave up two days to help organize
the Pub 32 Competition. "

DAVID ARMARIO
ART DIRECTOR, MEN'S JOURNAL

RICHARD BAKER
ART DIRECTOR, US

SPOTS

The SPOTS competition was established in 1987 in order to allow smaller illustrations to compete against others of a similar dimension. The SPOTS competition recognizes the oversized messages communicated by these little masterpieces in small spaces. A jury of four top art directors judged over 900 entries from the United States and abroad in four categories and selected 105 winners, included for the first time in this year's design annual.

JUDGES

INA SALTZ, COMPETITION CHAIRPERSON, PRINCIPAL-SALTZ DESIGN
JOHN KORPICS, DESIGN DIRECTOR-ENTERTAINMENT WEEKLY
ELIZABETH BETTS, DESIGN DIRECTOR-MEN'S HEALTH
MARY ZISK, ART DIRECTOR-ART & ANTIQUES

SPECIAL THANKS TO:

DONALD PARTYKA, POINT FIVE DESIGN
ALISSA LEVIN, POINT FIVE DESIGN
RACHEL ERICSON, CHILDREN'S TELEVISION WORKSHOP

STUDENT COMPETITION

Established in 1995, this competition and award honors the life and work of B. W. Honeycutt. It recognizes exceptional design by a student and is made possible by a generous contribution from Condé Nast Publications, Inc.

JUDGES

PAUL ROELOFS, COMPETITION CHAIRPERSON, ART DIRECTOR-INSTYLE
CHRISTINE CURRY, ILLUSTRATION EDITOR, NEW YORKER

DESIGN

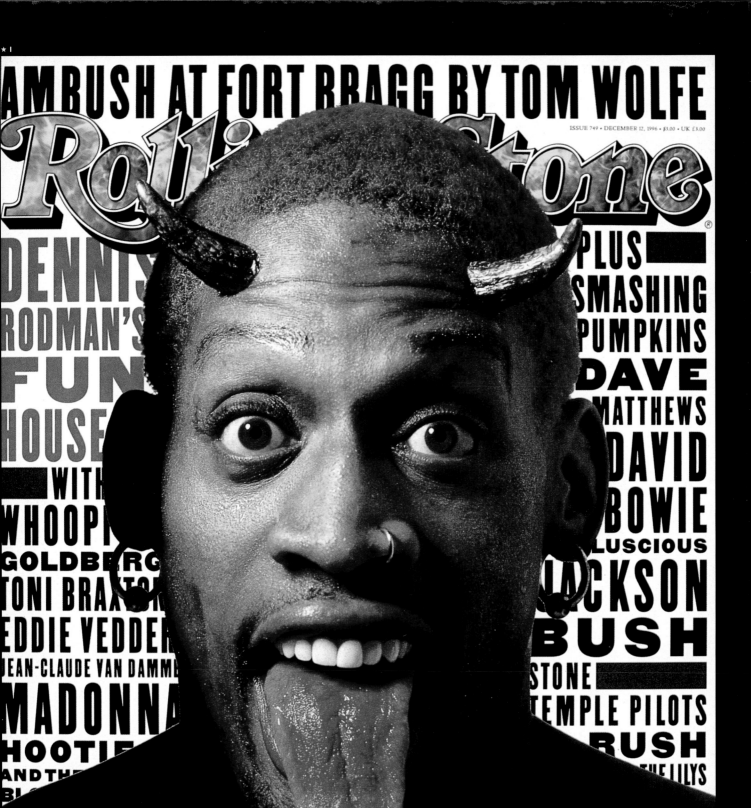

AMBUSH AT FORT BRAGG BY TOM WOLFE

Rolling Stone

ISSUE 749 • DECEMBER 12, 1996 • $3.00 • UK £3.00

DENNIS
RODMAN'S
FUN
HOUSE
WITH
WHOOPI
GOLDBERG
TONI BRAXTON
EDDIE VEDDER
JEAN-CLAUDE VAN DAMME
MADONNA
HOOTIE
AND THE
BLO

PLUS
SMASHING
PUMPKINS
DAVE
MATTHEWS
DAVID
BOWIE
LUSCIOUS
JACKSON
BUSH
STONE
TEMPLE PILOTS
RUSH
THE LILYS

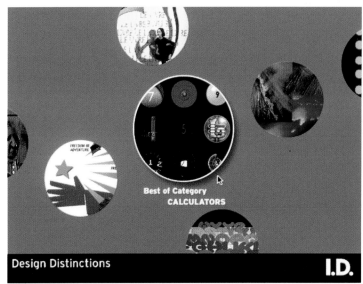

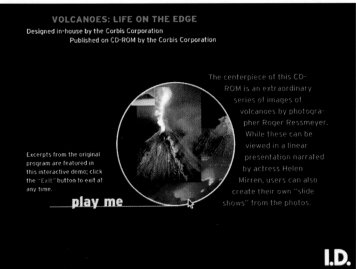

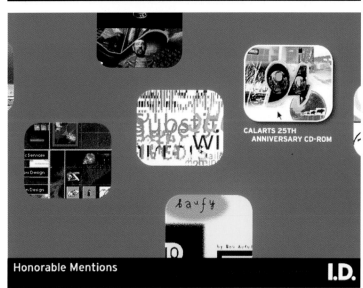

Publication I.D.
Art Directors Steve Simula, A. Arefin, Andrea Fella
Designers Sherie Bauer, Steve Simula,
Tony Ramos, Andrea Fella, Colette Moti, Floris Keizer
Photographer Chris Gallo
Studio Fitch Inc.
Publisher I.D. Magazine
Issue July 1996
Category Entire Issue

CHANCES THAT
THERE IS LIFE ON
ANOTHER PLANET.
1 IN 1,000,000,000

CHANCES THAT
YOUR NEXT PRODUCT
WILL BE A WINNER.
1 IN 10,000

**MAYBE GOOD DESIGN
ISN'T PRETTY**

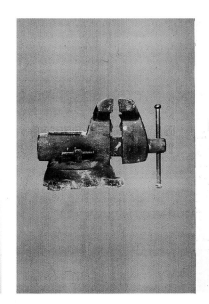

**MAYBE GREAT PRODUCTS
AREN'T ABOUT
BEAUTIFUL DESIGN**

3
Publication GVO Brochure
Creative Director Bill Cahan
Designers Bob Dinetz, Kevin Roberson
Illustrators Nick Dewar, Doug Aitken
Photographers Geof Kern, Holly Stewart
Studio Cahan & Associates
Issue August 1996
Category Overall Design

AND WE CAN TELL YOU THAT
THEY'RE _NOT_ ABOUT STYLE,
AND THEY DON'T COME FROM
R&D LABS OR FOCUS GROUPS
YET MOST COMPANIES FOCUS ON
THE PRODUCT, NOT THE PROBLEM
AND THAT'S THE PROBLEM

YOU COULD PLAY THE ODDS.
BUT GREAT PRODUCTS
DON'T HAVE TO BE
A GAMBLE.

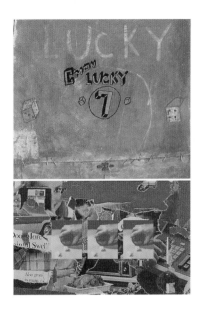

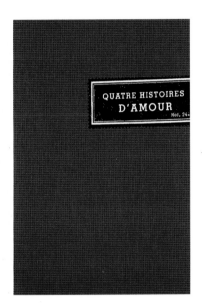

QUATRE HISTOIRES
D'AMOUR
Mod. 24-

It's an old story:
a guy takes his
wife to Paris for
their anniversary,
without finding out
what she wants.
The next year he
does. She falls
in love with him
all over again.

MAYBE THEY'RE
ABOUT EMOTION

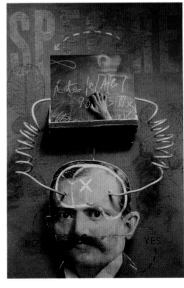

FIGURING OUT WHAT
DRIVES PEOPLE CRAZY

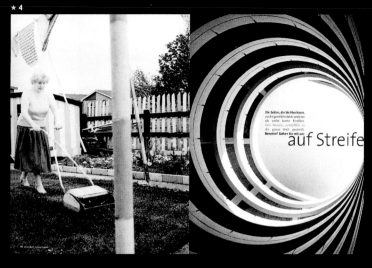

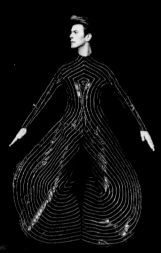

auf Streife

★ 4
Publication Sueddeutsche Zeitung Magazin
Art Director Markus Rasp
Designers Anne Blaschke, Otto Dzemla, Wilhelm Raffelsberger
Photo Editors Eva Ernst, Claudia Mueller
Photographers Julias Shulman, Herb Ritts, Henriette Grindat, Bernd & Hilla Becher, Ettore Sottsass, James Nachtwey, William Klein, Arino Eimu, Christoph Valentien, Julian Germain
Publisher Magazin Verlagsges. Sueddeutsche Zeitung mbh
Issue April 4, 1996
Category Feature Story

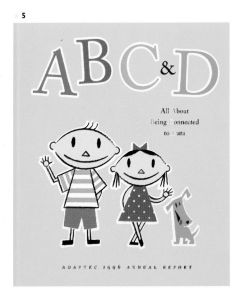

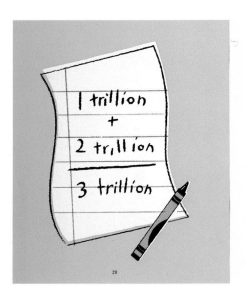

Financial Contents

5
Publication Adaptec 1996 Annual Report
Creative Director Bill Cahan
Designer Kevin Roberson
Illustrator Richard McGuire
Studio Cahan & Associates
Issue June 1996
Category Entire Issue

● 6
Publication Condé Nast House & Garden
Art Director Robert Priest
Designer Robert Priest
Photo Editor Deborah Needleman
Photographer Ilan Rubin
Publisher Condé Nast Publications Inc.
Issue September 1996
Category Cover

● 7
Publication Vanity Fair
Design Director David Harris
Art Director Gregory Mastrianni
Designer Gregory Mastrianni
Photo Editor Susan White
Photographer Mario Testino
Publisher Condé Nast Publications Inc.
Issue November 1996
Category Cover

● 8
Publication The Observer Life
Designer Wayne Ford
Photo Editor Jennie Ricketts
Photographer Nigel Parry
Publisher The Observer
Issue December 1,1996
Category Cover

● 9
Publication Metropolis
Art Directors Carl Lehmann-Haupt, William van Roden
Publisher Bellerophon Publishing
Issue March 1996
Category Cover

● 10

How We Eat: An America Divided

A SPECIAL ISSUE

● 10
Publication The New York Times Magazine
Art Director Janet Froelich
Designer Lisa Naftolin
Photo Editor Sarah Harbutt
Photographer Kenji Toma
Publisher The New York Times
Issue March 10, 1996
Category Cover

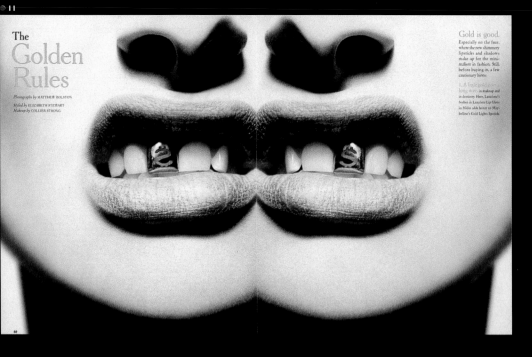

The
Golden
Rules

Photographs by MATTHEW ROLSTON.
Styled by ELIZABETH STEWART
Makeup by COLLIER STRONG

Gold is good. Especially on the face, where the new shimmery lipsticks and shadows make up for the minimalism in fashion. Still, before buying in, a few cautionary hints:

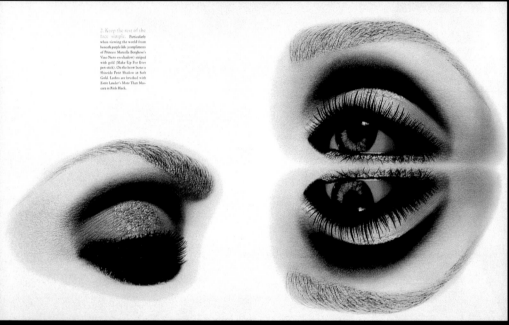

● 11

Publication The New York Times Magazine
Art Director Janet Froelich
Designers Janet Froelich, Paul Jean
Stylist Elizabeth Stewart
Photographer Matthew Rolston
Publisher The New York Times
Issue September 8, 1996
Category Feature Story
Merit Photography Fashion/Beauty Story

NICHOLAS LEMANN
on the end of
meritocracy.
RONALD STEEL
on America's
dominance.
MARTHA STEWART
in the kitchen.
A. M. HOMES and
DAVID FOSTER WALLACE
on young love.
GARRISON KEILLOR
on nostalgia.
PAUL KRUGMAN on
economic upheaval.
DAVID IVES
on the weekend.
JAMES GLEICK
on privacy.
ANN DOUGLAS
on the collapse of
the culture wars.

The New York Times Magazine

SEPTEMBER 29, 1996 / SECTION 6

The Next Hundred Years

Looking Forward, Looking Back: A Centennial Issue

THE DALAI LAMA
on faith.
JOHN TIERNEY
on good.
VERLYN
KLINKENBORG
on evil.
REM KOOLHAAS
on the skyline.
STANLEY CROUCH
on the raceless
society.
CHARLES SIEBERT
on the small.
TIMOTHY FERRIS
on the weird.
PERRI KLASS
on artificial wombs.
JOHN GALLIANO, REI
KAWAKUBO, ISAAC
MIZRAHI, MARIE-ANNE
OUDEJANS and THE GAP
on what we'll wear.
MICHAEL LEWIS
on futures.
JANE AND MICHAEL
STERN on what's
worth collecting.
VICTOR NAVASKY
on fatuous forecasts.

CONTENTS. Page 38

The New York Times Magazine / SEPTEMBER 29, 1996

This Way to the Future

The Optimists Are Right

So why do so many people think things are going to hell?

By John Tierney

The Flight

The Ideal

● 12
Publication The New York Times Magazine
Art Director Janet Froelich
Designers Lisa Naftolin, Joel Cuyler
Photo Editor Jody Quon
Publisher The New York Times
Issue September 29, 1996
Category Entire Issue

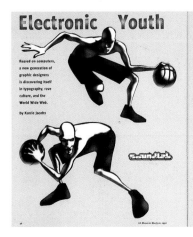

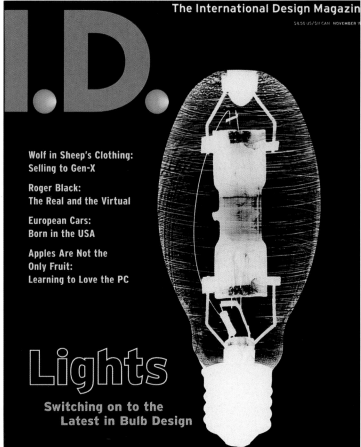

● 13
Publication I.D.
Creative Director A. Arefin
Art Director Andrea Fella
Photographers James Wojcik, Chris Gallo, David Bashaw
Publisher I.D. Magazine
Issue May/June 1996, July/August 1996, November 1996
Category Overall Design

ONE OF THE PRODUCTS CHOSEN for recognition in the Consumer Products category this year was a projection TV that is a svelte 12 inches deep. Which begs the question: how long before electronic products disappear entirely – into the wall, into the guts of your computer, into cyberspace? In the years to come, many of the products that were reviewed by jurors Tibor Kalman, Sam Lucente and Murray Moss may not even exist as objects in the tangible sense. As a result, "user interface" is becoming not just an aspect of design but the better part of it for some products.

This phenomenon led to a kind of division between traditional, tangible products and electronic items with more ethereal functions. As Kalman put it, "interface design was just not an issue when you designed a hammer." The jurors were more enthusiastic about low-tech and no-tech entries – the crank-powered portable radio they chose as Best of Category, a vacuum cleaner, a set of plastic bowls, an ergonomic toilet seat – than the electronic equipment, which Kalman said represented "a crisis of interface design." Lucente agreed: "It's rare that good hardware design and good interface design come together. We need to work with hardware and software as if it's one medium."

The problem, said Kalman, is one of integration: industrial designers, interface designers, graphic designers and package designers "have specialized themselves into separate corners of the process of bringing products to market." This issue was especially clear in the case of graphic design – the jurors frequently complained about a product being "attacked" by graphics that looked like an afterthought. But the seeming dissonance between a product's form and its function also came up often, especially in the case of the FreePlay Clockwork Radio, which the jurors nevertheless chose as Best of Category. Said Moss of the radio, "If the intent was to look like what it is, it's not successful. The design and technology appear to be at cross-purposes."

The jurors' prescription? Better integrated teams of designers working on products from the outset. "We need generalization, not specialization," declared Kalman. "Specialization is destroying many of these products."

Consumer
Products

Murray Moss, noting the number of products described as "ergonomic" and "user-friendly," complained that too many didn't live up to the description. The jury developed a healthy skepticism about "ergonomic" claims, preferring to reward products that addressed a clear ergonomic need – the toilet seat, for example.

Moss said that many of the products that claimed to be "user-friendly" weren't, and wondered if it was appropriate to expect a new technology to be instantly cozy and familiar. "When the telephone was invented," he said, "it would have been inappropriate for people to be comfortable with it instantly." Lucente suggested that it was a matter of priorities: "We're willing to invest time in learning to drive a car or to use QuarkXPress, but you want to be able to walk into someone else's house and know how to use the toilet seat."

JURORS: Murray Moss, Sam Lucente, Tibor Kalman
MODERATOR: Mark Alden Branch

I.D. ANNUAL DESIGN REVIEW 1996

67

HIGH-INTENSITY DISCHARGE

High-intensity discharge (HID) is the umbrella name for a family of lighting types that produce light by passing an electrical current through a gas or vapor under pressure. They range from the eerie amber glow of low-pressure sodium, which has virtually no ability to render color and is mostly used for lighting warehouses, tunnels and roadways, to the intense white light of metal halide. The oldest use of this technology dates back to 1901, when the first mercury-vapor lamp was invented. Long used for street lights, mercury vapor has largely been replaced by more efficient high-pressure sodium (left). The comer in the HID family is metal halide, whose white light and relatively good color rendering is popular for such uses as stadium lighting (far left). Further improvements in color rendering and a dramatic miniaturization of metal halide bulbs have made them increasingly popular for indoor uses, typically in high-ceilinged spaces.

The oldest and most familiar light sources, incandescent bulbs are available in thousands of shapes, sizes and configurations for the narrowest of specialized uses. Chrome-top bulbs (right) are used in open fixtures to prevent glare (in pendant lights in restaurants, for example). Sylvania makes a shatter-resistant and moisture-resistant bulb for outdoor use (center right) and a two-watt "flicker bulb" with a two-dimensional cartoonlike flame inside that glows and flickers when turned on (bottom). On the more utilitarian end of the spectrum, a small company called Bulbrite makes a nine-watt exit-lamp bulb (left) composed of ten smaller bulbs linked together.

INCANDESCENT

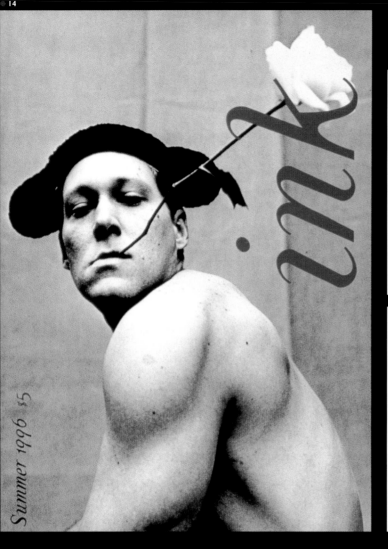

ink

Summer 1996 $5

Bon sai

gafner

boal

photographs, Andrea Fischer

• 15

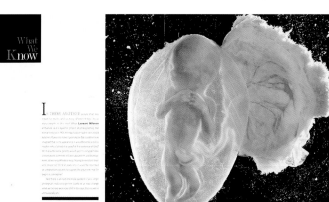

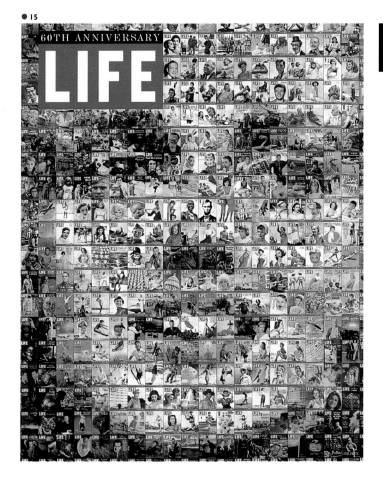

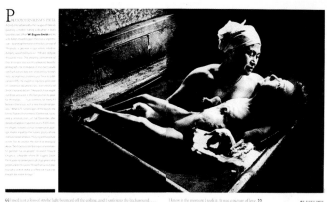

WHAT WE KNOW

SILVER SCREEN
DREAMS

Hard times are hard to forget, especially when there's no end in sight. But in 1936 escape could always be found at the movies, to which more than 11 million repaired each day. Theaters were lush with velvet, and often you got a door prize just for surrendering a ticket. Saturday matinees were cinematic banquets: a newsreel, a travelogue and, of course, a cliff-hanger, featuring a detective like Ace Drummond or a space traveler like Flash Gordon. There were cartoons with names like *Coo Coo Nut Grove*. There were syrup-sweet flicks, perhaps featuring a seven-year-old Shirley Temple in *Dimples* or an 11-year-old Freddie Bartholomew in *The Devil Is a Sissy*. And there were the features, including two Cole Porter musicals: *Anything Goes*, starring Bing Crosby, and *Born To Dance*, with Jimmy Stewart and Eleanor Powell. But the year's most enduring films were not musicals; indeed, unlike most movies of the time, they were not escapist fare. Frank Capra's *Mister Deeds Goes to Town* and Charlie Chaplin's *Modern Times* were rough-edged classics about vulnerable heroes making their way through a brutal, indifferent world with honesty, perseverance and humor. Such films reminded Americans of their inner dignity, which even hard times could never extinguish.

The Movies
Average Cost of a Movie Ticket
1936: $0.21
1996: $4.35

Megastar Salaries
1936: Mae West (for entire year)
$323,000
1996: Demi Moore (for Striptease)
$12,500,000

▲ The musical was Hollywood's cash cow, and **Fred Astaire's twinkle-toes** were priceless. He was able to spurn a million dollar contract from RKO.

1996

An unidentified man and woman are trussed and beaten in an episode involving gasoline, a noose, pliers aimed at teeth and knives in faces. Then into this fray comes John Kruger (Arnold Schwarzenegger), wearing a ski mask. Kruger is so tough he can haul two corpses across the lawn at the same time. What a guy."
■ JANET MASLIN, REVIEW OF ERASER IN THE NEW YORK TIMES

• 14
Publication Dance Ink
Design Director J. Abbott Miller
Designers Luke Hayman, Paul Carlos
Photo Editor Katherine Schlesinger
Publisher Dance Ink Foundation
Studio Design/Writing/Research
Issue May 1996
Category Entire Issue

• 15
Publication LIFE
Design Director Tom Bentkowski
Art Director Mimi Park
Designer Mimi Park
Illustrator Rob Silvers
Photo Editors Bobbi Baker Burrows, David Friend
Photographers Alfred Eisenstaedt, Martin Munkacsi, Lennart Nilsson, W. Eugene Smith
Publisher Time Inc.
Issue October 1996
Category Entire Issue

WITH A RÉSUMÉ
THAT BOASTS
'PULP FICTION,'
'GET SHORTY' AND
THIS MONTH'S
'MATILDA,' THE
ACTOR/DIRECTOR/
PRODUCER IS
SLOWLY TAKING
OVER HOLLYWOOD

Interview:
FRED
SCHRUERS
Photograph:
MARK
SELIGER

DANNY DEVITO

is proof that American movies will never be totally taken over by the musclebound, the husky and the blandly handsome. We think of him as action klutz — and sometimes as glowering — but we never think of him as someone we can sum up in an eye blink. Though *Other People's Money* was far from his biggest hit, the centrally insensitive businessman he portrayed in it somehow epitomized DeVito's slightly dark

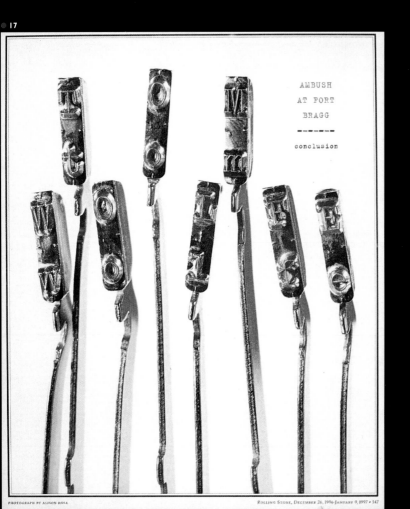

AMBUSH
AT FORT
BRAGG
----
conclusion

16
Publication US
Art Director Richard Baker
Designer Richard Baker
Photo Editor Jennifer Crandall
Photographer Mark Seliger
Publisher US Magazine Co., L.P.
Issue August 1996
Category Feature Spread

17
Publication Rolling Stone
Creative Director Fred Woodward
Designer Fred Woodward
Photo Editor Fiona McDonagh
Photographer Alison Rosa
Publisher Wenner Media
Issue December 1996/January 1997
Category Feature Single Page

18
Publication Quest
Creative Director Michael Grossman
Art Director Carla Frank
Photo Editor Catherine Talese
Publisher Meigher Communications
Issue June 1996
Category Redesign

CHESSY RAYNER'S NEW YORK STYLE • HOMING IN ON GREGOR VON REZZORI • JUNE 1996 $4.00

QUEST

NEW YORK FROM THE INSIDE

A Private Eye

CONFESSIONS OF A SOCIETY SPY

THAT CERTAIN NEW YORK
STYLE

Chessy Rayner's Got It—Indeed, She Always Has.
By Brooke Peters • Photographs by Michael O'Brien

Touchstones

Victorian Secrets

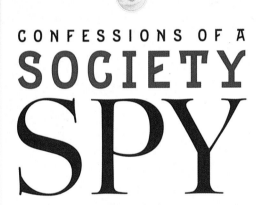

CONFESSIONS OF A
SOCIETY
SPY

DAVID PATRICK COLUMBIA REVEALS THE SECRET
ADVENTURES OF TOP PRIVATE EYE FRANK MONTE

When I was growing up I always thought I'd make a good private eye. I was nosy enough; I still am. I had a mother who used to go through my sisters' drawers, which I thought was an interesting habit—until she started going through mine and asking too many questions that I considered none of her business. Eventually the notion seemed childish. Jack Nicholson in *Chinatown* walking around with a sliced-up nose; who needs a sliced-up nose? If you need a detective, call the police. ◆ Several years ago, however, that notion was altered when a bilious and crusty-looking elderly Englishman, who in his youth had been married to an Astor, told me that his former in-laws and others like them (i.e., the very rich) used private eyes all the time. Detec-

Hollywood glamorized private eyes in films like The Keyhole, *1933, at right, starring George Brent. But the adventures of world-class spies like Monte are anything but make-believe.*

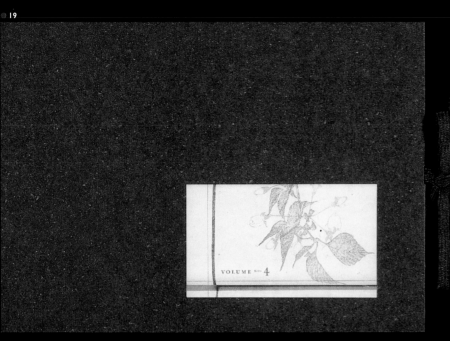

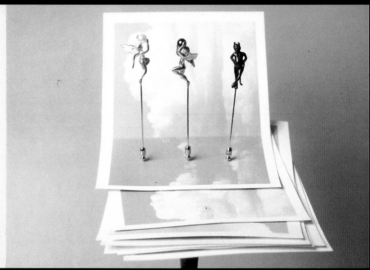

FOR THOSE
WHO WERE NICE
AND THE
NAUGHTY ONE

PLATE N° 3 Your list always includes both. And although the good guys are more worthy, we think even bad deeds shouldn't go unrecognized. This year, the punishment can fit the crime. Heavenly stickpins from American jewelry designer Gabrielle Kiss. The angels in sterling silver with a cultured pearl (3A) $195, or 24kt gold over bronze with a black cultured pearl (3B) $195. The devil in oxidized bronze (3C) $135. 1½" ornaments atop 2½" pins.

1.800.753.2038

BEAUTY
APPEARS WHEREVER
YOU CAN
DISCOVER IT

PLATE N° 17 In the eye of a stranger. On a screen, under a table, over breakfast. Perhaps after dinner, when a bitter espresso is brought to you in one of these cups. Porcelain demitasse cups and saucers with high-fired variegated glazes in a range of subtly distinct colors that complement one other. Clockwise, from top left: orchid (17A), sky (17B), lapis (17C), marine (17D), midnight (17E) or leaf (17A). $65. each. France. Our silverplated spoons, a clever design from the 1920s, have little faux coffee bean handles. Set of 6, (17G) $65.

1.800.753.2038

19
Publication Takashimaya Catalog
Creative Directors Allison Muench Williams, J. Phillips Williams
Designers Peter Phong, Allison Muench Williams
Photographer Geof Kern
Studio Design: M/W
Issue Vol. 4, 1996
Category Entire Issue

20
Publication Slant
Design Director Howard Brown
Art Director Mike Calkins
Designers Chip Kidd, Howard Brown, Mike Calkins
Illustrators Michael Witte, Dan Grzeca, Mark Dancey, David Sandlin
Photographer Chip Kidd
Publisher Urban Outfitters Inc.
Issue March 20, 1996
Category Entire Issue

PLEASE TRY AGAIN

Dino

by Nick Tosches

...YESTERDAY and TODAY

The PHANTOM HIGH ROLLER of GLITTER GULTCH

REPORTED BY JOHN MARR · ILLUSTRATED BY DAN GRECA

{ LAST LOOK }

EXCERPTS FROM THE BOOK
IN THE UNLIKELY EVENT OF A WATER LANDING:
A GEOGRAPHY OF GRIEF, BY CHRISTOPHER NÖEL

{ EXCERPTS }

On an icy January morning in 1992, Christopher Noel, half-asleep, glimpsed his fiancee, Brigid Clark, as she stood beside their bed, smiling. "Oh, your hair is sticking up there," she said, reaching affectionately for his head. Hours later, Noel was on a hospital pay phone, calling family members, as Clark, the victim of a car crash, was wheeled past him on a stretcher. Even before Clark had died, she had become "a huge and cloudy notion, a sudden, aggressive brainteaser in too many pieces," Noel would later write. His recent book, excerpted here, represents his attempt to rebuild her shattered memory-- and his life.

{ Q&A WITH THE AUTHOR }

{ FORUM: COPING WITH LOSS }

{ GRIEF-RELIEF WEB SITES }

{ ORDER THE BOOK NOW }

{ RECOMMENDED READING }

● 21

Publication Swoon
Art Director Warren Corbitt
Designer Warren Corbitt
Photo Editor Tyler Pappas
Publisher Condé Net
Online Address www.swoon.com/b_lovers/09_water/
Category Feature Story

DURING THE FIRST YEAR,

MANY PEOPLE SAID, "YOU MUST BE WRITING ABOUT THIS, AREN'T YOU?" BUT NO, IT'S TAKEN THESE SIXTEEN MONTHS FOR ME TO CATCH UP TO WHERE I AM. JUST HERE, JUST NOW. IN THIS TRANQUIL BETWEEN, THEN, I'M PERHAPS FINALLY SITUATED TO TRY TO DESCRIBE A FEW OF THE TEN THOUSAND FACETS OF WHAT IT IS AND HAS BEEN TO LOSE BRIGID CLARK.

>>

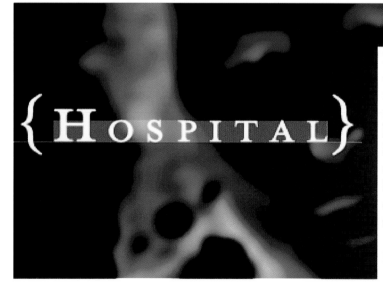

{ HOSPITAL }

MYTHOLOGIZING IS NO SURPRISE, of course, except that it begins immediately, from the moment I walk up to the hospital's front desk, ready to hear she has a broken this or that, and hear instead, in tones of reassurance, that she still has a pulse. I am not allowed to see her because her spleen needs to be sewn back together, and her left leg is broken, and her left lung is punctured and collapsed, all of which are "small potatoes" next to the head injury.

I sit down on the plastic chair against the wall.

HIS
ITE

DD
OUR
ORY

ORIES :

ARCH

ALOG

legacy

country

memorial

trauma

return

RE: VIETNAM
STORIES SINCE THE WAR

truth

family

perspective

connection

activism

..
**The space
doesn't exist
without you.**
..

● 22
Publication Re:Vietnam-Stories Since The War
Creative Directors Alison Cornyn, Sue Johnson, Chris Vail
Design Director Marc Weiss
Publisher Picture Projects
Studio Picture Projects
Client POV/PBS
Online Address www.picture-projects.com
Issue November 27, 1996
Category Entire Issue

● 23

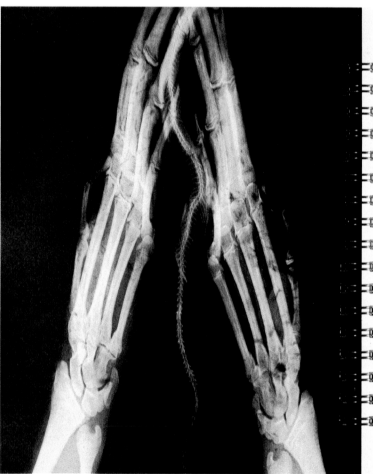

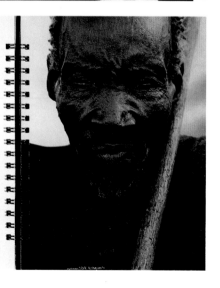

exploring peace

● 23
Publication mÂp
Creative Director Robert Bergman-Ungar
Art Director Giles Dunn
Designer Robert Bergman-Ungar
Illustrators Minoru Nomata, Mark Tansey
Photographers Nikolay Zurek, Simon Obarzanek, Hibiki Kobayashi, Lynne Cohen, Anne Barnard, Olivia Parker, Richard Burbridge, Andrew Macpherson, Mark Laita, Kevin Kerslake, Seiju Toda, Eamonn J. McCabe, NASA
Publisher mÂp Publications Inc./Verlag Bergman-Ungar Associates
Issue September 1996
Category Entire Issue

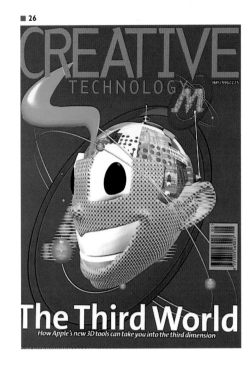

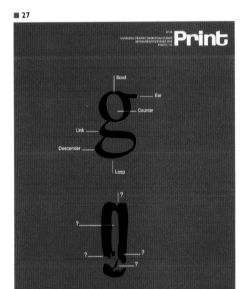

■ **24**
Publication BravoRichards
Creative Director Jurek Wajdowicz
Designers Lisa LaRochelle, Jurek Wajdowicz
Photographer Eugene Richards
Studio Emerson, Wajdowicz Studios
Client Island Paper Mills/E.B. Eddy Forest Products, Ltd.
Issue September 1996
Category Cover

■ **25**
Publication American Salon
Design Director Saralynne Lowrey
Art Directors Kathy Nestor, Lisa Realmuto
Photographer Kenneth Willardt
Publisher Advanstar Communications
Issue January 1996
Category Cover

■ **26**
Publication Creative Technology
Art Director Wayne Ford
Designer Wayne Ford
Illustrator Me Company
Publisher
Haymarket Trade & Leisure Publications Limited
Issue May 1996
Category Cover

■ **27**
Publication Print
Creative Director Andrew Kner
Designer Daniel Conlan
Publisher RC Publishing
Issue November/December 1996
Category Cover

■ **28**
Publication Clark Memorandum
Creative Director Linda Sullivan
Designer Linda Sullivan
Illustrator Rob Blackard
Publisher Brigham Young University
Studio BYU Publications & Graphics
Client J. Reuben Clark Law School
Issue Fall 1996
Category Cover

■ **29**
Publication AIA/NY Oculus
Creative Director Michael Gericke
Designers Michael Gericke, Edward Chiquitulto
Photographer Lydia Gould
Publisher Mohawk Paper Mills, Inc.
Studio Pentagram Design, Inc.
Client American Institute of Architects, NY
Issue January 1997
Category Cover

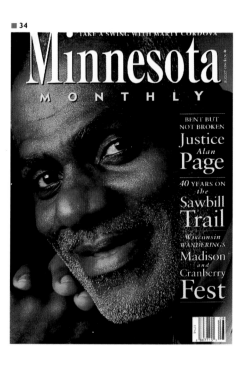

■ 30
Publication Casa Vogue Brazil
Creative Director Mariana Ochs
Art Director Toshio Yamasaki
Photographer Tuca Reinés
Publisher Carta Editorial Ltd.
Studio Mariana Ochs Design
Issue November 1996
Category Cover

■ 31
Publication Computerwoche Extra
Art Director Horst Moser
Designer Horst Moser
Photo Editor Horst Moser
Photographer Johan DeBoer
Publisher Independent
Issue November 29, 1996
Category Cover

■ 32
Publication Ecrivain
Design Directors Walter Bernard, Milton Glaser
Designer Milton Glaser
Photographer Matthew Klein
Studio WBMG
Client Alpha Presse
Issue October/November 1996
Category Cover

■ 33
Publication France
Creative Director Kelly Doe
Art Director John Lineberger
Illustrator Paul Cezanne
Publisher French Embassy
Issue Spring 1996
Category Cover

■ 34
Publication Minnesota Monthly
Art Director Mark Shafer
Designer Brian Donahue
Photo Editor Mark Shafer
Photographer Thomas Strand
Publisher Minnesota Monthly Publishers
Issue August 1996
Category Cover

■ 35
Publication Stick
Design Director Scott Clum
Designer Jason Selander
Illustrator Jennifer Briggs
Photo Editor Trevor Graves
Photographer Trevor Graves
Publisher Ray Gun Publishing
Studio Ride
Client Ray Gun
Issue December 1996/January 1997
Category Cover

■ 36

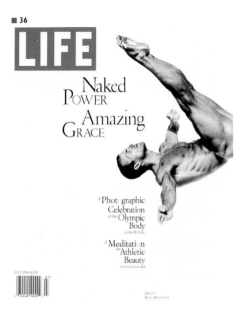

■ 37

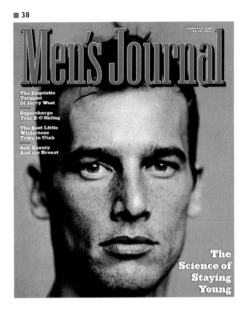

■ 38

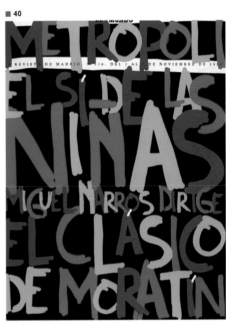

■ 39

■ 40

■ 41

■ 36
Publication LIFE
Design Director Tom Bentkowski
Designer Mimi Park
Photo Editor David Friend
Photographer Joe McNally
Publisher Time Inc.
Issue July 1996
Category Cover

■ 37
Publication Martha Stewart Living
Creative Director Gael Towey
Design Director Eric Pike
Designers Eric Pike, Frances Boswell
Photo Editor Heidi Posner
Photographer Anita Calero
Publisher Time Inc.
Issue July/August 1996
Category Cover

■ 38
Publication Men's Journal
Art Director David Armario
Designer David Armario
Photo Editor Deborah Needleman
Photographer José Picayo
Publisher Wenner Media
Issue February 1996
Category Cover

■ 39
Publication Esquire
Design Director Diana LaGuardia
Art Directors Rockwell Harwood, Michael Mrak
Photo Editor Marianne Butler
Photographer Wayne Maser
Publisher The Hearst Corporation-Magazines Division
Issue March 1996
Category Cover

■ 40
Publication Metropoli El Mundo
Design Director Carmelo Caderot
Art Director Rodrigo Sanchez
Designers Rodrigo Sanchez, Maria González, Javier Sanz
Publisher Unidad Editorial S.A.
Issue November 1, 1996
Category Cover

■ 41
Publication Guardian Weekend
Art Director Mark Porter
Designer Mark Porter
Photographer Martin Parr
Publisher Guardian Media Group
Issue October 5, 1996
Category Cover

31

■ 42

■ 43

■ 44

■ 42
Publication The Observer Life
Designer Wayne Ford
Photo Editor Jennie Ricketts
Photographer Ian McKinnell
Publisher The Observer
Issue September 8, 1996
Category Cover

■ 43
Publication The Observer Life
Designer Wayne Ford
Photo Editor Jo Adams
Photographer Gavin Bond
Publisher The Observer
Issue December 8, 1996
Category Cover

■ 44
Publication Sueddeutsche Zeitung Magazin
Art Director Markus Rasp
Designers Anne Blaschke, Otto Dzemla,
Wilhelm Raffelsberger
Photo Editors Eva Ernst, Claudia Mueller
Photographer Juergen Teller
Publisher Magazin Verlagsges.
Sueddeutsche Zeitung mbh
Issue March 15, 1996
Category Cover

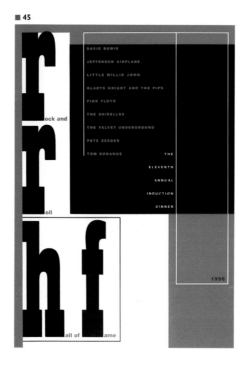

■ 45

■ 46

■ 45
Publication Rock & Roll Hall Of Fame
Creative Director Terry Koppel
Designer Terry Koppel
Photo Editor Danny Fields
Publisher The Rock & Roll Hall of Fame
Studio Terry Koppel Design
Issue January 17, 1996
Category Cover

■ 46
Publication Rock & Roll Hall Of Fame
Creative Director Terry Koppel
Designer Terry Koppel
Photo Editor Danny Fields
Publisher The Rock & Roll Hall of Fame
Studio Terry Koppel Design
Issue January 17, 1996
Category Cover

■ 47
Publication Metropolis
Art Directors Carl Lehmann-Haupt,
William van Roden
Publisher Bellerophon Publishing
Issue January/February 1996
Category Cover

■ 47

■ 48
Publication Rolling Stone
Creative Director Fred Woodward
Designer Fred Woodward
Photo Editor Jodi Peckman
Photographer Mark Seliger
Publisher Wenner Media
Issue September 19, 1996
Category Cover

■ 49
Publication Rolling Stone
Creative Director Fred Woodward
Designer Fred Woodward
Photo Editor Jodi Peckman
Photographer Mark Seliger
Publisher Wenner Media
Issue July 11-25 1996
Category Cover

■ 50
Publication Rolling Stone
Creative Director Fred Woodward
Designer Fred Woodward
Photo Editor Jodi Peckman
Photographer Montalbetti Campbell
Publisher Wenner Media
Issue May 16, 1996
Category Cover

■ 51
Publication Vibe
Art Director Lee Ellen Fanning
Designer Lee Ellen Fanning
Illustrators Ryan Jones,
Lee Ellen Fanning
Photographers Nathaniel S. Butler,
Andrew D. Bernstein, Greg Foster
Publisher Time Inc.
Issue August 1996
Category Cover

The New York Times Magazine
THE SOPHISTICATED TRAVELER®
PART 2/MARCH 3, 1996

SPRING ADVENTURES

The New York Times Magazine
FEBRUARY 11, 1996 / SECTION 6

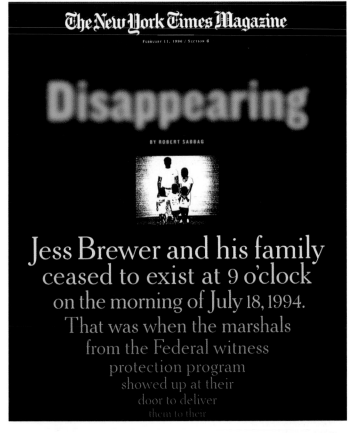

Disappearing
BY ROBERT SABBAG

Jess Brewer and his family
ceased to exist at 9 o'clock
on the morning of July 18, 1994.
That was when the marshals
from the Federal witness
protection program
showed up at their
door to deliver
them to their

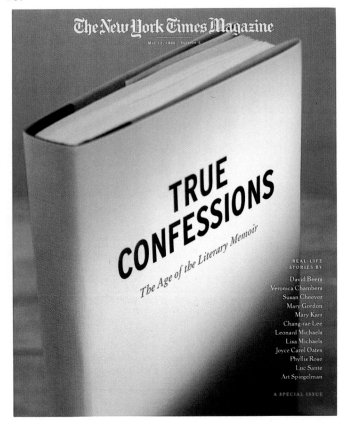

The New York Times Magazine
MAY 12, 1996 / SECTION 6

TRUE CONFESSIONS
The Age of the Literary Memoir

REAL-LIFE STORIES BY

David Beers
Veronica Chambers
Susan Cheever
Mary Gordon
Mary Karr
Chang-rae Lee
Leonard Michaels
Lisa Michaels
Joyce Carol Oates
Phyllis Rose
Luc Sante
Art Spiegelman

A SPECIAL ISSUE

The New York Times Magazine
JULY 7, 1996 / SECTION 6

Blepharoplasty
Brow Lift
Chemical Peel
Rhinoplasty
Mammoplasty
Otoplasty
Rhytidectomy
Calf Implants
Brachioplasty
Mastopexy
Phalloplasty
Dermabrasion
Liposuction
Gynecomastia
Buttock Augmentation

Effacing Ourselves
By Charles Siebert

■ 52
Publication
The New York Times Magazine
Art Director Ken McFarlin
Illustrator Brian Cronin
Publisher The New York Times
Issue March 3, 1996
Category Cover

■ 53
Publication
The New York Times Magazine
Art Director Janet Froelich
Designer Catherine Gilmore-Barnes
Photo Editor Sarah Harbutt
Publisher The New York Times
Issue February 11, 1996
Category Cover

■ 54
Publication
The New York Times Magazine
Art Director Janet Froelich
Designer Lisa Naftolin
Photo Editor Kathy Ryan
Photographer Victor Schrager
Publisher The New York Times
Issue May 12, 1996
Category Cover

■ 55
Publication
The New York Times Magazine
Art Director Janet Froelich
Designer Joel Cuyler
Photo Editor Kathy Ryan
Photographers
Rimma Gerlovina, Valeriy Gerlovin
Publisher The New York Times
Issue July 7, 1996
Category Cover

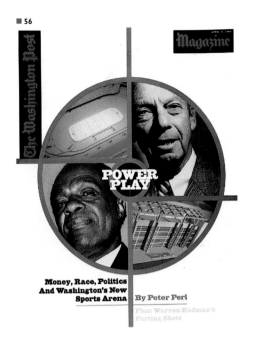

■ 56

■ 57

■ 58

■ 56
Publication The Washington Post Magazine
Art Director Kelly Doe
Designer Kelly Doe
Photo Editor Karen Tanaka
Photographers David Peterson, David Sharpe
Publisher The Washington Post Co.
Issue April 21, 1996
Category Cover

■ 57
Publication The Washington Post Magazine
Art Director Kelly Doe
Designer Kelly Doe
Photo Editor Karen Tanaka
Photographer Rei Taka
Publisher The Washington Post Co.
Issue April 28, 1996
Category Cover

■ 58
Publication The Washington Post Magazine
Art Director Kelly Doe
Designer Kelly Doe
Publisher The Washington Post Co.
Issue August 4, 1996
Category Cover

■ 59
Publication The Washington Post Magazine
Art Director Kelly Doe
Designer Kelly Doe
Photo Editor Karen Tanaka
Photographers Sylvia Plachy, Will Thompson,
Dale Boyer, Martin Chambi
Publisher The Washington Post Co.
Issue October 20, 1996
Category Cover

■ 60
Publication The Washington Post Magazine
Art Director Kelly Doe
Designer Kelly Doe
Photo Editor Karen Tanaka
Photographer Alan Richardson, Archive Photos
Publisher The Washington Post Co.
Issue November 3, 1996
Category Cover

■ 59

■ 60

■ 61

■ 61
Publication The Boston Globe
Art Director Thomas Lauder
Designer Thomas Lauder
Illustrator Thomas Lauder
Publisher The Boston Globe
Issue October 10, 1996
Category Front Page

■ 62

■ 63

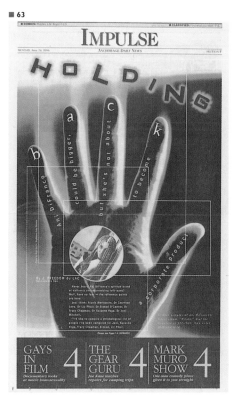

■ 65

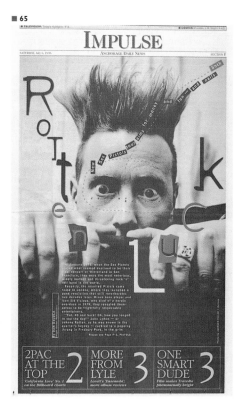

■ 64

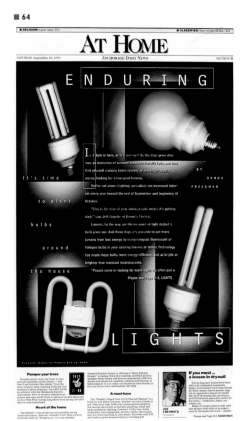

■ 66

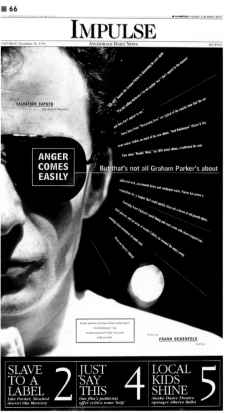

■ 62
Publication Anchorage Daily News
Design Director Lance Lekander
Designer Lance Lekander
Publisher Anchorage Daily News
Issue January 19, 1996
Category Front Page

■ 63
Publication Anchorage Daily News
Creative Director Dee Boyles
Designer Dee Boyles
Illustrator Dee Boyles
Photographer Mark Vans
Publisher Anchorage Daily News
Issue June 24, 1996
Category Front Page

■ 64
Publication Anchorage Daily News
Creative Director Pamela Dunlap-Shohl
Designer Pamela Dunlap-Shohl
Illustrator Pamela Dunlap-Shohl
Publisher Anchorage Daily News
Issue September 28, 1996
Category Front Page

■ 65
Publication Anchorage Daily News
Creative Director Dee Boyles
Designer Dee Boyles
Photographer Juergen Teller
Publisher Anchorage Daily News
Issue July 6, 1996
Category Front Page

■ 66
Publication Anchorage Daily News
Creative Director Lance Lekander
Designer Lance Lekander
Photographer Frank W. Ockenfels 3
Publisher Anchorage Daily News
Issue November 30, 1996
Category Front Page

■ 67

Adobe
PUBLISHING, DESIGN, AND DIGITAL MEDIA
magazine
Volume 8, Number 2, December 1996 • $5.00

the sixth annual design contest

THE
1996
ADOBE MAGAZINE
DESIGN CONTEST

Contest photography by Jim Linna

■ 67
Publication Adobe
Art Directors Jenna Ashley,
Kathleen Koeneman
Designers Jenna Ashley,
Kathleen Koeneman
Photographers Jim Linna,
Rosanne Olson, Kim Zumwalt
Publisher Adobe Systems Inc.
Issue December 1996
Category Entire Issue

BEST OF SHOW

CROSSING **BOUNDARIES**
MULTIMEDIA,
< < <

At DNA Multimedia, a 'cross-cultural approach' gives rise to award-winning CD-ROMs

■ 68

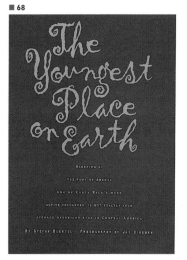

The Youngest Place on Earth

SLEEPING AT
THE FOOT OF ARENAL,
ONE OF COSTA RICA'S MOST
ACTIVE VOLCANOES, IS NOT EXACTLY YOUR
AVERAGE OVERNIGHT STAY IN CENTRAL AMERICA

BY STEFAN BECHTEL • PHOTOGRAPHY BY JAY DICKMAN

■ 69

Pontiffs and Jobs
be Damned,
even
Grown-up
Surfers
Never Quit
Chasing
Perfect
Waves

By Ken McAlpine ● Photography by Jay Dickman

■ 70

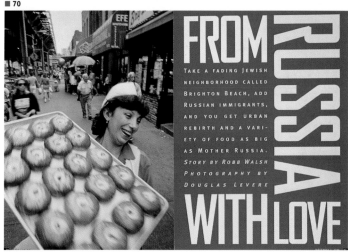

FROM RUSSIA

TAKE A FADING JEWISH
NEIGHBORHOOD CALLED
BRIGHTON BEACH, ADD
RUSSIAN IMMIGRANTS,
AND YOU GET URBAN
REBIRTH AND A VARI-
ETY OF FOOD AS BIG
AS MOTHER RUSSIA.
STORY BY ROBB WALSH
PHOTOGRAPHY BY
DOUGLAS LEVERE

WITH LOVE

■ 68
Publication American Way
Design Director Scott Feaster
Designer John May
Photographer Jay Dickman
Publisher
American Airlines Inflight Media
Issue April 15, 1996
Category Feature Spread

■ 69
Publication American Way
Design Director Scott Feaster
Designer John May
Photographer Jay Dickman
Publisher
American Airlines Inflight Media
Issue June 1, 1996
Category Feature Spread

■ 70
Publication American Way
Design Director Scott Feaster
Designer John May
Photographer Douglas Levere
Publisher
American Airlines Inflight Media
Issue November 1, 1996
Category Feature Spread

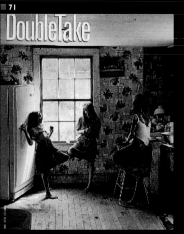

DoubleTake

Contents

■ **71**
Publication DoubleTake
Design Director Molly Renda
Designer Molly Renda
Photo Editor Alex Harris
Publisher
Center for Documentary Studies
Issue Fall 1996
Category Entire Issue

STEALING HOME PHOTOGRAPHS BY MARGARET SARTOR

WESTERN STATES

■ **72**
Publication Fast Company
Art Director Patrick Mitchell
Designer Patrick Mitchell
Publisher Fast Company
Issue Premiere Issue
Category Feature Single Page

■ **73**
Publication Fast Company
Art Director Patrick Mitchell
Designer Patrick Mitchell
Illustrator Ralph Steadman
Publisher Fast Company
Issue August/September 1996
Category Feature Spread

FAST COMPANY

WORKISPERSON

We've *tried* command-and-control. It doesn't work. We've *tried* reengineering. It failed. We've tried *everything* except the one thing that's been staring us in the face: TRUST THE PEOPLE.

ALCOMPUTING

THE NEW RULES: Processes don't do work, *people* do. Learning is about work, work is about learning — both are social. Organizations are webs of participation.

ISSOCIALKNOWL

Change the patterns of participation, you change the organization. Personal computing is giving way to *social* computing.

EDGEISPOWER

These new rules connect those who *get it* — and separate those who don't.

THIS IS WHAT COMES AFTER REENGINEERING.

As America gears up for the last election of the Industrial Age, the new economic order is overthrowing the old politics. Meet the Cyber-Libertarians and Techno-Communitarians— business parties for the 21st century.

RAGE AGAINST the POLITICAL MACHINE

This is the month when pundits and politicians are liplocked to network microphones. Republicans gather in San Diego. Democrats convene in Chicago. Both sides wave signs, wear silly hats, talk through boring speeches, drink bartenders to their knees, and grind out their mechanical nominations. [The men and women creating the new economy won't be watching.] After the conventions, Bob Dole and Bill Clinton will continue to declare that Americans face a crucial choice. "The differences are profound and fundamental," says Dole. "We now have two very different visions of change before the American people," says Clinton. [The new and anxious creating the new economy aren't buying it.] "Dole is settled in his thinking," says Ralph Miller, president and CEO of APX International, an advanced engineering company that designs prototypes for auto companies around the world. "He's General Motors."

By Ronald Brownstein
ILLUSTRATIONS BY RALPH STEADMAN

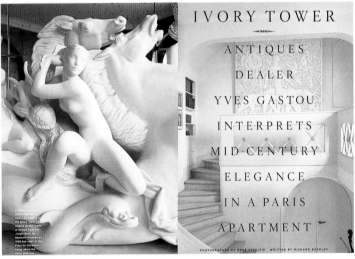

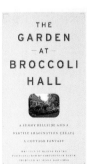

■ 74
Publication Condé Nast House & Garden
Art Director Robert Priest
Designers Debra Bishop, Ruth Diener
Photo Editor Deborah Needleman
Publisher Condé Nast Publications Inc.
Issue October 1996, September 1996, December 1996
Category Overall Design

Object Lesson
Power Ranges
RESTAURANT STOVES NEWLY TAILORED FOR THE HOME AND
RESIDENTIAL STOVES WITH PROFESSIONAL AIRS OFFER THE
AMBITIOUS COOK MANY CHOICES AND NO EXCUSES

COOKIE FORTUNE

■ 75
Publication Condé Nast House & Garden
Art Director Robert Priest
Designer Robert Priest
Photo Editor Deborah Needleman
Publisher Condé Nast Publications Inc.
Issue October 1996
Category Feature Story

■ 76
Publication Condé Nast House & Garden
Art Director Robert Priest
Designer Debra Bishop
Photo Editor Deborah Needleman
Photographer Ilan Rubin
Publisher Condé Nast Publications Inc.
Issue December 1996
Category Feature Story

KALEIDOSCOPE

TRICIA GUILD BRINGS HER PRISMATIC PALETTE TO THE URBAN DWELLER

CONDÉ NAST
House & Garden

SEPTEMBER 1996 $4.95

Home Again

BORDERS FOR A NEW WORLD

"I don't want to buy anyone else's decoration. When you walk into a house, you look for the little bit of spirit you can make yours"

Tricia's World

green links

limes and chartreuses
are driving us to distraction

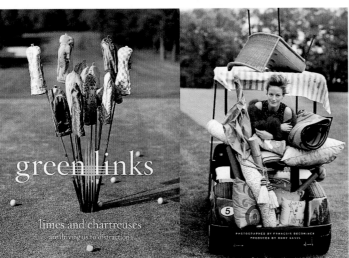

■ 78
Publication Condé Nast House & Garden
Art Director Robert Priest
Designer Debra Bishop
Photo Editor Deborah Needleman
Photographer Gilles De Chabaneix
Publisher Condé Nast Publications Inc.
Issue Summer 1996
Category Feature Story

■ 77
Publication Condé Nast House & Garden
Art Director Robert Priest
Designers Debra Bishop, Ruth Diener
Publisher Condé Nast Publications Inc.
Issue September 1996
Category Redesign

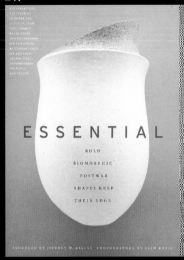

ESSENTIAL GESTURES

BOLD
BIOMORPHIC
POSTWAR
SHAPES KEEP
THEIR EDGE

PRODUCED BY JEFFREY W. MILLER PHOTOGRAPHED BY ILAN RUBIN

Above and Beyond

Marilyn Bridges showcases America from the air.

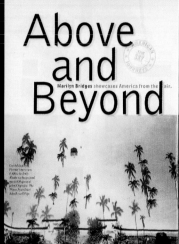

NOW AND ZEN

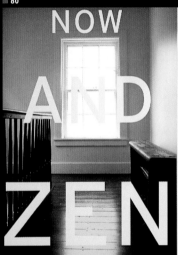

A CONNECTICUT FARMHOUSE IS RESTORED WITH A SIMPLICITY THAT IS AT ONCE MODERN AND TIMELESS BY SUZANNE SLESIN PHOTOGRAPHED BY ANITA CALERO

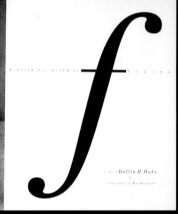

f

Dallin H. Oaks

79
Publication
Condé Nast House & Garden
Art Director Robert Priest
Designer Debra Bishop
Photo Editor Deborah Needleman
Photographer Ilan Rubin
Publisher Condé Nast Publications Inc.
Issue October 1996
Category Feature Spread

80
Publication
Condé Nast House & Garden
Art Director Robert Priest
Designer Debra Bishop
Photo Editor Deborah Needleman
Photographer Anita Calero
Publisher Condé Nast Publications Inc.
Issue October 1996
Category Feature Spread

81
Publication Clark Memorandum
Creative Director Linda Sullivan
Designer Linda Sullivan
Illustrator Rob Blackard
Publisher Brigham Young University
Client J. Reuben Clark Law School
Issue Fall 1996
Category Feature Spread

82
Publication Condé Nast Traveler
Design Director Robert Best
Art Director Carla Frank
Designer Robert Best
Photo Editor Kathleen Klech
Photographer Marilyn Bridges
Publisher Condé Nast Publications Inc.
Issue September 1996
Category Feature Story

■ 83

ROCK OF AGES

NAVEL OF THE MEDITERRANEAN, MALTA IS A PUZZLE OF THE GRANDIOSE AND THE INTRICATE. STEPHEN FENICHELL PRIES OPEN AN ISLAND OF INTRIGUE AND ARDOR

a Ride on the Wild Side

■ 84

MALTA'S UR-BUILDINGS, THE OLDEST FREESTANDING STRUCTURES ON EARTH, LIE EXPOSED TO A CLEAR MID-MEDITERRANEAN SKY: THE BONES OF SHELTER—WALL, FLOOR, WINDOW, HEARTH

THE MOCK-GOTHIC CATHEDRAL IS NO RELIC, BUT THE FANTASY OF A PARISH PRIEST WHO WON THE NATIONAL LOTTERY IN THE 1970S

"May I make a request?" my driving partner said. "Tonight, we don't sleep in a motel right on a highway, with the cars going whoosh! whoosh!"

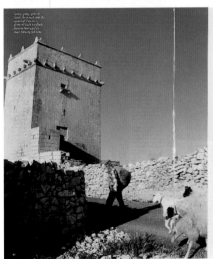

I PENETRATE A DIMLY LIT TUNNEL WALLED WITH LIMESTONE THAT HAS ATTAINED THE MOIST, CRUMBLY SOFTNESS OF FRESH LEMON CAKE

"You don't want to go to Lenoir," a woman said. I asked her what they did for fun in Lenoir. "Shoot each other," she said

■ 83
Publication Condé Nast Traveler
Design Director Robert Best
Art Director Carla Frank
Designer Robert Best
Photo Editor Kathleen Klech
Photographer Xavier Lambours
Publisher Condé Nast Publications Inc.
Issue July 1996
Category Feature Story

■ 84
Publication Condé Nast Traveler
Design Director Robert Best
Art Director Carla Frank
Designer Robert Best
Photo Editor Kathleen Klech
Photographer Moshe Brakha
Publisher Condé Nast Publications Inc.
Issue September 1996
Category Feature Story

A Giant Awakes

The past is hoarded like treasure in Beijing, but China is a nation in training, flexing its muscles and banking on its cities. John Krich went back and found the old capital bristling with construction cranes and ever-wider ring roads. Welcome to the once and future Beijing

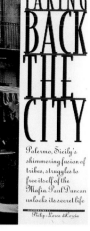

TAKING BACK THE CITY

Palermo, Sicily's shimmering fusion of tribes, struggles to free itself of the Mafia. Paul Duncan unlocks its secret life

IT ISN'T DIFFICULT TO CONJURE HEARTBREAKING BEAUTY FROM THE MADNESS OF PALERMO: THAT STRANGE

THIS ISN'T ITALY. JUDGE PALERMO BY THE STANDARDS OF OTHER ITALIAN CITIES AND YOU'LL END UP HATING IT. THIS IS BARELY EVEN EUROPE

■ 85
Publication Condé Nast Traveler
Design Director Robert Best
Art Director Carla Frank
Designer Robert Best
Photo Editor Kathleen Klech
Photographer Antonin Kratochvil
Publisher Condé Nast Publications Inc.
Issue November 1996
Category Feature Story

■ 86
Publication Condé Nast Traveler
Design Director Robert Best
Photo Editor Kathleen Klech
Photographer Phillip Lorca Di Corcia
Publisher Condé Nast Publications Inc.
Issue December 1996
Category Feature Story

■ 87
Publication Condé Nast Traveler
Design Director Robert Best
Art Director Carla Frank
Designer Robert Best
Photo Editor Kathleen Klech
Photographer William Abranowicz
Publisher Condé Nast Publications Inc.
Issue September 1996
Category Feature Story

■ 88
Publication Condé Nast Traveler
Design Director Robert Best
Art Director Carla Frank
Designer Carla Frank
Photo Editor Kathleen Klech
Photographer Hakan Ludwigson
Publisher Condé Nast Publications Inc.
Issue November 1996
Category Feature Story

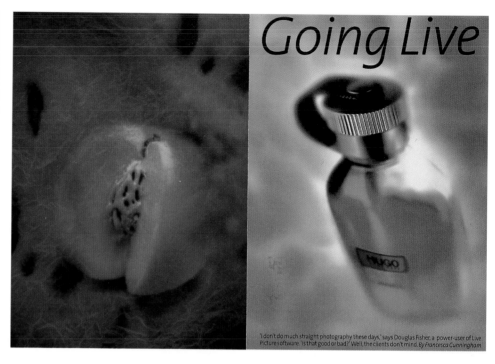

CREATIVE
TECHNOLOGY
MARCH 1996 £2.75

Going Live

Live Studies
WHY PHOTOGRAPHER DOUGLAS FISHER IS CHAMPIONING THE LIVE PICTURE CAUSE

VIRTUAL REALITY-IT'S ALMOST HERE ● DIGITAL CAMERAS IN ACTION ● HOW TO BUY A MONITOR

'I don't do much straight photography these days,' says Douglas Fisher, a power-user of Live Picture software. 'Is that good or bad?' Well, the clients don't mind. By Francesca Cunningham

A Question of Style

Sometimes a designer's style can run out of substance. Francesca Cunningham asks if you can have too much of a good thing. Portraits by Colin Stout

spiderman

■ 89
Publication Creative Technology
Art Director Wayne Ford
Designer Wayne Ford
Photo Editor Wayne Ford
Photographers Douglas Fisher, Robert Wilson, Colin Stout
Publisher Haymarket Trade & Leisure Publications Limited
Issue March 1996
Category Entire Issue

Creating 3D on a Mac is hard work. Ask Me Company, who made these characters. But new tools and technologies are on the way to take us all closer to the third dimension. David Cook reports

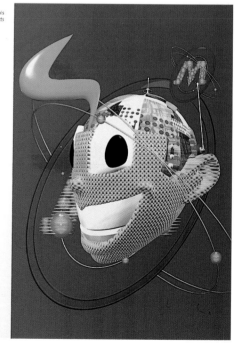

Deep Space

■ 90
Publication Creative Technology
Art Director Wayne Ford
Designer Wayne Ford
Illustrator Me Company
Publisher Haymarket Trade & Leisure Publications Limited
Issue May 1996
Category Feature Spread

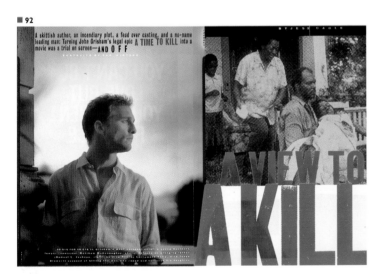

■ 91
Publication Entertainment Weekly
Design Director John Korpics
Publisher Time Inc.
Issues October 25, 1996
November 29, 1996
December 27, 1996
Category Overall Design

■ 92
Publication Entertainment Weekly
Design Director John Korpics
Designer John Korpics
Photo Editor Doris Brautigan
Photographer Dan Winters
Publisher Time Inc.
Issue July 27, 1996
Category Feature Spread

■ 93
Publication Entertainment Weekly
Design Director John Korpics
Designer John Korpics
Photo Editor Doris Brautigan
Photographer Ruven Afanador
Publisher Time Inc.
Issue October 18, 1996
Category Feature Spread

■ 94
Publication Entertainment Weekly
Design Director John Korpics
Art Director Michael Picon
Designer Michael Picon
Illustrators Tim Gabor, Anita Kunz, Georgeanne Dean
Photo Editor Alice Babcock
Photographers Kevin Irby, Mathew Rolston
Publisher Time Inc.
Issue November 29, 1996
Category Feature Story

■ 95
Publication Entertainment Weekly
Design Director John Korpics
Art Director Joe Kimberling
Designer Joe Kimberling
Illustrators CSA Design, Mark Summers, Christoph Neiman
Photo Editor Julie Mihaly
Publisher Time Inc.
Issue October 25, 1996
Category Feature Story

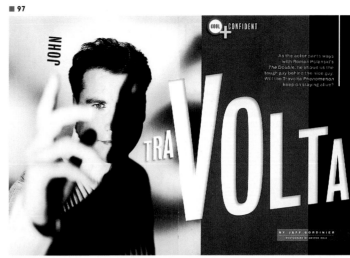

■ 96
Publication Entertainment Weekly
Design Director John Korpics
Art Directors Rina Migliaccio, Joe Kimberling
Designer Rina Migliaccio
Illustrators Mark Ryden, Greg Clarke
Photo Editor Doris Brautigan
Photographer Firooz Zahedi
Publisher Time Inc.
Issue November 22, 1996
Category Feature Story
   ■ **A** Feature Spread

■ 97
Publication Entertainment Weekly
Design Director John Korpics
Art Director Michael Picon
Designers Michael Picon, Stacie Reistetter
Photo Editors Doris Brautigan, Ramiro Fernandez
Publisher Time Inc.
Issue June 28, 1996
Category Feature Story

■ 98
Publication Entertainment Weekly:
The 100 Greatest Movie Stars
of All Time
Art Director Don Morris
Designers Don Morris, Josh Klenert,
James Reyman, Jennifer Starr
Photo Editor Julie Mihaly
Publisher Time Inc.
Studio Don Morris Design
Issue 1996 Special Issue
Category Entire Issue

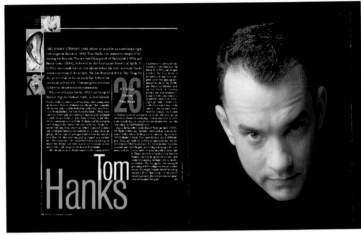

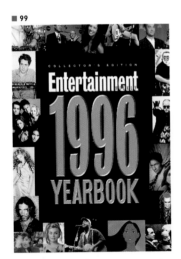

■ 99
Publication Entertainment Weekly:
1996 Yearbook
Design Director Robert Newman
Art Director Don Morris
Designers Don Morris, Josh Klenert,
James Reyman, Jennifer Starr
Photo Editor Julie Mihaly
Publisher Time Inc.
Studio Don Morris Design
Issue February/March/April
Category Entire Issue

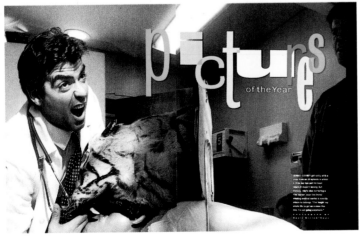

COMME DES GARÇONS

ART COUTURE

BY DEBORAH DRIER

■ 100
Publication Guggenheim Magazine
Creative Director J. Abbott Miller
Designers Luke Hayman, Jonathan Hoefler
Publisher Dance Ink Foundation
Studio Design/Writing/Research
Issue October , 1996
Category Entire Issue

GIANNI BERENGO GARDIN

Piccole figure

■ 101
Publication Leica World
Art Director Horst Moser
Designers Nina Simson, Sabine Hetzer, Horst Moser
Photo Editors Michael Koetzle, Horst Moser
Photographers Penn W. McBride, Henri Cartier-Bresson
Publisher Independent
Issue November 1996
Category Entire Issue

ALEXANDER LIBERMAN

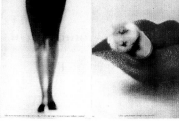

EIN GESPRÄCH MIT ALEXANDER LIBERMAN

»Mich hat der Zufall interessiert«

GISÈLE FREUND

Bilder aus bewegter Zeit

FROM SHORTS TO SUITS, THIS SEASON THE MILANESE OFFER US A STUNNING VISION—BOLDLY UNADORNED CLOTHES IN A DRAMATIC PALETTE OF BLACK AND WHITE

SPRING PREVIEW 2

THE ITALIAN COLLECTIONS

PHOTOGRAPHS BY FRANCOIS HALARD

Photographs by DEWEY NICKS

AND FOR YOU TO MAKE THE SEASIDE SCENE IN STYLE, THE THREE B'S ARE KEY: BOLD COLORS, BAGGY SHORTS AND, NATURALLY, PLENTY OF BIKINIS—ON THE GIRLS, OF COURSE

Surf's up

CATCH A WAVE: GET YOURSELF INTO SOME AUTHENTIC BOARD SHORT

BEACH REGULATIONS: SIMPLE, LIGHTWEIGHT LAYERS TO PEEL OFF WHEN TEMPERATURES RISE

■ 102
Publication GQ
Design Director John Korpics
Designer John Korpics
Photo Editor Karen Frank
Photographer Francois Halard
Publisher Condé Nast Publications Inc.
Issue March 1996
Category Feature Story

■ 103
Publication GQ
Design Director John Korpics
Designer Rina Migliaccio
Photo Editor Karen Frank
Photographer Dewey Nicks
Publisher Condé Nast Publications Inc.
Issue May 1996
Category Feature Story

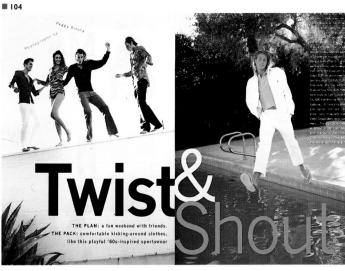

Twist&
Shout

THE PLAN: a fun weekend with friends.
THE PACK: comfortable kicking-around clothes,
like this playful '60s-inspired sportswear

HOW
MINIMAL
CAN
YOU GO?

YOUR SUMMER GOAL: TO WEAR
AS LITTLE MAKEUP AS POSSIBLE

First step: Figure out your own absolute minimum. We asked makeup artist Vincent Longo to leave half of each model's face completely naked to show that makeup can be barely perceptible *and* still very flattering. With the right products and techniques, anyone—including *you*—can pare down to almost nothing.

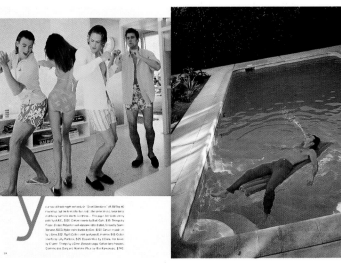

IamNot

Afraid

For years I've kept my panic attacks a secret.
Now I am going public with my fear. By Barbara Grizzutti Harrison

Right now, the most striking way to dress up is to pare down. Keep the lines simple, letting fabric textures and makeup tones—both with a warm, burnished luster—cast their own soft glow

• high impact style

delicate sparkle at your fingertips

second-skin shimmer

the textured chignon

it's not what you reveal, it's how you reveal it boldly and simply

cut velvet

■ 104
Publication GQ
Design Director John Korpics
Designer John Korpics
Photo Editor Karen Frank
Photographer Peggy Sirota
Publisher Condé Nast Publications Inc.
Issue May 1996
Category Feature Story

■ 105
Publication Health
Art Director Jane Palecek
Designer Jane Palecek
Photographer Exum
Publisher Time Inc.
Issue May/June 1996
Category Feature Spread

■ 106
Publication Glamour
Art Director Kati Korpijaakko
Designer Kati Korpijaakko
Photographers Ben Watts, Len Delessio
Publisher Condé Nast Publications Inc.
Issue August 1996
Category Feature Story

■ 107
Publication Glamour
Art Director Kati Korpijaakko
Designer Russel Labosky
Photographers Hiromasa
Publisher Condé Nast Publications Inc.
Issue December 1996
Category Feature Story

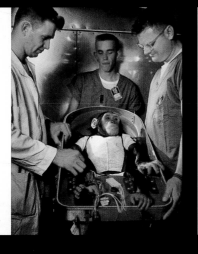

■ 107
Publication
Luna Moonshots Brochure
Design Director Mark Geer
Designers Mark Geer, Karen Malnar
Photo Editor Mark Geer
Publisher The Beasley Company, Inc.
Issue October 1, 1996
Category Entire Issue

a NOSE for ROSES

To read the essays of the acclaimed poet and naturalist Diane Ackerman is to recognize the soul of a true gardener—one in which unflinching empiricism is filtered through empathy and memory. "I've gardened for decades," she says, "starting with small raised beds, and gradually getting more ambitious. I may be writing about the ways of raccoons or bees, but I am part of the garden and the garden is part of me. Both appear in my books." This is nowhere more apparent than in Ackerman's erudite and passionate writing on roses, from her best-selling collection of essays. *From the book A Natural History of the Senses by Diane Ackerman. Copyright © 1990 by Diane Ackerman. Reprinted by permission of Random House, Inc. See THE SOURCE, page 110.*

TEXT BY DIANE ACKERMAN • ILLUSTRATIONS BY JEFF FISHER

deer in the roses

■ 108
Publication Garden Design
Creative Director Michael Grossman
Art Director Christin Gangi
Designer Christin Gangi
Illustrator Jeffrey Fisher
Photo Editor Susan Goldberger
Publisher Meigher Communications
Issue June/July 1996
Category Feature Story

■ 109
Publication Garden Design
Creative Director Michael Grossman
Art Director Christin Gangi
Designer Toby Fox
Illustrator Benoit
Photo Editor Susan Goldberger
Publisher Meigher Communications
Issue December 1996/January 1997
Category Feature Spread

Sugared leather dipped in honey

This Old Garden Renovation is hell. Life is chaos, budgets are shot, marriages are strained, and the hand-beveled French doors still won't open on humid days. But if you think it's painful to come home after work and see the refrigerator sitting in the entrance hall covered with a drop cloth and an inch of noxious plaster dust, you should try living through the kind of renovation we're doing. Ours is much harder—fraught with emotion, filled with the kind of heart-wrenching decisions that keep you up nights: Let the silver maple die a natural death or take it down? Is there too

By Stephanie Pierson Illustration by Benoit

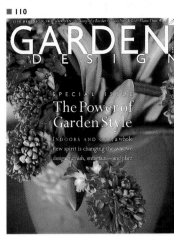

GARDEN
DESIGN

SPECIAL ISSUE

The Power of
Garden Style

INDOORS AND OUT, a whole
new spirit is changing the way we
design, furnish, entertain—and plant

DIRT

Sakura Season

For Mower Mavens

Natural
Seduction

THE BIRDS, THE BEES
AND THE BLOSSOMS

GROWIN G

EXPANDING VIOLETS

THE POWER OF THE GARDEN
TOUCHES EVERYTHING WE
TOUCH TODAY ■ BY CAROL HELMS

THIS IS GARDEN STYLE

TRANSPLANTS

A NOVICE GARDENER DISCOVERS A TIMELESS DESIGN THAT CONTAINS HER PASSION

AN ORDERLY RETREAT

BY BARBARA H. SEEBER ■ PHOTOGRAPHS BY LEONARD G. PHILLIPS

WHAT DO PLANTS
REALLY WANT?

GOODWIN'S DESIGNS ECHO THE
ELEGANTLY COMPLEX RHYTHMS
OF PLANTS AS THEY BREATHE,
FEED, BREED, AND REPRODUCE

ANATOMY OF A
BORDER

SIX BIG DESIGN LESSONS EMERGE FROM A SMALL GARDEN

LESSON ONE: *the repetition and contrast to unify a border and make it flow.*

BY HARRIET HEYMAN ■ PHOTOGRAPHS BY ROBERT HOLMES

■ 110
Publication Garden Design
Creative Director Michael Grossman
Art Director Christin Gangi
Designer Toby Fox
Photo Editor Susan Goldberger
Publisher Meigher Communications
Issue April/May 1996
Category Entire Issue

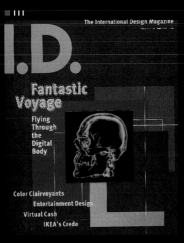

The International Design Magazine

I.D.

Fantastic Voyage

Flying
Through
the
Digital
Body

Color Clairvoyants

Entertainment Design

Virtual Cash

IKEA's Credo

Uncovering
the design
intricacies beneath
the humble coffee-cup
lid: from pasteboard
to polystyrene, and from
cup of joe to
cappuccino.

 TOP THIS

by Phil Patton

Photography by James Wojcik

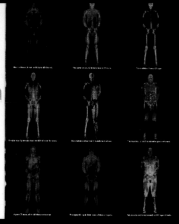

Life Beyond Death

A look at the origins and implications of Alexander Tsiaras's *Anatomical Travelogue*, a series of animated journeys through human anatomy on CD-ROM, the Web, TV and even a 3-D IMAX movie.
By Peter Hall

Cup lids dispose of a problem — a small one, to be sure — while the world around them remains ragged and uncertain.

For most designers, to be included in the IKEA catalogue ranks higher than coverage in the glossiest magazine.

If you look at them without touching or lifting, lids can seem as stately as sculpted plaster or marble.

■ 112

Publication I.D.
Art Directors A. Arefin, Andrea Fella
Photographer James Wojcik
Publisher I.D. Magazine
Issue May/June 1996
Category Feature Story

RECOVERY   TOLERANCE

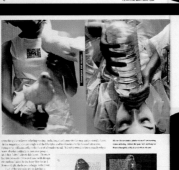

■ 111

Publication I.D.
Creative Director A. Arefin
Art Director Andrea Fella
Publisher I.D. Magazine
Issue March/April 1996
Category Entire Issue

■ 113

■ 113
Publication La Revista
Design Director Carmelo Caderot
Art Director Rodrigo Sanchez
Designers Rodrigo Sanchez,
Miguel Buckenmeyer, Maria González,
Amparo Redondo
Illustrator Ulises Culebro
Photo Editor Chema Conesa
Photographer Chema Conesa
Publisher Unidad Editorial S.A.
Issue March 17, 1996
Category Entire Issue

■ 114

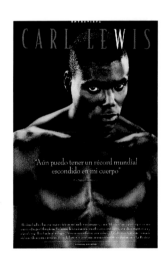

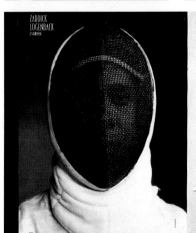

■ 114
Publication La Revista
Design Director Carmelo Caderot
Art Director Rodrigo Sanchez
Designers Rodrigo Sanchez, Miguel Buckenmeyer,
Maria González, Amparo Redondo
Photo Editor Chema Conesa
Photographers Chema Conesa,
Annie Leibovitz, Jose Ayma
Publisher Unidad Editorial S.A.
Issue July 7, 1996
Category Entire Issue

LIFE

A Photographic
Celebration
of the Olympic
Body
by Joe McNally

Naked
POWER

A Meditation
on Athletic
Beauty
by Lisa Grunwald

Amazing
GRACE

THE
U.S.
WATER
POLO
TEAM

JULY 1996/$3.95

0 72440 10099 2

LIFE SPECIAL

THESE ARE THE PEOPLE OF *CITIUS, ALTIUS,*

NAKED
POWER

FORTIUS— FASTER, HIGHER, STRONGER. BUILT

FOR PERFORMANCE, THEY ARE AS ASTONISHING

AMAZING

IN ASPECT AS THEY ARE ON THE FIELD OF PLAY.

GRACE

PHOTOGRAPHY BY JOE McNALLY

THE
SHADOW
WORLD
OF THE
SUICIDE
BOMBERS

Living
with
DEATH

Photography by **Larry Towell** Text by **Kenneth Miller**

Fighting
Back

Quick
as a
Cat

Grand
Old Man

The
Bod Squad

Firm
Equals
Form

Folded Dreams

By Charles Hirshberg Photography by Gregory Heisler

■ 115
Publication LIFE
Design Director Tom Bentkowski
Designers Tom Bentkowski, Mimi Park,
Marti Golon, Jean Andreuzzi,
Photo Editor David Friend
Publisher Time Inc.
Issue July 1996
Category Entire Issue

■ 116
Publication LIFE
Design Director Tom Bentkowski
Designer Tom Bentkowski
Photo Editor David Friend
Photographer Joe McNally
Publisher Time Inc.
Issue July 1996
Category Feature Story

It all began

with a television set,

a 16-inch, black-and-white Zenith that arrived in our apartment in Brooklyn in 1949 like a creature from another planet. I was only two at the time, too young to comprehend much beyond the picture tube's eerie light, but that electronic pod—and for an Eisenlike it—contained the seeds from which my generation, the baby boom generation, grew. Television talked to us, nurtured us, brought us together. It gave us our myths and our dreams. It set us apart from all who had come before.

Of course, before television there was sex. And plenty of it, 76 million Americans were born between 1946 and 1964, the years that have come to define the demographic anomaly known as the baby boom, the most fertile period in U.S. history. Postwar prosperity had much to do with it, as did faith in the future, and an ideology of reproduction that pushed women out of the wartime workforce and into labor. Ours was the largest generation ever, accounting for almost a third of the nation's population by the 1980s. And we made our presence felt: 15 million homes built in the 1970s, 30,000 shopping centers created in 1992 alone; 1.3 million canned baby food sold in 1953; and, of course, TV sets, seven million of them manufactured in 1951, up from 6,000 in 1946.

By ROBERT FRIEDMAN, Photographs by ULF SKOGSBERGH

April 19, 1995.

Oklahoma City

614 injured.

169 dead.

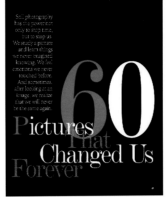

Still photography has the power not only to stop time, but to teach us. We study a picture and learn things we never imagined knowing. We feel emotions we never touched before. And sometimes, after looking at an image, we realize that we will never be the same again.

60
Pictures
That
Changed Us
Forever

■ 119
Publication LIFE
Design Director Tom Bentkowski
Art Director Mimi Park
Designer Mimi Park
Photo Editors David Friend,
Bobbi Baker Burrows
Publisher Time Inc.
Issue October 1996
Category Feature Story

■ 117
Publication LIFE
Design Director Tom Bentkowski
Art Director Mimi Park
Designer Mimi Park, Tom Bentkowski
Photo Editors David Friend,
Vivette Porges
Photographer Ulf Skogsbergh
Publisher Time Inc.
Issue Summer 1996
Category Feature Spread

■ 118
Publication LIFE
Design Director Tom Bentkowski
Designer Marti Golon
Photo Editor David Friend
Photographer James Balog
Publisher Time Inc.
Issue January 1996
Category Feature Story

Publication Martha Stewart Living
Creative Director Gael Towey
Design Director Eric Pike
Art Directors Agnethe Glatved, Claudia
Bruno, Scot Schy, James Dunlinson
Designers Eric Pike, Britta Steinbrecht,
Agnethe Glatved, Claudia Bruno, Scot
Schy, James Dunlinson, Anne-Marie Midi,
Illustrator Rodica Prado
Photo Editor Heidi Posner
Photographers William Abranowicz,
Christopher Baker, Todd Eberle, Davies
and Starr, Stephen Lewis, Victor Schrager,
Anita Calero, Jonelle Weaver, Evan Sklar,
Lisa Hubbard, Mathew Septimus
Publisher Time Inc.
Issue October 1996
Category Overall Design

apple desserts

felt

Publication Martha Stewart Living
Creative Director Gael Towey
Design Director Eric Pike
Designers Eric Pike, Hannah Milman
Photo Editor Heidi Posner
Photographer Victoria Pearson
Publisher Time Inc.
Issue April 1996
Category Feature Story

Publication Martha Stewart Living
Creative Director Gael Towey
Design Director Eric Pike
Art Director Agnethe Glatved
Designers Agnethe Glatved, Jodi Levine
Photo Editor Heidi Posner
Photographer Carlton Davis
Publisher Time Inc.
Issue December 1996
Category Feature Spread

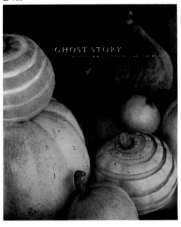

GHOST STORY

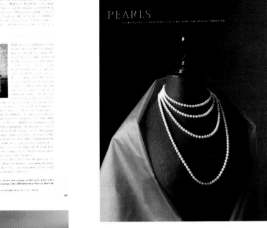

PEARLS

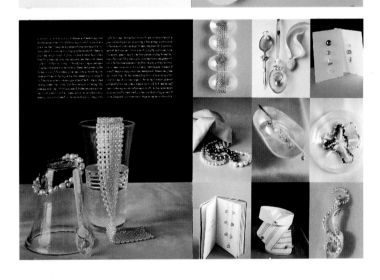

■ 123
Publication Martha Stewart Living
Creative Director Gael Towey
Design Director Eric Pike
Art Director Claudia Bruno
Designers Claudia Bruno,
Britta Steinbrecht, Ayesha Patel
Photo Editor Heidi Posner
Photographer William Abranowicz
Publisher Time Inc.
Issue October 1996
Category Feature Story

■ 124
Publication Martha Stewart Living
Creative Director Gael Towey
Design Director Eric Pike
Designers Eric Pike, Hannah Milman,
Ayesha Patel
Photo Editor Heidi Posner
Photographer Gentl & Hyers
Publisher Time Inc.
Issue Winter 1996/Spring 1997
Category Feature Story

■ 125

MERINGUE

■ 125
Publication Martha Stewart Living
Creative Director Gael Towey
Design Director Eric Pike
Designers Eric Pike, Robert Fisher,
Susan Spungen
Photo Editor Heidi Posner
Photographer Victoria Pearson
Publisher Time Inc.
Issue December 1996/Jan.1997
Category Feature Spread

LETTER PERFECT

shelves

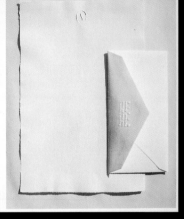 

ground covers

MELONS

glossary

DAHLIAS

■ 129
Publication Martha Stewart Living
Creative Director Gael Towey
Design Director Eric Pike
Art Director Claudia Bruno
Designers Claudia Bruno,
Margaret Roach
Photo Editor Heidi Posner
Photographer Christopher Baker
Publisher Time Inc.
Issue June 1996
Category Feature Story

■ 130
Publication Martha Stewart Living
Creative Director Gael Towey
Design Director Eric Pike
Designers Eric Pike, Frances Boswell
Photo Editor Heidi Posner
Photographer Anita Calero
Publisher Time Inc.
Issue July/August 1996
Category Feature Story

■ 131
Publication Martha Stewart Living
Creative Director Gael Towey
Design Director Eric Pike
Art Directors Claudia Bruno, Page Marchese
Designers Claudia Bruno, Page Marchese
Photo Editor Heidi Posner
Photographer Todd Eberle
Publisher Time Inc.
Issue October 1996
Category Feature Spread

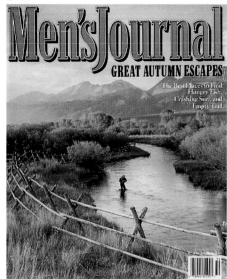

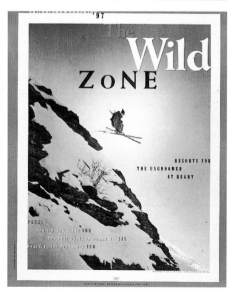

■ 132
Publication Men's Journal
Art Director David Armario
Designers David Armario, Tom Brown,
Dirk Barnett, Eva Spring
Photo Editors Denise Sfraga, Kim Gougenheim
Publisher Wenner Media
Issue October, November, December 1996
Category Overall Design

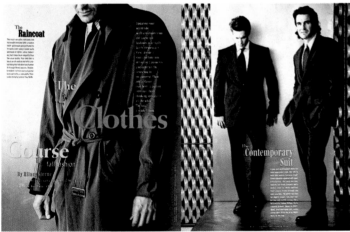

■ 133
Publication Men's Journal
Art Director David Armario
Designers David Armario, Tom Brown, Dirk Barnett, Eva Spring
Photo Editors Denise Sfraga, Kim Gougenheim
Publisher Wenner Media
Issue September 1996
Category Redesign

■ 134
Publication Men's Journal
Art Director David Armario
Designers David Armario,
Tom Brown, Dirk Barnett, Eva Spring
Photo Editors Denise Sfraga, Kim Gougenheim
Photographers Robert Paul Maxwell, Troy Word,
Tony Diziniro, David Barry, Andy Anderson
Publisher Wenner Media
Issue October 1996
Category Entire Issue

Blood
Sport
By Lamar Graham

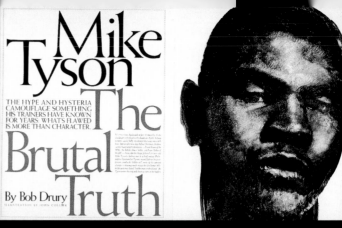

Mike Tyson
The Brutal Truth
THE HYPE AND HYSTERIA
CAMOUFLAGE SOMETHING
HIS TRAINERS HAVE KNOWN
FOR YEARS: WHAT'S FLAWED
IS MORE THAN CHARACTER.

By Bob Drury

GREAT
White
COMEBACK

By David Helvarg

Silently stalking the seas, America's boomer subs are the ultimate necessary evil. And one hell of a ride.

THE BiG STICK

By Fred Schruers

135
Publication Men's Journal
Art Director David Armario
Designers Tom Brown, David Armario
Photo Editor Deborah Needleman
Photographer Marc Asnin
Publisher Wenner Media
Issue June/July 1996
Category Feature Spread

136
Publication Men's Journal
Art Director David Armario
Designers Tom Brown, David Armario
Photographer Christian Witkin
Publisher Wenner Media
Issue June/July 1996
Category Feature Story

137
Publication Men's Journal
Art Director David Armario
Designer David Armario
Illustrator John Collier
Photo Editor Denise Sfraga
Publisher Wenner Media
Issue March 1996
Category Feature Spread

138
Publication Men's Journal
Art Director David Armario
Designers Tom Brown, David Armario
Photo Editor Denise Sfraga
Photographer Antonin Kratochvil
Publisher Wenner Media
Issue October 1996
Category Feature Spread

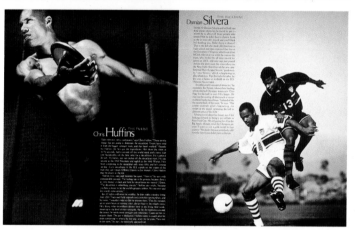

■ 139
Publication Men's Journal
Art Director David Armario
Designer David Armario
Photo Editor Deborah Needleman
Photographer John Huet
Publisher Wenner Media
Issue April 1996
Category Feature Story

■ 140
Publication Men's Journal
Art Director David Armario
Designer David Armario
Photo Editor Deborah Needleman
Photographer John Huet
Publisher Wenner Media
Issue May 1996
Category Feature Story

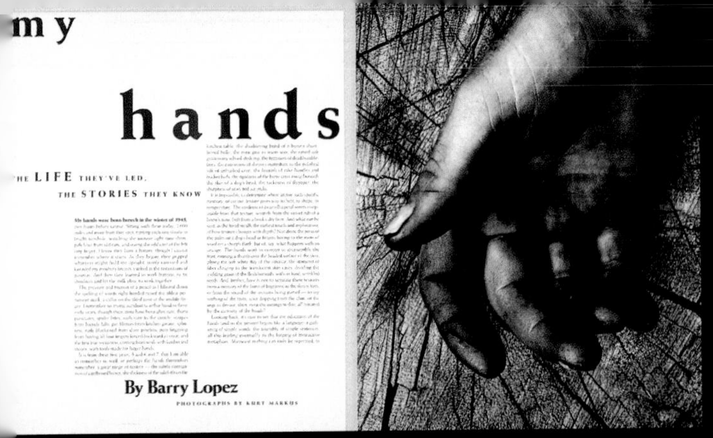

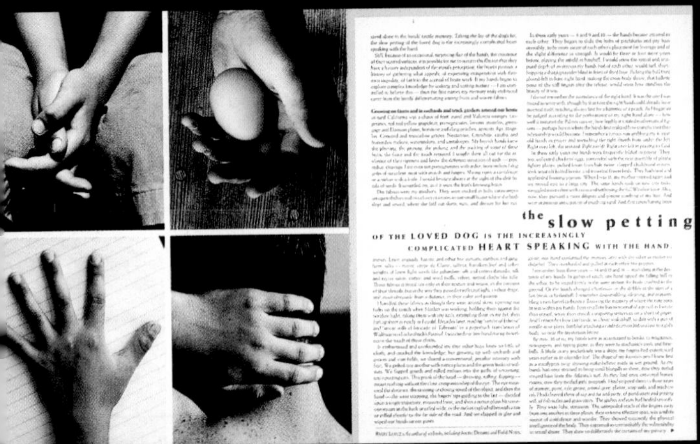

my
hands

THE **LIFE** THEY'VE LED.
THE **STORIES** THEY KNOW

[body text column — illegible]

By Barry Lopez

PHOTOGRAPHS BY ADDY MARKUS

the **slow petting**

OF THE **LOVED DOG** IS THE INCREASINGLY
COMPLICATED **HEART SPEAKING** WITH THE HAND.

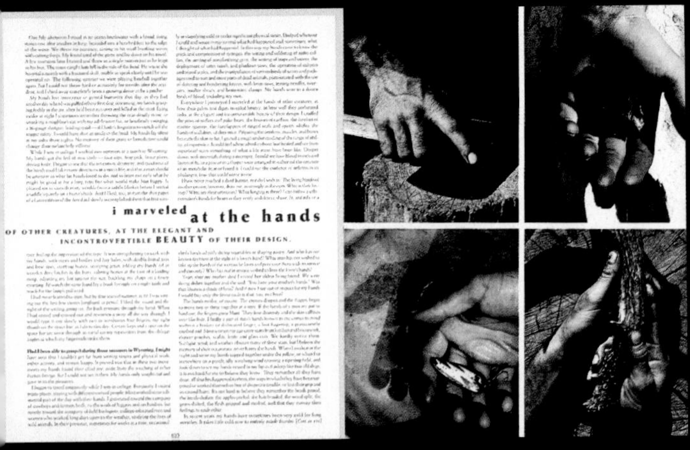

i marveled at the hands

OF OTHER CREATURES, AT THE ELEGANT AND
INCONTROVERTIBLE **BEAUTY** OF THEIR DESIGN.

142

The
PLAYERS
By Bob Spitz

141   142

7
technology & nature

technovation

■ 143

Publication mÂp
Creative Director
Robert Bergman-Ungar
Photographers
Andrew Macpherson, Santi Caleca
Publisher Map Publications Inc.
Verlag Bergman-Ungar Associates
Studio Bergman-Ungar Associates
Issue January 1996
Category Entire Issue

interview: Issey Miyake

mÂp: Can you discuss the balance between nature and technology in your work?

[interview body text — partly illegible]

photographs by Andrew Macpherson

INTERIOR DESIGN '96

New York

INTERIORS

STAINLESS STEEL HAS ITS MOMENT AND THE MELTING POT WAS NEVER HOTTER

1996

SUDDENLY, EVERYTHING IS **STAINLESS STEEL.**

THE LIVING IS EASY

HEAVY METAL

FOR STATUS KITCHENS, BRAWNY COMMERCIAL APPLIANCES

THE SHINING

FOR MACHINE-AGE MINDED METALHEADS, A VERITABLE CATALOGUE OF ALL THAT GLITTERS

ANDREW WYLIE'S GREAT INVENTION A failure as a writer, he re-made himself as a cartoon villain of an agent: The Jackal, scourge of publishers, hijacker of other agents' writers. Is Wylie serious about the role he is playing? By Rebecca Mead

THE PARK AVE. STATE DEPARTMENT

AT THE COUNCIL ON FOREIGN RELATIONS, WHERE KENNAN AND KISSINGER STRATEGIZED **THE COLD WAR,** A NEW GENERATION OF ASPIRING WISE MEN **STRUGGLES** TO STAY RELEVANT—WITH THE HELP OF AN IN-HOUSE P.R. MAN. BY ERIC KONIGSBERG

■ 144
Publication New York
Design Director Robert Newman
Art Director Deanna Lowe
Designers Vita Parrino, Ellene Wundrok
Photo Editors Michael Green, Jordan Schaps
Publisher K-III Publications
Issue October 14, 1996
Category Entire Issue

■ 145
Publication New York
Design Director Robert Newman
Art Director Syndi Becker
Photo Editor Jordan Schaps
Publisher K-III Publications
Issue May 27, 1996
Category Feature Spread

■ 146
Publication New York
Design Director Robert Newman
Photo Editors Margery Goldberg, Sabine Meyer
Photographer Frank W. Ockenfels 3
Publisher K-III Publications
Issue August 5, 1996
Category Feature Spread

■ 147
Publication New York
Design Director Robert Newman
Designer Florian Bachleda
Photo Editor Margery Goldberg
Photographer David Barry
Publisher K-III Publications
Issue October 7, 1996
Category Feature Spread

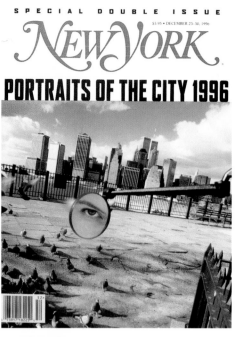

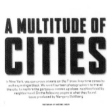

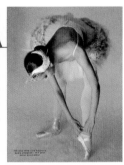

■ 148
Publication New York
Design Director Robert Newman
Art Directors Florian Bachleda, Deanna Lowe
Designers Andrea Dunham, Jennifer Gilman, Pino Impastato,
Vita Parrino, Robert Perrino, Jennifer Procopio,
Eugene Todman, Ellene Wundrok
Photo Editors Margery Goldberg, Sabine Meyer,
Nakyung Han, Yvonne Stender
Publisher K-III Publications
Issues April 15, December 23-30, September 9, 1996
Category Overall Design

■ 149
Publication New York
Design Director Robert Newman
Art Director Deanna Lowe
Designers Vita Parrino,
Ellene Wundrok
Photo Editors Margery Goldberg,
Sabine Meyer, Nakyung Han,
Yvonne Stender
Publisher K-III Publications
Issue September 9, 1996
Category Entire Issue

■ 150
Publication New York
Design Director Robert Newman
Designer Deanna Lowe
Photo Editors Margery Goldberg,
Sabine Meyer
Photographer Dan Chavkin
Publisher K-III Publications
Issue August 12, 1996
Category Feature Spread

■ 151
Publication New York
Design Director Robert Newman
Designer Deanna Lowe
Photo Editors Margery Goldberg,
Sabine Meyer
Photographer Norman Jean Roy
Publisher K-III Publications
Issue October 21, 1996
Category Feature Spread

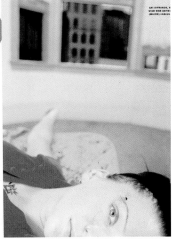

■ 152
Publication New York
Design Director Robert Newman
Art Director Deanna Lowe
Photo Editors Margery Goldberg, Nakyung Han
Publisher K-III Publications
Issue September 9, 1996
Category Feature Spread

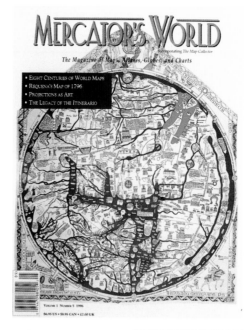

■ 153
Publication Mercator's World
Design Director Stephen Stanley
Illustrator James Carpenter
Publisher
Aster Publishing Corporation
Issue November/December 1996
Category Overall Design

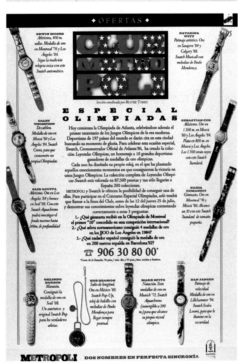

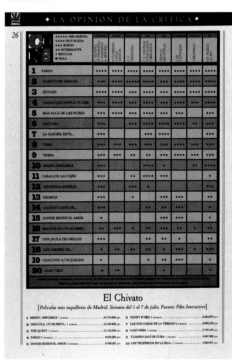

■ 154
Publication Metropoli El Mundo
Design Director Carmelo Caderot
Art Director Rodrigo Sanchez
Designers Rodrigo Sanchez, Miguel Buckenmeyer,
Maria González, Javier Sanz
Publisher Unidad Editorial S.A.
Issue May 1996
Category Redesign

■ 155
Publication Mojo
Creative Director Andy Cowles
Art Director Stephen Fawcett
Designer Stephen Fawcett
Photo Editor Susie Hudson
Photographer Richard Creamer
Publisher EMAP Metro
Issue April 1996
Category Feature Spread

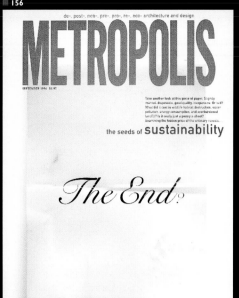

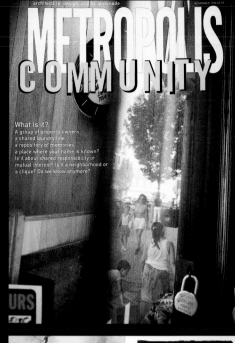

■ 156
Publication Metropolis
Art Directors Carl Lehmann-Haupt, William van Roden
Publisher Bellerophon Publishing
Issue September 1996, October 1996, November 1996
Category Overall Design

■ 157

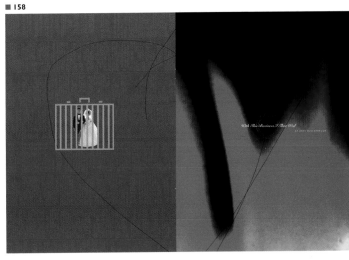

IN THE MONSOON

■ 158

■ 159

■ 160

■ 157
Publication Outside
Creative Director Susan Casey
Designer Susan Casey
Photo Editor Susan B. Smith
Photographer James Delano Whitlow
Publisher Mariah Media
Issue December 1996
Category Feature Story

■ 158
Publication Oz
Art Director Ted Fabella
Designer Ted Fabella
Studio The Office of Ted Fabella
Category Feature Spread

■ 159
Publication Private Clubs
Design Director Steve Connatser
Designer Steve Connatser
Photographer Alan Richardson
Publisher ACPI
Issue July/August 1996
Category Feature Spread

■ 160
Publication P.O.V.
Design Director Lynette Cortez
Designer Lynette Cortez
Illustrator Katherine Streeter
Publisher Byob/Freedom Ventures, Inc.
Studio Lynette Cortez Design Inc.
Issue November 1996
Category Feature Spread

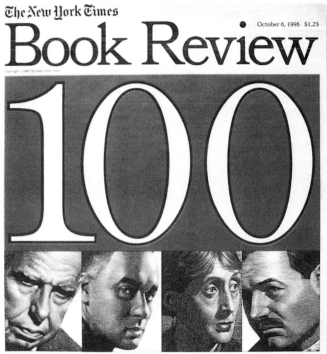

■ 161
Publication The New York Times/Book Review
Art Director Steven Heller
Illustrator Mark Summers
Publisher The New York Times
Issue October 6, 1996
Category Entire Issue

■ 162
Publication The New York Times Magazine/Men's Fashion
Art Director Michael Valenti
Photographer Phillip Dixon
Publisher The New York Times
Issue March 24, 1996
Category Entire Issue

The New York Times Magazine

APRIL 14, 1996 / SECTION 6

A CELEBRATION OF

100

ONE HUNDRED YEARS

1896 W.E.B. DU BOIS on big-city Negroes WILBUR WRIGHT on his flying machine
WINSTON CHURCHILL on hunting lions MARY LEE on Hitler's believers ANNE O'HARE MCCORMICK
on F.D.R. HAROLD DENNY on horror at Buchenwald GRANDMA MOSES on Thanksgiving
CLELLON HOLMES on the Beats GAY TALESE on Frisbees DAVID HALBERSTAM on when there
was hope in Vietnam FRANCES FITZGERALD on when there was not NEIL SHEEHAN
on Robert McNamara SYDNEY SCHANBERG on the killing fields THE TIMES CRITICS on Broadway
JAMES BALDWIN on blacks and Jews VICTOR S. NAVASKY on the Kennedys TOM WICKER
on Chicago '68 IRVING KRISTOL on the cold war RICHARD REEVES on Woodstock GLORIA STEINEM
on stockings SUSAN BROWNMILLER on sisterhood MERLE MILLER on being homosexual
JOYCE MAYNARD on being 18 J. ANTHONY LUKAS on Watergate SARA DAVIDSON on Patty Hearst
ORIANA FALLACI on Qaddafi NORMAN MAILER on Jimmy Carter ANTHONY LEWIS on apartheid
BARBARA GRIZZUTI HARRISON on Oprah NAN ROBERTSON on toxic shock THOMAS L. FRIEDMAN
on Beirut WEI JINGSHENG on Mao's China MAUREEN DOWD on Dan Quayle BILL KELLER
on glasnost HOWELL RAINES on growing up with Grady JEFFREY SCHMALZ on AIDS
MATUSCHKA on her breast JAMES GLEICK on Microsoft ROGER COHEN on Bosnia **1996**

CONTENTS, PAGE 38

The Early Years

1950's

The Newport Of Long Island

The Most Gifted Demagogue Ever

Embattled Infidel

Living With the Violence of Beirut

The New York Times Magazine

JUNE 9, 1996 / SECTION 6

A Celebration of One Hundred Years

PICTURES

1896-1996

PERILS

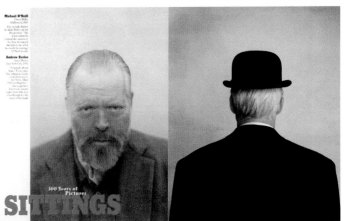

SITTINGS

■ 163
Publication The New York Times Magazine
Art Director Janet Froelich
Designer Catherine Gilmore-Barnes
Photo Editor Kathy Ryan
Publisher The New York Times
Issue April 14, 1996
Category Entire Issue

■ 164
Publication The New York Times Magazine
Art Director Janet Froelich
Designer Joel Cuyler
Photo Editor Kathy Ryan
Publisher The New York Times
Issue June 9, 1996
Category Entire Issue

DESIGN ENTIRE ISSUES & FEATURES ■ MERIT

165
Publication The New York Times Magazine
Art Director Janet Froelich
Designer Nancy Harris
Photo Editor Kathy Ryan
Publisher The New York Times
Issue June 23, 1996
Category Entire Issue

166
Publication The New York Times Magazine
Art Director Janet Froelich
Designer Joel Cuyler
Photo Editor Kathy Ryan
Publisher The New York Times
Issue November 24, 1996
Category Entire Issue

A DIGITAL SALON

A CALL FOR ENTRIES

An exhibit of all media using the newest digital technology

*Photography   ***Computer generated imagery**

*Modeling and Rendering   ***Animation**

An exhibit at the **High Road Gallery,** 12 E Stafford Ave. in Worthington, Ohio

Show dates: January 8 to January 29
Take in: January 6, 6-8 PM at High Road Gallery
Opening reception: Sunday, January 9, 2-4 PM 2005
Take down: January 29, 4-6 PM

To submit images for consideration: Each artist may submit up to five works for consideration and at least two will be selected to be displayed. Artists must live in Ohio. Send contact sheets, slides, or prints to Randy Jones, Digital Salon, High Road Gallery, 12 E Stafford Ave, Worthington, OH 43085. Please include the entry form below, and a $15.00 entry fee made out to High Road Gallery. All entries will be returned. Deadline for submission is November 15, 2004. A juror will select awards to be given at the opening reception. Questions may be directed to Randy Jones, chairman, 486-5105.

The gallery asks exhibiting artists to volunteer one day during open hours of the exhibit to help staff the gallery. Artists will contribute light food for the opening reception. The gallery takes a 10 percent commission on sales.

Pieces included in the show must be framed for hanging with wire and glass or plexi, no sawtooth. No work shown previously at High Road is acceptable, and all work should be for sale. Artists are asked to insure their own works.

---detach---

Artist name_____   email_____

Address_____   phone_____

_____

_____

_____

■ 167
Publication The New York Times Magazine
Art Director Janet Froelich
Designer Nancy Harris
Stylist Franciscus Ankoné
Photographer Serge Lutens
Publisher The New York Times
Issue October 6, 1996
Category Feature Story

■ 168
Publication The New York Times Magazine
Art Director Janet Froelich
Designer Julie Weiss
Stylist Franciscus Ankoné
Photographer Dominique Isserman
Publisher The New York Times
Issue November 10, 1996
Category Feature Story

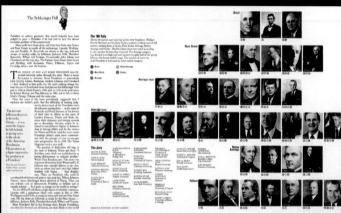

169
Publication The New York Times Magazine
Art Director Janet Froelich
Designers Lisa Naftolin, Susan Dazzo
Illustrator Daniel Adel
Publisher The New York Times
Issue December 15, 1996
Category Feature Story

170
Publication The New York Times Magazine
Art Director Janet Froelich
Designer Nancy Harris
Photo Editor Kathy Ryan
Photographers Rimma Gerlovina, Valeriy Gerlovin
Publisher The New York Times
Issue July 7, 1996
Category Feature Story

■ 171

On one side of the battle over rap:
Bob Dole and the cultural right.

On the other: a record mogul from
South-Central Los Angeles who
takes winning very, very seriously.

Does a SugarBear Bite?

SUGE KNIGHT AND HIS POSSE

By Lynn Hirschberg

■ 173

Some arresting developments in swimwear.

Photographs by Enrique Badulescu
Styled by Elizabeth Stewart

In the Tank

■ 172

Artist and Animal

Female wrestlers, coming on strong.

Photographs by Kurt Markus. Text by Mary Martin.

■ 173
Publication The New York Times Magazine
Art Director Janet Froelich
Designer Janet Froelich
Stylist Elizabeth Stewart
Photographer Enrique Badulescu
Publisher The New York Times
Issue May 5, 1996
Category Feature Story

■ 171
Publication The New York Times Magazine
Art Director Janet Froelich
Designer Joel Cuyler, Lisa Naftolin
Photo Editor Kathy Ryan
Photographer Michael O'Neill
Publisher The New York Times
Issue January 14, 1996
Category Feature Spread

■ 172
Publication The New York Times Magazine
Art Director Janet Froelich
Designer Joel Cuyler
Photo Editor Kathy Ryan
Photographer Kurt Markus
Publisher The New York Times
Issue March 3, 1996
Category Feature Story

true colors

translucent reds and subtle apricots

true colors

true colors

african violet and fuchsia tones

■ 175
Publication Salon News
Creative Director Victoria Maddocks
Design Director Jean Griffin
Designer Victoria Maddocks
Photographer Paul Sunday
Publisher Fairchild Publications
Issue May 1996
Category Feature Story

■ 174
Publication The New York Times Magazine
Art Director Janet Froelich
Designer Joel Cuyler
Stylist Franciscus Ankoné
Photographer Javier Vallhonrat
Publisher The New York Times
Issue April 21, 1996
Category Feature Story

■ 176

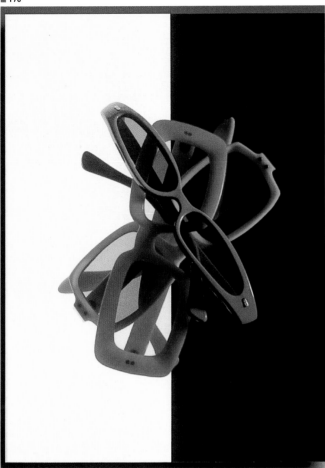

■ 178

■ 177

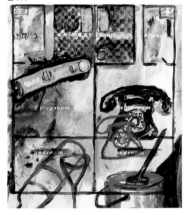

BOUND

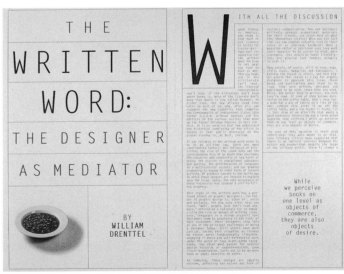

■ 176
Publication Strobe
Creative Director Cheryl Heller
Design Director Carole Freehauf
Designer Veronica Oh
Photographers Geof Kern, Michael Lewis,
Judith Joy Ross, P. L. de Corcia,
Francois Robert, Christian Witkin
Publisher S.D. Warren
Studio Siegel & Gale
Client S.D. Warren
Issue October 1996
Category Entire Issue

■ 177
Publication Scenario
Creative Director Andrew Kner
Designer Andrew Kner
Illustrator Karen Caldicott
Publisher RC Publishing
Issue September 1996
Category Feature Spread

■ 178
Publication Speaking Volumes
The World of the Book:
Mohawk Rethinking Design #3
Designers Michael Bierut, Lisa Anderson
Publisher Mohawk Paper Mills, Inc.
Studio Pentagram Design, Inc.
Client Mohawk Paper Mills, Inc.
Issue December 1996
Category Entire Issue

SURVIVAL
OF THE FITTEST
RAPID ADAP
TATION IS THE KEY
IN THE TO EVOLUTION
INFORMATION AGE

THE CUSTOMER IS

King

Jefferson Airplane were America's greatest and most idiosyncratically unique rock band. From late 1966 to 1970 – roughly from *Surrealistic Pillow* to Marty Balin's decision to leave the band that was his brainchild – the Airplane were an unstoppable machine, idolized by fans, respected by peers and critics as the purest distillation of San Francisco's rock aesthetic, and were allowed their eccentricities by their blue-chip record label, RCA Victor, because they sold vast amounts of records.

For five albums – *Surrealistic Pillow, After Bathing at Baxter's, Crown of Creation, Bless Its Pointed Little Head* and *Volunteers* – the

jefferson airplane

the shirelles

■ 179
Publication Profit
Creative Director Bill Cahan
Designer Kevin Roberson
Illustrators Bob Dinetz, Coco Masuda
Photographers Robert Schlatter, Tony Stromberg, Douglas Bros.
Studio Cahan & Associates
Client Oracle Corp.
Issue September 1996
Category Entire Issue

■ 180
Publication Rock & Roll Hall of Fame 1996
Creative Director Terry Koppel
Designer Terry Koppel
Photo Editor Danny Fields
Publisher The Rock & Roll Hall of Fame
Studio Terry Koppel Design
Issue January 17, 1996
Category Entire Issue

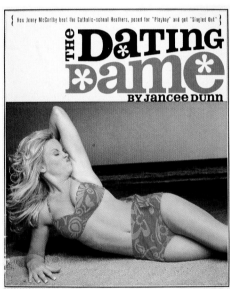

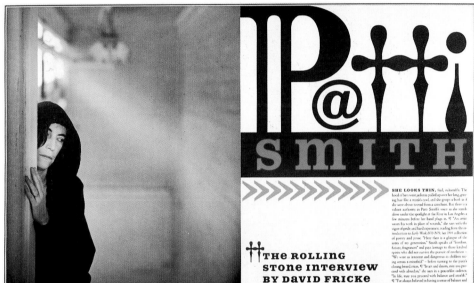

■ 181
Publication Rolling Stone
Creative Director Fred Woodward
Designers Fred Woodward, Gail Anderson, Lee Bearson,
Geraldine Hessler, Eric Siry
Photo Editors Jodi Peckman, Fiona McDonagh
Publisher Wenner Media
Issue October 17, 1996, July 11, 1996, December 26, 1996
Category Overall Design

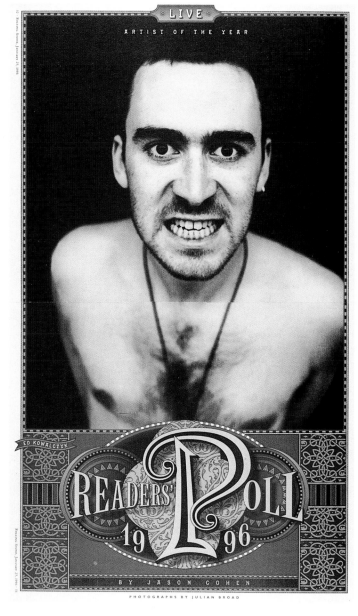

LIVE

ARTIST OF THE YEAR

ED KOWALCZYK

READERS' POLL 1996

BY JASON COHEN

PHOTOGRAPHS BY JULIAN BROAD

FAMOUS BY ASSOCIATION

VIC CHESNUTT

...HIS ROCK & ROLL HEROES IN THE SPOTLIGHT YOU...

BY MARY ELLEN MARK

BY MARK KEMP

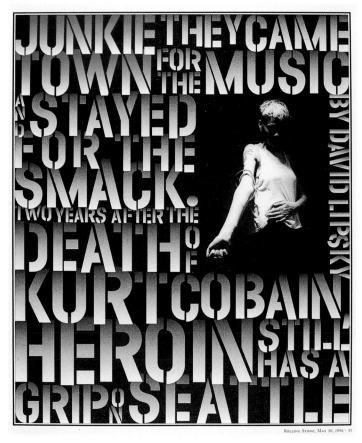

JUNKIE TOWN AND STAYED FOR THE SMACK. THEY CAME FOR THE MUSIC TWO YEARS AFTER THE DEATH OF KURT COBAIN, HEROIN STILL HAS A GRIP ON SEATTLE BY DAVID LIPSKY

ROLLING STONE, MAY 30, 1996 · 35

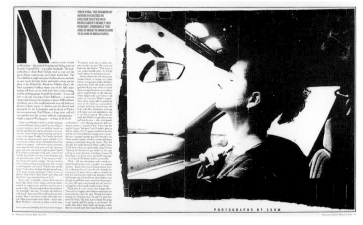

N

PHOTOGRAPHS BY EXUM

"SEATTLE IS JUST A VERY JUNKIE-FRIENDLY PLACE," SAYS ONE YOUNG HEROIN USER. "HERE, THERE'S ALMOST NO REASON NOT TO USE."

■ 182
Publication Rolling Stone
Creative Director Fred Woodward
Designer Lee Bearson
Photo Editor Jodi Peckman
Photographer Julian Broad
Publisher Wenner Media
Issue January 25, 1996
Category Feature Spread

■ 183
Publication Rolling Stone
Creative Director Fred Woodward
Designers Lee Bearson,
Fred Woodward
Photo Editor Jodi Peckman
Photographer Mary Ellen Mark
Publisher Wenner Media
Issue September 19, 1996
Category Feature Spread

■ 184
Publication Rolling Stone
Creative Director Fred Woodward
Designer Gail Anderson
Photo Editor Jodi Peckman
Photographer Exum
Publisher Wenner Media
Issue May 30, 1996
Category Feature Story

■ 185

LEADERS OF THE NEW COOL

BY ALEC FOEGE

"OH, MY GOODNESS, ROY ROGERS IS GONE!" ✤ So exclaims Lauryn Hill as she swerves around a familiar corner near her suburban New Jersey neighborhood. It's a sultry night in July, and the Fugees' singer is driving me back from Sony Music Studios, in midtown Manhattan, in her mom's wheels, a brand-new sport utility vehicle with all the add-ons. The recent disappearance of a local landmark like the boarded-up fast-food emporium is yet one more reminder that life for Hill has been moving ahead at warp speed. ✤ "We used to be No. 10, now we perma-

FROM LEFT:
PRAKAZREL
MICHEL,
LAURYN HILL,
WYCLEF JEAN

PHOTOGRAPHS BY MATTHEW ROLSTON

ROLLING STONE, SEPTEMBER 7, 1996 · 4?

■ 185

Publication Rolling Stone
Creative Director Fred Woodward
Designer Fred Woodward
Photo Editor Jodi Peckman
Photographer Matthew Rolston
Publisher Wenner Media
Issue September 5, 1996
Category Feature Spread

■ 186

RUSSIAN ROULETTE

apart as Patti Smith albums. The endless apartment blocks seemed blacked out. Could it be that no one lived in Russia? Or was there just not much living to be done? Red Square was shadowy. The Kremlin was dim. The river was an opaque trough beneath dismal bridges. The U.S.S.R. was very dark, considering it was still daytime.

»»»»»» I came to Russia for the first time in July 1982, arriving at the twilight of the Brezhnev era and also, literally, at twilight. Dusk is prolonged and shining in midsummer at 55 degrees of latitude, but nothing shone in Moscow. Storefronts weren't lit, and there were very few storefronts. No headlights were visible. More to the point, no cars were. The city had streetlamps, but as far

THE NEW RUSSIA HAS CAPITALISM, GANGS, BIG MACS AND NOW THE FIRST-FREE PRESIDENTIAL ELECTIONS IN ITS 1,100-YEAR HISTORY. IF ONLY THE VOTERS HAD FOUND A CANDIDATE THEY LIKED

ROURKE

■ 186

Publication Rolling Stone
Creative Director Fred Woodward
Designer Geraldine Hessler
Publisher Wenner Media
Issue September 19, 1996
Category Feature Single Page

■ 187

KIND OF BLUE

by LORRAINE ALI

Photograph by JON RAGEL

■ 187

Publication Rolling Stone
Creative Director Fred Woodward
Designers Fred Woodward,
Geraldine Hessler
Photo Editor Jodi Peckman
Photographer Jon Ragel
Publisher Wenner Media
Issue October 3, 1996
Category Feature Spread

■ 188

COOL JERK

SEAN PENN

by CHRIS MUNDY

■ 188

Publication Rolling Stone
Creative Director Fred Woodward
Designers Gail Anderson,
Fred Woodward
Photo Editor Jodi Peckman
Photographer Mark Seliger
Publisher Wenner Media
Issue April 4, 1996
Category Feature Spread

189
Publication Rolling Stone
Creative Director Fred Woodward
Designers Fred Woodward,
Geraldine Hessler
Photo Editor Jodi Peckman
Photographer Anton Corbijn
Publisher Wenner Media
Issue October 17, 1996
Category Feature Spread

190
Publication Rolling Stone
Creative Director Fred Woodward
Designers Fred Woodward,
Gail Anderson
Photo Editor Jodi Peckman
Photographer Albert Watson
Publisher Wenner Media
Issue October 17, 1996
Category Feature Spread

191
Publication Rolling Stone
Creative Director Fred Woodward
Designers Fred Woodward,
Gail Anderson
Illustrator Al Hirschfeld
Publisher Wenner Media
Issue November 14, 1996
Category Feature Spread

192
Publication Rolling Stone
Creative Director Fred Woodward
Designer Lee Bearson
Illustrator Istvan Banyai
Publisher Wenner Media
Issue November 14, 1996
Category Feature Spread

193
Publication Rolling Stone
Creative Director Fred Woodward
Designer Geraldine Hessler
Photo Editor Jodi Peckman
Photographer Nitin Vadukul
Publisher Wenner Media
Issue December 1996/January 1997
Category Feature Single Page

LEGENDS OF COUNTRY MUSIC

PORTFOLIO BY MARK SELIGER

■ 194

Publication Rolling Stone
Creative Director Fred Woodward
Designers Fred Woodward, Gail Anderson
Photo Editor Jodi Peckman
Photographer Mark Seliger
Publisher Wenner Media
Issue December 1996/January 1997
Category Feature Story
　　■ **A** Feature Spread

■ 195

■ 196

■ 197

■ 198

■ 195
Publication Rolling Stone
Creative Director Fred Woodward
Designer Geraldine Hessler
Publisher Wenner Media
Issue June 13, 1996
Category Department

■ 196
Publication Rolling Stone
Creative Director Fred Woodward
Designer Gail Anderson
Illustrator James Pendergrast
Publisher Wenner Media
Issue December 1996/January 1997
Category Department

■ 197
Publication Rolling Stone
Creative Director Fred Woodward
Designer Gail Anderson
Photo Editor Jodi Peckman
Publisher Wenner Media
Issue December 1996/January 1997
Category Department

■ 198
Publication Rolling Stone
Creative Director Fred Woodward
Designer Lee Bearson
Illustrator C.F. Payne
Publisher Wenner Media
Issue October 3, 1996
Category Department

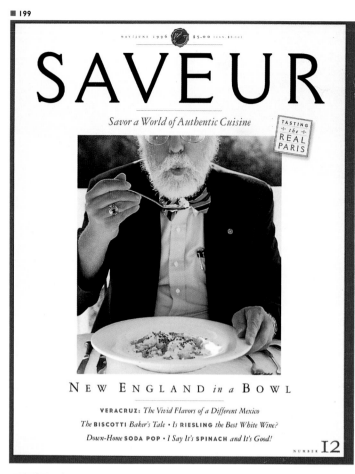

■ 199
Publication Saveur
Creative Director Michael Grossman
Art Director Jill Armus
Designers Jill Armus, Toby Fox
Photo Editor Susan Goldberger
Publisher Meigher Communications
Issue February/March 1996, March/April 1996, May/June 1996
Category Overall Design

MEMPHIS TRADITIONS RUN DEEP AND
TRUE, IN COOKING AS IN THE BLUES

THE BELLY OF SOUL

BY MARY ANN EAGLE • PHOTOGRAPHS BY BEN FINK

MEMPHIS SOUL FOOD

SECRET RECIPES *are
passed down in Memphis
like a dead man's legacy*

MEMPHIS SOUL FOOD

ITS USED *by slaves to
roast leftovers were the
first Memphis barbecues*

COOKING FROM A LOST EGYPT

*A New York food authority rediscovers
the flavors of her exotic Cairo childhood*

BY COLETTE ROSSANT • PHOTOGRAPHS BY TRIA GIOVAN

*Grandmothers
made daily trips
to the dusty and
bustling market
to handpick the
best ingredients*

*Farmas road
my sweet
potatoes in coffee
grounds, as I
listened and ate
scalant cookies*

■ 200

Publication Saveur
Creative Director Michael Grossman
Art Director Jill Armus
Designer Jill Armus
Photo Editor Susan Goldberger
Photographer Ben Fink
Publisher Meigher Communications
Issue March/April 1996
Category Feature Story

■ 201

Publication Saveur
Creative Director Michael Grossman
Art Director Jill Armus
Designer Jill Armus
Photo Editor Susan Goldberger
Photographers Tria Giovan, Henri Cartier-Bresson
Publisher Meigher Communications
Issue November/December 1996
Category Feature Story

Makeover Mania

A MASSIVE MOVEMENT OF PLAYERS DURING
THE OFF-SEASON HAS RESULTED IN SOME
STARTLING FACE-LIFTS FOR SEVERAL TEAMS

BY TIM CROTHERS

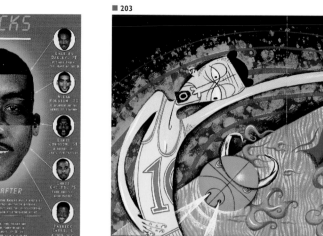

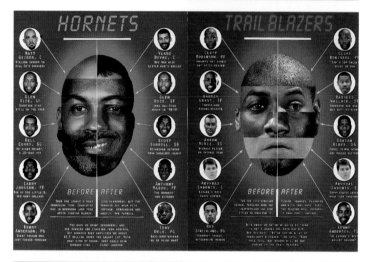

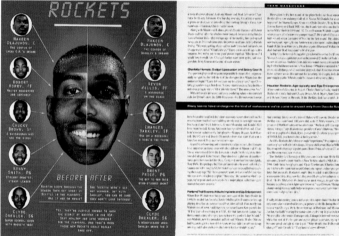

Olé!

THEY CALL THEM MATADORS: THE BAD DEFENDERS WHO PLAY THEIR MEN JUST AS THEY WOULD A CHARGING BULL. BY JACK McCALLUM

■ 202
Publication Sports Illustrated Presents
Design Director F. Darrin Perry
Art Directors Luis Grullon, Michael Schinnerer
Designer Bruce Glase
Photo Editor Jeffrey Weig
Publisher Time Inc.
Issue October 1996
Category Feature Story

■ 203
Publication Sports Illustrated Presents
Design Director F. Darrin Perry
Art Directors Luis Grullon, Michael Schinnerer
Designer Bruce Glase
Illustrator Chris Pyle
Photo Editor Jeffrey Weig
Publisher Time Inc.
Issue October 1996
Category Feature Story

■ 204

SWM, tall, handsome, 29, professional football player, seeks beautiful,. intelligent young woman to help design dream house and create family equivalent of America's Team. Must like quiet evenings at home, either cruising America Online or admiring tropical fish tank. Must spend Sundays in crowded stadiums rooting for Dallas Cowboys. Dislike of 49ers and Redskins a plus, but not required.

■ 205

singin' the blue

IF BOXING HAS A SOUL, IT MAY RESIDE IN A PLACE THAT'S A THROWBACK TO THE DAYS OF SMOKY CLUBS AND FRIDAY-NIGHT FIGHTS: PHILADELPHIA'S BLUE HORIZON

BY BILL BARICH / PHOTOGRAPHS BY ANTONIN KRATOCHVIL

■ 206

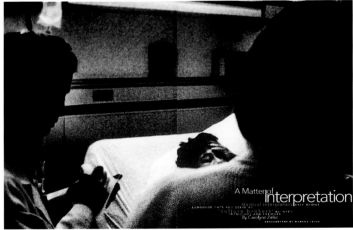

A Matter of Interpretation

■ 207

that old COLLEGE TRY

a heir-raising DILEMMA

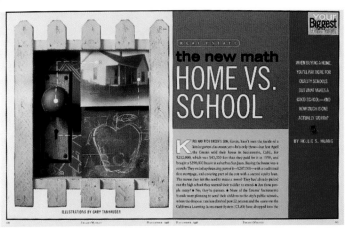

the new math HOME VS. SCHOOL

■ 204
Publication Sports Illustrated
Design Director Steven Hoffman
Art Director Craig Gartner
Publisher Time Inc.
Issue January 15, 1996
Category Feature Spread

■ 205
Publication Sports Illustrated
Design Director Steven Hoffman
Art Director Catherine Gillespie
Publisher Time Inc.
Issue December 9, 1996
Category Feature Spread

■ 206
Publication Stanford Medicine
Art Director David Armario
Designer David Armario
Photographer Marcus Lusan
Publisher Stanford Medicine
Issue Fall 1996
Category Feature Spread

■ 207
Publication Smart Money
Art Director Amy Rosenfeld
Designers Amy Rosenfeld, Donna Agajanian, Robin Terra, Julie Lazarus, Doris Downes Jewett
Illustrators Brian Cairns, Gary Baseman, Gary Tanhauser
Photo Editors Jane Clark, Heidi Yockey
Photographers Len Irish, Kevin Irby
Publisher Dow Jones & Hearst Corp.
Issue December 1996
Category Entire Issue

93

Model

Moral?

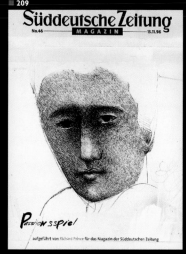

Passionsspiel

aufgeführt von Richard Prince für das Magazin der Süddeutschen Zeitung

■ 208
Publication
Sueddeutsche Zeitung Magazin
Art Director Markus Rasp
Designers Anne Blaschke, Otto Dzemla, Wilhelm Raffelsberger
Photographers Norbert Schoerner, Johannes Muggenthaler, David LaChapelle, Juergen Teller
Publisher Magazin Verlagsges. Sueddeutsche Zeitung mbh
Issue March 15, 1996
Category Entire Issue

■ 209
Publication
Sueddeutsche Zeitung Magazin
Art Director Markus Rasp
Designers Anne Blaschke, Otto Dzemla, Wilhelm Raffelsberger, Richard Prince
Photo Editors Eva Ernst, Claudia Mueller
Publisher Magazin Verlagsges. Sueddeutsche Zeitung mbh
Issue November 15, 1996
Category Entire Issue

das Glück, nicht ich sein zu.. müssen

Ein Gespräch mit dem slowenischen Philosophen und Psychoanalytiker Slavoj Zizek über Mode. Fünf Thesen hat der Photograph Schoerner in Bilder umgesetzt.

»Vielleicht sind die Frivolität der Mode und ihr konstanter Wechsel in die menschliche Natur eingeschrieben.«

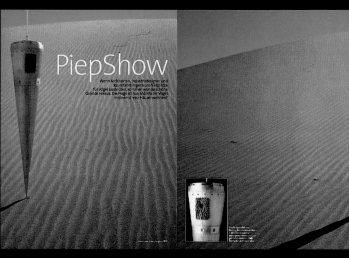

Scheingefechte

Der Soldat ist doch noch Vorbild. Seine Uniform inspiriert ... die Modedesigner.

PiepShow

Wenn Architekten, Industriedesigner und Raumfahrtingenieure Nistplätze für Vögel ausbrüten, kommen wunderschöne Gebilde heraus. Die Frage ist nun: Möchte Ihr Vogel in einem dieser Häuser wohnen?

»Ich werde einfach immer schöner«

Pamela Anderson über plastische Chirurgie, Sex-Appeal und Diamanten.

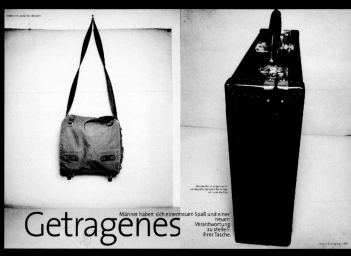

Männer haben sich einen neuen Spaß und einer neuen Verantwortung zu stellen: ihrer Tasche.

Getragenes

do it
yourself

FRAGILE

XULY.BËT

Designer T-Shirts sind unverschämt teuer. Aber nicht für die Leser des SZ-Magazins. Exklusiv für Sie entwarfen berühmte Modemacher Vorlagen, die man sich auf's weiße T-Shirt drucken lassen kann – im nächsten Copy-Shop.

CORINNE COBSON

BOGNER

JEAN COLONNA

GIORGIO ARMANI

JIL SANDER

KARL LAGERFELD

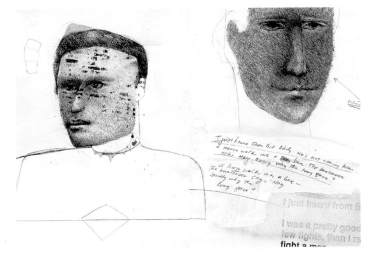

DESIGN ENTIRE ISSUES & FEATURES ■ MERIT

■ 210
Publication Sueddeutsche Zeitung Magazin
Art Director Markus Rasp
Designers Anne Blaschke, Otto Dzemla, Wilhelm Raffelsberger
Illustrators Xuly Bët, Corinne Cobson, Willy Bogner, Martin Margiela, Donna Karan, Jil Sander, Karl Lagerfeld, Jean Colonna, Giorgio Armani
Photo Editors Eva Ernst, Claudia Mueller
Publisher Magazin Verlagsges. Sueddeutsche Zeitung mbh
Issue June 28, 1996
Category Feature Story

■ 211
Publication Sueddeutsche Zeitung Magazin
Art Director Markus Rasp
Designer Richard Prince
Photo Editors Eva Ernst, Claudia Mueller
Publisher Magazin Verlagsges. Sueddeutsche Zeitung mbh
Issue November 15, 1996
Category Feature Story

This Old House

JANUARY/FEBRUARY 1996

pullout guide to **Savannah,** site of the **Spring TV Project**

PLUS: Hammers, Heating and Insulation, Sanders, Driveways, Phone Wiring, Cedar Clapboard

USA $3.50 CANADA $4.50

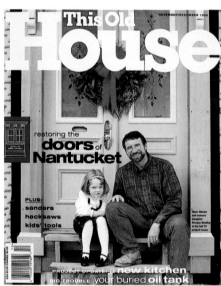

This Old House

NOVEMBER/DECEMBER 1996

restoring the **doors of Nantucket**

PLUS: sanders hacksaws kids' tools

PROJECT UPDATE: a **new kitchen**

BIG TROUBLE: your buried **oil tank**

This Old House

MAY/JUNE 1996

Secrets of a **brick pathway**

A perfect **treehouse** for kids

Steve Thomas takes the measure of the **Savannah project**

USA $3.50 CANADA $4.50

Publication This Old House
Design Director Matthew Drace
Art Director Timothy Jones
Designers Diana Haas, Marcus Villaca
Publisher Time Inc.
Issue May/June 1996, Nov./Dec. 1996, Jan./Feb. 1996
Category Overall Design

cedar siding

From the forest through the mill

By Thomas Baker
Photographs by Pete Eckert

Publication This Old House
Design Director Matthew Drace
Art Director Timothy Jones
Designers Diana Haas, Marcus Villaca
Publisher Time Inc.
Issue January/February 1996
Category Entire Issue

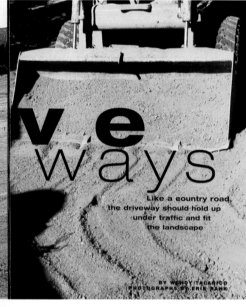

Driveways

Like a country road, the driveway should hold up under traffic and fit the landscape

BY WENDY TALARICO
PHOTOGRAPHS BY ERIK RANK

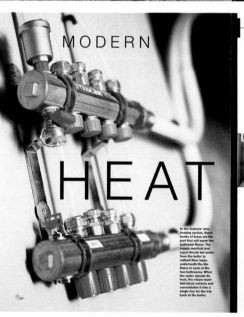

MODERN HEAT

THE WAY PLUMBING and heating expert Richard Trethewey sees it, most of America's home-heating systems are oversized reproductions of technology that's half a century old. "For decades, we've been sizing systems to handle what's called the 'design temperature,' then adding 20 to 100 percent more capacity on top of that," he says. "The design temperature for Boston is minus 10 degrees, but it's only that cold less than 1 percent of the time. The rest of the time, you've got boilers and furnaces running at maximum output to meet much lower heat requirements. That's like running your car with the pedal down and constantly fitting the brakes!"

Richard has a few other peeves about the way homes are heated and cooled,

The two Richards, Trethewey and Bile, ready the new microprocessor-controlled boiler for Drive functions: warm air, warm floors and hot water.

but he can also point to readily available solutions. Many are included in the new systems at 124 Federal. For example, an exterior temperature sensor raises and lowers the water temperature in the boiler, and the hot water is continuously circulated—not started and stopped—to provide just the right amount of heat and greater comfort. "For every three degrees you lower the boiler water temperature, you burn 1 percent less fuel," says Richard. "If the average temperature is 150 instead of 210, that's a 20 percent savings right there." Better controls like this, he says, are "the next quantum leap in energy efficiency."

HEATING: SOMETHING OLD, SOMETHING NEW

Illustrations by Brian Garrigan

This Old Furnace
Before the Guinzes bought it, the house on Federal Street was hardly heated at all, and what heat there was was limited to a first-floor bathroom... forced-air system powered by a gas-fired furnace...

High-Velocity Heat
Compared with the old furnace, the new heating system seems positively state-of-the-art...

Warm Floors, Hot Showers
In the second-floor bathrooms, the heating is directly underfoot, thanks to a radiant-floor system...

Today's Homeowner

Expert Advice On Improving Your Home

November 1996

Overcoming The Blues
Simple Tips On Reading Plans

Hot Shower Controls

Work-Saving Yard Tools

FIRST FLOOR PLAN

■ 214
Publication Today's Homeowner
Design Director Murray Greenfield
Designers Milton Glaser,
Walter Bernard
Publisher Times Mirror Magazines
Issue November 1996
Category Redesign

Overcoming The Blues

A homeowner's guide to understanding blueprint basics. by Paul J. Donio

EXISTING KITCHEN

EXISTING DINING

LINE UP WALLS

homeowner's digest

Fast And Loose Flooring

REDUCE YOUR Payments

money matters

HOUSE POLITICS

HAVE IT THREE WAYS

technology

LEAD ALERT

November 1996

An expert's notes on choosing the best hand tools for working around your yard.
by Lynn Ocone

TOOLING UP

KIDS' STUFF

WHAT IS THE LATEST IN CHILDREN'S PROGRAMS? LOTS OF NEW TITLES FOR GIRLS, MORE MATH AND EVEN THE CHANCE TO SAVE THE EARTH FROM A WAYWARD COMET.

THE YEAR IN SOFTWARE

BY B. J. SIGESMUND

A YEAR AGO, ANY PARENT WOULD HAVE SAID THAT THE MOST FAMOUS character in his kid's CD-ROM library was Carmen Sandiego or a tiny, talkative car named Putt-Putt. But these days, parents might feel like they've been plopped smack into the middle of their child's video collection. Or toy box.

The best-selling new titles are the Walt Disney Co.'s stars, ranging from Pocahontas and Winnie the Pooh to the gang from "Toy Story." (Disney Interactive's Animated StoryBook Toy Story sold a whopping 270,000 copies in the eight-month period that ended in August.) Even Barbie and the Fox network's Simpsons are in the CD-ROM business.

The scramble to recruit recognizable characters is an outgrowth of the frenetic competition among software developers. But parents worried about their children's being exposed to a computer version of the Cartoon Network should rest easy. There are a number of encouraging trends. For example: there are more titles for girls, better and more

EDITORS' CHOICE

HERE ARE THE BEST NEW KIDS' CD-ROMS FROM MASTERPIECE MANSION AND THE LAND BEFORE TIME TO DRACULA'S SECRET

OUR TOP FIFTY

THE NEWSWEEK editors' choice selection begins when software publishers nominate their best titles—this year, a total of more than 400 CD-ROMs. The nominees fall into six categories: Adventure (educational games and mysteries), Creativity (writing, painting and music via computer), Learning (drills and lessons in particular areas), Problem Solving (spatial relationships and memory), Reading (storybooks, early alphabet

EDUCATION

THEY'LL NEVER REPLACE DEDICATED TEACHERS, BUT UNDER THE RIGHT CONDITIONS PERSONAL COMPUTERS CAN BECOME EXTREMELY VALUABLE CLASSROOM TOOLS

TO THE HEAD OF THE CLASS

BY BARBARA KANTROWITZ

FARHIA HERSI'S TINY FINGERS TAP OUT COMPUTER CODE. MAGICALLY, A CIRcle and then a square appear on the screen in front of her. All around 5-year-old Farhia, third graders at the Gwendolyn Powell Brown Computer School in Harlem are creating their own multicolor designs: stars, flowers, even what looks like a butterfly. The director of the school, Donna Brewster, likes to joke that some of the computers—mostly vintage Apples and Ataris—are older than the kids. But few of these students have a computer at home; without the school, they would never get near a keyboard. They're happy just to get a chance to learn—no matter how ancient the equipment. And Farhia and her classmates have all got the message: the future is digital, and they want to be part of it.

Few people would question why older kids need computers. But what about preschoolers and children in early elementary grades? Many of these youngsters haven't

■ 215
Publication Newsweek: Computers & The Family
Art Director Miriam Campiz
Designer Miriam Campiz
Illustrators Nickelodeon, Paul Corio, Gary Panter, Edward Fatheringham, Carol Lay, Chris Pyle
Photo Editor Jessica De Witt
Photographers George Lange, Bart Nagel, Carrie Boretz, Joseph Pluchino, John Eder, John Wilkes, Andrew Brusso
Publisher Newsweek
Studio M. Campiz Design
Issue Fall 1996
Category Overall Design

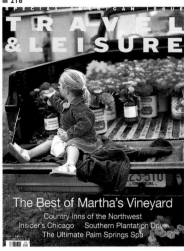

SPECIAL AMERICAN ISSUE
TRAVEL & LEISURE

The Best of Martha's Vineyard
Country Inns of the Northwest
Insider's Chicago   Southern Plantation Drive
The Ultimate Palm Springs Spa

Springtime in Acadiana
A car, some friends, a bevy of plantation houses: the ultimate Louisiana drive. **By Brooke Hayward** Photographed by Simon Watson

■ 216
Publication Travel & Leisure
Design Director Pamela Berry
Designers Pamela Berry,
Gaemer Gutierrez, Daniel Josephs
Photo Editors
Jim Franco, Fran Gealer
Photographers Christopher Baker,
Simon Watson, Eika Aoshima,
Stewart Ferebee, Ken Kochey
Publisher American Express Publishing
Issue April 1996
Category Entire Issue

Parlange lacks one treasure it could have claimed: the 1884 John Singer Sargent portrait of 'Madame X.' Its subject was born on the plantation

chicago
special three-part report
the many sides of the second city: james atlas returns to a changed hometown • how to get the most out of a long weekend • west town, the next great neighborhood

SURPRISE: WHERE TO FIND GREAT AMERICAN FOOD
TRAVEL & LEISURE

taking the plunge in Bonaire

Hidden Pleasures in the Italian Alps
New York Now: SoHo à Go-Go
One Family's Trip Around the World

shops restaurants bars galleries markets hotels

soho: what's new now

■ 217
Publication Travel & Leisure
Design Director Pamela Berry
Designers Pamela Berry, Dina White,
Daniel Josephs
Photo Editors Jim Franco, Fran Gealer
Photographers Daniella Stallinger,
Stewart Shining, Steven Sebring,
Gentl & Hyers, Luca Trovato
Publisher American Express Publishing
Issue November 1996
Category Entire Issue

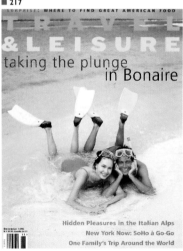

Way Beyond Black

party dresses   noble trains   steak birdcages   hottest pin

easing into east africa

EIGHT FAMILY-STYLE GUESTHOUSES THAT EMBRACE
THE LANDSCAPE OF KENYA AND TANZANIA BY JOHN HEMINWAY
PHOTOGRAPHED BY GENTL & HYERS

TRAVEL & LEISURE
a country holiday in Scotland

Jamaica's
Undiscovered
Shore

The Best of
Aspen, On and
Off the Slopes

Love Affair
with Buenos Aires

Tango
Argentino

Listening to the rhythms of
Buenos Aires, a city of opera
and soccer, psychotherapy and
the occult, Borges and Eva
Perón • By Gabriella De Ferrari
Photographed by Daniela Stallinger

Best of ASPEN

■ 218
Publication Travel & Leisure
Design Director Pamela Berry
Designers Pamela Berry,
Dina White, Daniel Josephs
Photo Editors Jim Franco,
Fran Gealer, Katie Dunn
Photographers Simon Watson,
Eika Aoshima, Daniella Stallinger
Publisher American Express Publishing
Issue December 1996
Category Entire Issue

And God Created
Hawaii

Stephen Drucker discovers
the best of the Big Island

Photographed by Gentl & Hyers

■ 219
Publication Travel & Leisure
Design Director Pamela Berry
Designer Gaemer Gutierrez
Photo Editor Jim Franco
Photographer Gentl & Hyers
Publisher American Express Publishing
Issue January 1996
Category Feature Single Page Spread

catching the current in amsterdam

gabriella de ferrari

follows the canals and cobbled walkways of the old world's most enduring city

photographed by john huba

THE ART OF
EATING WELL IN VENICE

FORGET WHAT THEY TOLD YOU:
A SUPERB MEAL CAN BE HAD, AND YOU DON'T HAVE TO STORM A COMPANY.

YOU JUST HAVE TO KNOW WHERE

BY PAUL LEVY. PHOTOGRAPHED BY SIMON WATSON

because they couldn't build upward, dutch architects instead mirrored their creations in the waters of the canals. the town appears to be standing not on the earth but on its own reflection

VENETIANS DO DINE WELL AT HOME—AND NOT JUST ON FISH—BUT SURPRISINGLY FEW RESTAURANTS HERE SERVE THE TRUE LOCAL SPECIALTIES. THOSE THAT DO ARE COVETED BY VISITORS LUCKY ENOUGH TO HAVE FOUND THEM.

the warm sound of amsterdam's many carillons keeps me company as i scan the skyline. on any street a house with simple straight lines may sit next to one with trapezoidal gables, while another as decorative as a wedding cake proudly perches near a postmodern apparition

AFTER A VISIT TO THE ACCADEMIA AND A CANAL-SIDE LUNCH AT RISTORANTE RIVIERA, STROLL OVER TO NICO'S FOR THE FINEST GELATI IN TOWN—THEN CROSS THE CANAL AND LINGER UNTIL TWILIGHT AT ONE OF PIAZZA SAN MARCO'S CAFÉS

■ 220

Publication Travel & Leisure
Design Director Pamela Berry
Designer Pamela Berry
Photo Editor Jim Franco
Photographer John Huba
Publisher American Express Publishing
Issue February 1996
Category Feature Story

■ 221

Publication Travel & Leisure
Design Director Pamela Berry
Designer Pamela Berry
Photo Editor Jim Franco
Photographer Simon Watson
Publisher American Express Publishing
Issue May 1996
Category Feature Story

Beyond the sober façade is a surprisingly
seductive
city so why is
zurich
so misunderstood?

by john russell   photographed by luca travato

HOW TO AFFORD
LONDON

BY NATE KOECHLEY

zurich
has no "beautiful people,"
and it has no
conspicuous
people, either

Hotels

a

down by the
lake
is a bathing place which
in high summer turns into
a subdepartment of tahiti

ten affordable london outings

■ 222
Publication Travel & Leisure
Design Director Pamela Berry
Designer Katherine Timme
Photo Editor Jim Franco
Photographer Luca Travato
Publisher American Express Publishing
Issue June 1996
Category Feature Story

■ 223
Publication Travel & Leisure
Design Director Pamela Berry
Designers Dina White, Pamela Berry
Photo Editor Jim Franco
Photographers Daniela Stallinger, Henry Bourne
Publisher American Express Publishing
Issue August 1996
Category Feature Story

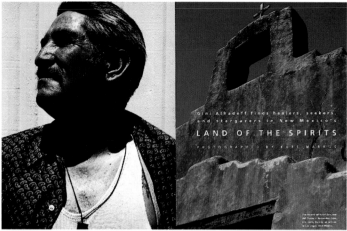

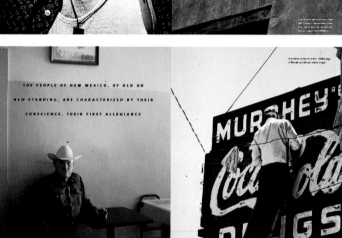

THE PEOPLE OF NEW MEXICO, OF OLD OR

NEW STANDING, ARE CHARACTERIZED BY THEIR

CONSCIENCE, THEIR FIRST ALLEGIANCE

COKES
ICE
CREAM
TAMALES
CANDY

next great neighborhoods

The inside track on streets with a buzz in NEW YORK, LONDON, PARIS, L.A., and TOKYO

Photographed by Daniela Stallinger

NEW YORK

LONDON

PARIS

■ 224

Publication Travel & Leisure
Design Director Pamela Berry
Designer Pamela Berry
Photo Editor Jim Franco
Photographer Kurt Markus
Publisher American Express Publishing
Issue September 1996
Category Feature Story

■ 225

Publication Travel & Leisure
Design Director Pamela Berry
Designer Dina White
Photo Editor Jim Franco
Photographer Daniela Stallinger
Publisher American Express Publishing
Issue September 1996
Category Feature Story

■ 226

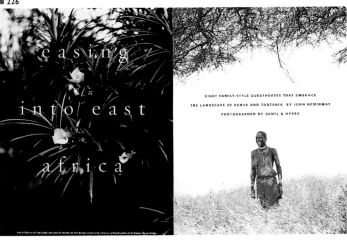

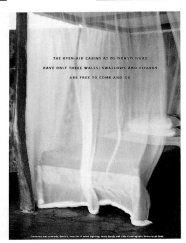

■ 226
Publication Travel & Leisure
Design Director Pamela Berry
Designers Pamela Berry, Daniel Josephs
Photo Editor Jim Franco
Photographer Gentl & Hyers
Publisher American Express Publishing
Issue November 1996
Category Feature Story

■ 227
Publication The Work
Creative Director Dana Arnett
Designers Jeff Breazeale,
Curtis Schreiber, Dan Kraemer
Studio VSA Partners, Inc.
Client Clio
Issue Winter 1996
Category Entire Issue

type

■ 228
Publication U&lc
Art Director Michael Ian Kaye
Designer Michael Ian Kaye
Publisher International Typeface Corp.
Issue Fall 1996
Category Entire Issue

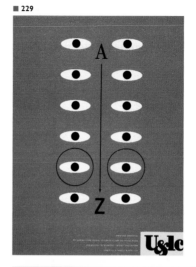

■ 229
Publication U&lc
Art Directors Michael Ian Kaye,
Carin Goldberg
Designers Michael Ian Kaye,
Carin Goldberg
Publisher International Typeface Corp.
Issue Winter 1996
Category Entire Issue

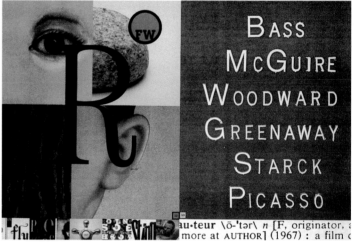

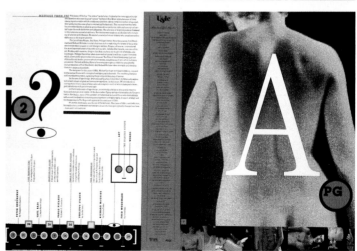

■ 230 ■ A

■ B

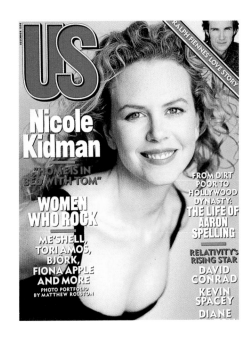

■ 231

■ 232

■ 230
Publication US
Art Director Richard Baker
Designers Richard Baker, Dan Stark, Bess Wong
Photo Editors Jennifer Crandall, Rachel Knepfer, Steve Warner, Kristin Dymitruk
Photographers Mark Seliger, Butch Belair, Andrew Southam
Publisher US Magazine Co., L.P.
Issues March 1996, August 1996, December 1996
Category Overall Design
　　■ A Entire Issue
　　■ B Entire Issue

■ 231
Publication US
Art Director Richard Baker
Designer Richard Baker
Photo Editor Jennifer Crandall
Photographer Mark Seliger
Publisher US Magazine Co., L.P.
Issue June 1996
Category Feature Spread

■ 232
Publication US
Art Director Richard Baker
Designer Richard Baker
Photo Editor Jennifer Crandall
Photographer Mathew Rolston
Publisher US Magazine Co., L.P.
Issue August 1996
Category Feature Spread

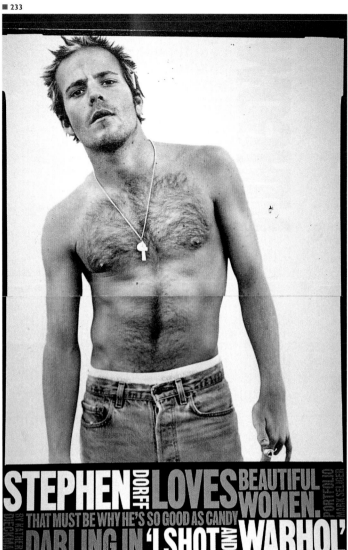

STEPHEN DORFF **LOVES** BEAUTIFUL **WOMEN.** THAT MUST BE WHY HE'S SO GOOD AS CANDY **DARLING IN 'I SHOT** ANDY **WARHOL'**

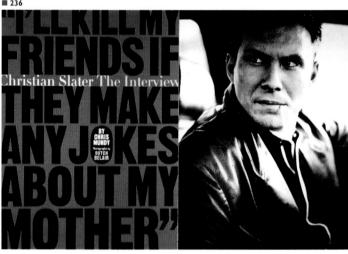

THIS YEAR'S "AS IF" GIRL AIMS HIGH AND SHOOTS STRAIGHT ABOUT BOYS, BRAS AND, LIKE, SWEAT

ALICIA SILVERSTONE By Margy Rochlin

PHOTOGRAPHS BY PEGGY SIROTA

"I'LL KILL MY FRIENDS IF THEY MAKE ANY JOKES ABOUT MY MOTHER"

Christian Slater The Interview

BY CHRIS MUNDY Photographs by BUTCH BELAIR

Will the supermodel from Down Under come out on top as an actress?

elle MACPHERSON

BY JANCEE DUNN

Photograph by Frank W. Ockenfels 3

INTERVIEW Mim Udovitch

PHOTOGRAPHS Max Vadukul

STING

■ 233
Publication US
Art Director Richard Baker
Designers Dan Stark, Richard Baker
Photo Editor Jennifer Crandall
Photographer Mark Seliger
Publisher US Magazine Co., L.P.
Issue May 1996
Category Feature Spread

■ 234
Publication US
Art Director Richard Baker
Designers Richard Baker, Megan Kingsbury
Photo Editor Jennifer Crandall
Photographer Frank W. Ockenfels 3
Publisher US Magazine Co., L.P.
Issue May 1996
Category Feature Spread

■ 235
Publication US
Art Director Richard Baker
Designer Richard Baker
Photo Editor Jennifer Crandall
Photographer Peggy Sirota
Publisher US Magazine Co., L.P.
Issue January 1996
Category Feature Spread

■ 236
Publication US
Art Director Richard Baker
Designer Richard Baker
Photo Editor Jennifer Crandall
Photographer Butch Belair
Publisher US Magazine Co., L.P.
Issue March 1996
Category Feature Spread

■ 237
Publication US
Art Director Richard Baker
Designer Richard Baker
Photo Editor Jennifer Crandall
Photographer Max Vadukul
Publisher US Magazine Co., L.P.
Issue April 1996
Category Feature Spread

WO-DY HARRELSON

The freewheeling actor contemplates abstinence, psychic moments, Courtney Love and marriage

INTERVIEW TOM O'NEILL • PHOTOGRAPH DAN WINTERS

BY AL WEISEL

Photograph by Andrew Southam

Jewel

◆ FROM ALASKAN DIVES TO VH1 DUETS, THIS FOLKIE SINGER SPINS HER HEART INTO A GOLD DEBUT

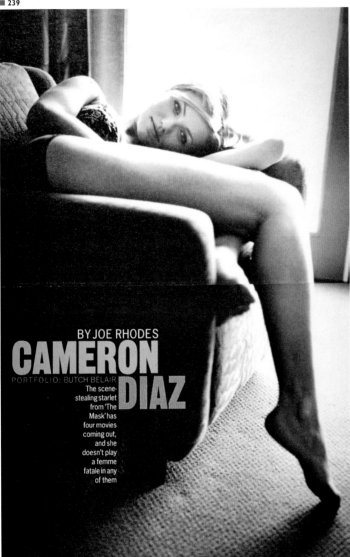

BY JOE RHODES

CAMERON DIAZ

PORTFOLIO: BUTCH BELAIR

The scene-stealing starlet from 'The Mask' has four movies coming out, and she doesn't play a femme fatale in any of them

ELIZABETH HURLEY

THE ACTRESS DIVULGES HER CAREER ASPIRATIONS, HER APATHY TOWARD MARRIAGE AND KIDS, AND WHY SHE FOR GAVE HUGH GRANT, THE MAN SHE WANTS TO GROW OLD WITH

BY JOE RHODES Portfolio: BRIGITTE LACOMBE

Photo Portfolio: MATTHEW ROLSTON

TRACY BONHAM

She ROCK

In the beginning, only boys got to play in the band. Then came Janis and Patti and others. Now, in the '90s, meet seven women who will rock your world — if they don't already

Tracy Bonham

■ 238
Publication US
Art Director Richard Baker
Designer Richard Baker
Photo Editor Jennifer Crandall
Photographer Dan Winters
Publisher US Magazine Co., L.P.
Issue July 1996
Category Feature Spread

■ 239
Publication US
Art Director Richard Baker
Designer Richard Baker
Photo Editor Jennifer Crandall
Photographer Butch Belair
Publisher US Magazine Co., L.P.
Issue March 1996
Category Feature Spread

■ 240
Publication US
Art Director Richard Baker
Designer Richard Baker
Photo Editor Jennifer Crandall
Photographer Andrew Southam
Publisher US Magazine Co., L.P.
Issue July 1996
Category Feature Spread

■ 241
Publication US
Art Director Richard Baker
Designer Richard Baker
Photo Editor Jennifer Crandall
Photographer Brigitte Lacombe
Publisher US Magazine Co., L.P.
Issue September 1996
Category Feature Spread

■ 242
Publication US
Art Director Richard Baker
Designer Richard Baker
Photo Editor Jennifer Crandall
Photographer Mathew Rolston
Publisher US Magazine Co., L.P.
Issue December 1996
Category Feature Spread

PHOTOGRAPHS BY MARK SELIGER

By MARGY ROCHLIN No longer just Tom Cruise's wife, the Aussie actress takes the lead in Jane Campion's moody 'Portrait of a Lady'

NICOLE
kidman

"Bee! Bee! Bee!" A fat bumblebee can't stay away from Nicole Kidman's face. Just when she settles into ➤

▶ "Around here, there's so much killing you've got to harden yourself from within," says 16-year-old reporter LEALAN JONES about his Chicago neighborhood. "If you don't, you'll be sobbing every day." Instead, he and his best friend, LLOYD NEWMAN, 17, took to the streets. Armed with a microphone, they let their community speak, turning up the volume for the nation to hear. National Public Radio aired the results: *The 14 Stories of Eric Morse*, which examines the life and death of a 5-year-old dropped from the 14th floor of a Chicago housing project, and *Ghetto Life 101*. Jones and Newman will continue their journalism careers, but they've already given us an earful. Listen up.   *Omoronke Idowu*

POWER MOVES

▶ He says he's lazy, but his ear is restless. TRICKY teases hip hop into dark, morbidly slow colors that seethe with paranoia, tenderness, and the skewed sexual dialogue he conducts with various female vocalists—Björk, Naneh Cherry, and mainstay Martina—who serve as foils for his own world-weary voice. Exuding the animated cool of a street alien, he opens doors by mixing races, genders, and incompatible moods. Tricky's self-described "hip hop blues," first witnessed on last year's *Maxinquaye*, evokes a spectrum of influences: Bilie's ennui, Bilie's low-fi spectral tone, the sly phrasings of Slick Rick, dub, and thrashy punk—all blended into a surreal urban rapscape. Tricky has dodged music biz red tape by marketing his collaborations under the monikers Nearly God and Drunkenstein. His mission: to maximize this output, in order to do as much damage as possible.
George Pitts

◀ You're a six-foot-ten, 240-pound basketball center from St. Croix whom people have compared to a young Kareem Abdul-Jabbar. You're a consensus first team All-American. You're a certain NBA lottery pick. But you have one year of college remaining. In a time when virtually every prep player over six-foot-three who can dunk a tennis ball is skipping college in favor of the pros, do you take the millions and run? TIM DUNCAN, a psychology major and college hoops' most dominant post player, took the road less traveled and will soon be enjoying his senior year at Wake Forest University. His most memorable power move may be that he didn't move at all.
CU Lima

140 VIBE

LAST MAN STANDING

After Dr. Dre's departure and Tupac's slaying, the Death Row empire is in need of rebuilding. It's time for Snoop Doggy Dogg to step up. By Smokey D. Fontaine. Photographs by Philippe McClelland

THE OSCAR-WINNING ACTRESS FOLLOWS UP THE HILARIOUS 'FIRST WIVES CLUB' WITH A HEART-WRENCHING PERFORMANCE IN 'MARVIN'S ROOM' BY LAURA MORICE

KEATON
DIANE

AS WEDNESDAY FUND. 89

■ 245

Publication Vibe
Art Director Lee Ellen Fanning
Designer Dwayne Shaw
Photo Editor George Pitts
Photographer Stephanie Sednaout
Publisher Time Inc.
Issue September 1996
Category Feature Single Page

■ 246

Publication Vibe
Art Director Lee Ellen Fanning
Designer Lee Ellen Fanning
Photo Editor George Pitts
Photographer Philippe McCelland
Publisher Time Inc.
Issue December 1996/January 1997
Category Feature Spread

■ 243

Publication US
Art Director Richard Baker
Designer Richard Baker
Photo Editors Jennifer Crandall,
Rachel Knepfer
Photographer Mark Seliger
Publisher US Magazine Co., L.P.
Issue December 1996
Category Feature Spread

■ 244

Publication US
Art Director Richard Baker
Designer Dan Stark
Photo Editor Jennifer Crandall
Photographer Brigitte Lacombe
Publisher US Magazine Co., L.P.
Issue December 1996
Category Department

■ 247

Publication ZooViews Newsletter
Designer Melanie Doherty
Photographer Caroline Kopp
Publisher Graphic Arts Center
Studio Melanie Doherty Design
Client
The San Francisco Zoological Society
Issue March/April 1996
Category Feature Spread

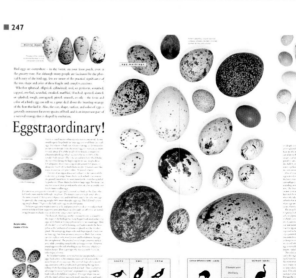

Eggstraordinary!

■ 248

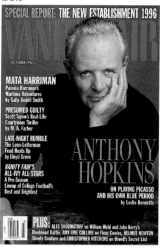

■ 249

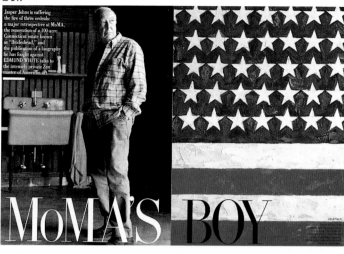

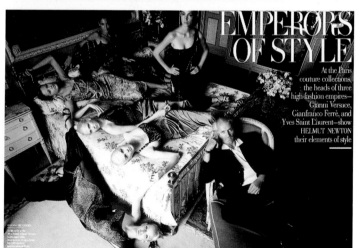

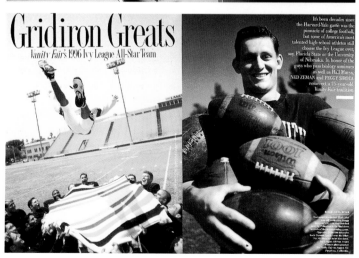

■ 248
Publication Vanity Fair
Design Director David Harris
Art Director Gregory Mastrianni
Designers David Harris, Gregory Mastrianni, Mimi Dutta, John Dixon, Chita Steinberg
Photo Editor Susan White
Photographers John Dixon, Chita Steinberg
Publisher Condé Nast Publications Inc.
Issue October 1996
Category Entire Issue

■ 249
Publication Vanity Fair
Design Director David Harris
Designer David Harris
Photo Editor Susan White
Publisher Condé Nast Publications Inc.
Issue September 1996
Category Feature Story

PhillyStyle

film noir

The best in black and white

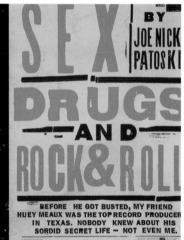

SEX DRUGS AND ROCK & ROLL

BY JOE NICK PATOSKI

BEFORE HE GOT BUSTED, MY FRIEND HUEY MEAUX WAS THE TOP RECORD PRODUCER IN TEXAS. NOBODY KNEW ABOUT HIS SORDID SECRET LIFE — NOT EVEN ME.

Thrill Killers

All over urban Texas, *young thugs* are committing a *vicious* new kind of crime: Find an unsuspecting victim, *rob him,* then *shoot him just for fun.* And most of the time, they're getting away with it.

by Jim Atkinson

■ 250
Publication Young Sisters and Brothers
Creative Director Lance A. Pettiford
Art Director Gregory Atkins
Designer Lance A. Pettiford
Photo Editor Stephen Chin
Photographer Marc Baptiste
Publisher Paige Publications
Issue July 1996
Category Feature Story

■ 251
Publication Philadelphia
Creative Directors Betsy Brecht,
Frank Baseman
Designers Betsy Brecht,
Frank Baseman
Photographer John Romeo
Publisher Metrocorp
Issue May 1996
Category Department

■ 252
Publication Texas Monthly
Creative Director D. J. Stout
Designers D. J. Stout, Nancy McMillen
Illustrator John Collier
Photo Editor D. J. Stout
Publisher Texas Monthly
Issue May 1996
Category Feature Spread

■ 253
Publication Texas Monthly
Creative Director D. J. Stout
Designers D. J. Stout, Nancy McMillen
Illustrator Hungry Dog Studio
Photo Editor D. J. Stout
Publisher Texas Monthly
Issue November 1996
Category Feature Spread

■ 254
Publication BravoRichards
Creative Director Jurek Wajdowicz
Designers Lisa LaRochelle,
Jurek Wajdowicz
Photographer Eugene Richards
Studio Emerson, Wajdowicz Studios
Client Island Paper Mills,
E.B. Eddy Forest Products, Ltd.
Issue September 1996
Category Entire Issue

■ 255
Publication
Dagens Nyheters Manadsmagasin
Art Directors Peter Alenas,
Pompe Hedengren
Photo Editor Hakan Lindgren
Publisher Dagens Nyheter
Issue November 30, 1996
Category Entire Issue

Billy Rubino

Aids drabbar alla

Jan-Olof "Nola" Morfeldt

■ 256
Publication
Dagens Nyheters Manadsmagasin
Art Directors Peter Alenas,
Pompe Hedengren
Illustrator Hakan Menfors
Photo Editor Hakan Lindgren
Photographer Mikael Jansson
Publisher Dagens Nyheter
Issue November 30, 1996
Category Feature Story

■ 258
Publication
Dagens Nyheters Manadsmagasin
Design Director John Bark
Art Director Anders Frelin
Designer Kerstin Wigstrand
Photographer Fredrik Funck
Issue November 17, 1996
Category Feature Single Page

■ 257
Publication
Dagens Nyheters Manadsmagasin
Design Director John Bark
Art Director Anders Frelin
Designer Anders Frelin
Illustrator Mats Johansson
Issue January 5, 1996
Category Feature Single Page

■ 259

■ 260

■ 261

Mark Henry, weightlifter

■ 259
Publication LIFE
Design Director Tom Bentkowski
Designer Jean Andreuzzi
Photo Editor David Friend
Publisher Time Inc.
Issue April 1996
Category Contents

■ 260
Publication LIFE
Design Director Tom Bentkowski
Designer Jean Andreuzzi
Photo Editor David Friend
Publisher Time Inc.
Issue November 1996
Category Contents

■ 261
Publication LIFE
Design Director Tom Bentkowski
Designer Jean Andreuzzi
Photo Editor David Friend
Photographer Joe McNally
Publisher Time Inc.
Issue July 1996
Category Contents

■ 262
Publication LIFE
Design Director Tom Bentkowski
Art Director Mimi Park
Designer Mimi Park
Photo Editors David Friend, Vivette Porges
Photographer Ulf Skogsbergh
Publisher Time Inc.
Issue July 15, 1996
Category Contents

■ 263
Publication LIFE
Design Director Tom Bentkowski
Art Director Mimi Park
Designer Mimi Park
Photo Editors David Friend, Bobbi Baker Burrows
Photographer John Loengard
Publisher Time Inc.
Issue October 1996
Category Contents

■ 262

Contents

■ 263

■ 264

■ 265

■ 264
Publication Musician
Art Director Robin Lee MaLik
Designer Robin Lee MaLik
Photographer Kristin Larsen
Publisher BPI Communications
Issue December 1996
Category Contents

■ 265
Publication New York
Design Director Robert Newman
Art Director Florian Bachleda
Designer Andrea Dunham
Illustrator Hanoch Piven
Publisher K-III Publications
Issue July 7, 1996
Category Contents

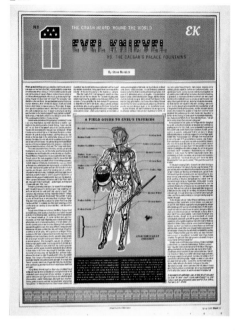

■ 266
Publication Slant
Creative Director Howard Brown
Designer Ward Sutton
Illustrator Ward Sutton
Publisher Urban Outfitters, Inc.
Client Urban Outfitters
Issue November 1996
Category Feature Single Page

■ 268
Publication Slant
Design Director Howard Brown
Art Director Mike Calkins
Designer Mike Calkins
Illustrator Mike Calkins
Publisher Urban Outfitters Inc.
Studio Urban Outfitters, In-House
Issue Spring 1996
Category Feature Single Page

■ 270
Publication Slant
Design Director Howard Brown
Art Director Mike Calkins
Designer Mike Calkins
Illustrator Mike Calkins
Publisher Urban Outfitters Inc.
Studio Urban Outfitters, In-House
Issue Fall 1996
Category Feature Single Page

■ 267
Publication Slant
Design Director Howard Brown
Art Director Mike Calkins
Designers Mike Calkins, Joe Morse
Illustrator Joe Morse
Publisher Urban Outfitters Inc.
Studio Urban Outfitters, In-House
Issue Spring 1996
Category Feature Single Page

■ 269
Publication Slant
Design Director Howard Brown
Art Director Mike Calkins
Designers Howard Brown, Steve Raskin
Illustrator Steve Raskin
Publisher Urban Outfitters Inc.
Studio Urban Outfitters, In-House
Issue Spring 1996
Category Feature Single Page

■ 271
Publication Slant
Design Director Howard Brown
Art Director Mike Calkins
Designer Mike Calkins
Illustrator Mike Calkins
Publisher Urban Outfitters Inc.
Studio Urban Outfitters, In-House
Issue November 23, 1996
Category Feature Single Page

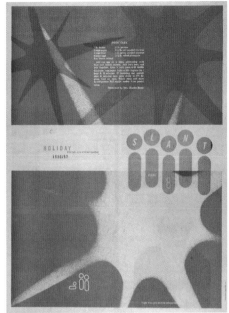

■ 272
Publication Slant
Design Director Howard Brown
Art Director Mike Calkins
Designers Laurant Clilluffo, Dave Bates, Jeff Kleinsmith, Art Chantry, Howard Brown, Mike Calkins
Illustrators Laurant Clilluffo, Dave Bates
Publisher Urban Outfitters Inc.
Studio Urban Outfitters, In-House
Issue Fall 1996
Category Entire Issue

■ 273
Publication Slant
Design Director Howard Brown
Art Director Mike Calkins
Designers Sharon Werner, Paul Howalt, Dave Bates, Howard Brown, Mike Calkins
Illustrators Dave Bates, Greg Ruth
Publisher Urban Outfitters Inc.
Issue November 23, 1996
Category Entire Issue

■ 274
Publication Slant
Design Director Howard Brown
Art Director Mike Calkins
Designer Mike Calkins
Illustrator Mike Calkins
Publisher Urban Outfitters Inc.
Studio Urban Outfitters, In-House
Issue November 23, 1996
Category Feature Single Page

■ 275

■ 276

■ 278

■ 275
Publication The Boston Globe
Designers Sue Dawson, Aldona Charlton
Publisher The Boston Globe
Issue February 11, 1996
Category Feature Single Page

■ 277

■ 279

■ 276
Publication The Boston Globe
Art Director Cindy Daniels
Designer Cindy Daniels
Illustrator Sean McNaughton
Publisher The Boston Globe
Issue March 4, 1996
Category Feature Single Page

■ 277
Publication The Boston Globe
Art Director Rena Sokolow
Designer Rena Sokolow
Publisher The Boston Globe
Issue October 27, 1996
Category Feature Single Page

■ 278
Publication The Boston Globe
Art Director Keith A. Webb
Designer Keith A. Webb
Illustrator Keith A. Webb
Publisher The Boston Globe
Issue July 19, 1996
Category Feature Single Page

■ 279
Publication The Boston Globe
Art Director Keith A. Webb
Designer Keith A. Webb
Publisher The Boston Globe
Issue November 14, 1996
Category Feature Single Page

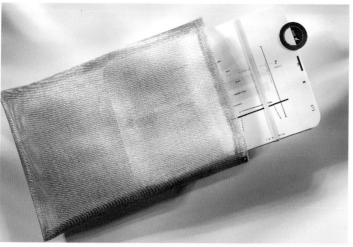

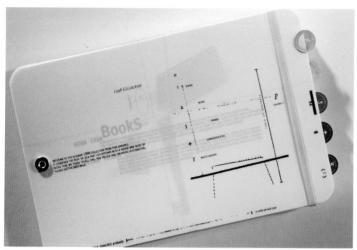

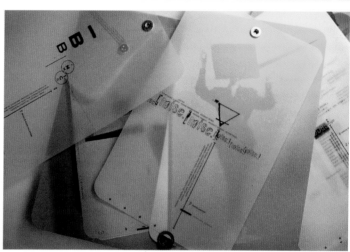

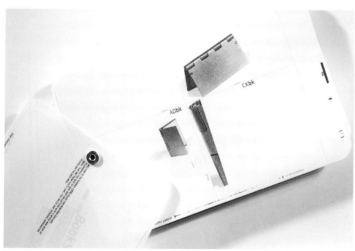

■ 280
Publication Pina Zangaro
Art Director Jennifer Sterling
Designer Jennifer Sterling
Illustrator Jennifer Sterling
Photographer Dave Magnusson
Publisher Logos Graphics
Studio Jennifer Sterling Design
Issue July 1996
Category Entire Issue

■ 281
Publication Sterling Design
Art Director Jennifer Sterling
Designer Jennifer Sterling
Illustrators Jennifer Sterling, Jonathan Rosan
Photographers Jennifer Sterling, Jonathan Rosan
Publisher Logos Graphics
Studio Jennifer Sterling Design
Issue June 1996
Category Entire Issue

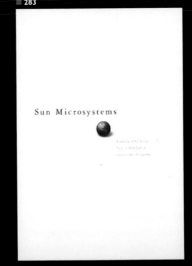

Sun Microsystems

WATCH

EXPERIENCE

Sun is a

global leader

in enterprise

network

computing.

EAK

UNDERSTAND

The Sun Wide
Area Network

Connected.

INTERACTIVE MULTIMEDIA HAS
FOSTERED NEW TRENDS IN
EDUCATION, ENTERTAINMENT
AND BUSINESS. IT HAS ALSO
LED TO NEW METHODS TO
DELIVER AND ACCESS INFOR-
MATION. OPTICAL STORAGE
TECHNOLOGY HAS MADE DELIV-
ERING MULTIMEDIA CONTENT
INEXPENSIVE AND EFFECTIVE.

■ 282
Publication Oak Technology 1995 Annual Report
Creative Director Bill Cahan
Designer Craig Clark
Studio Cahan & Associates
Issue September 1995
Category Entire Issue

■ 283
Publication Sun Microsystems Brochure
Creative Director Bill Cahan
Designer Sharrie Brooks
Photographers Tony Stromberg, Geof Kern, Marko Lavisha, Maria Robledo
Studio Cahan & Associates
Issue October 1996
Category Entire Issue

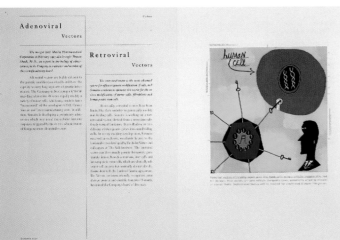

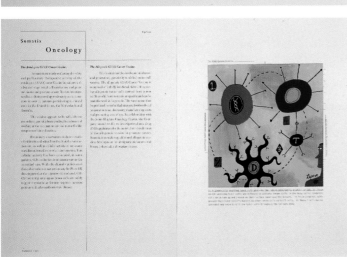

■ **284**
Publication Somatix 1996 Annual Report
Creative Director Bill Cahan
Designer Sharrie Brooks
Illustrator Calef Brown
Studio Cahan & Associates
Issue November 1996
Category Entire Issue

■ **285**
Publication Trident Microsystems 1995 Annual Report
Creative Director Bill Cahan
Designer Bob Dinetz
Studio Cahan & Associates
Issue October 1995
Category Entire Issue

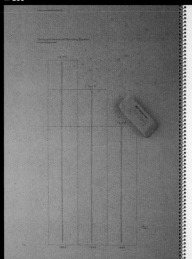

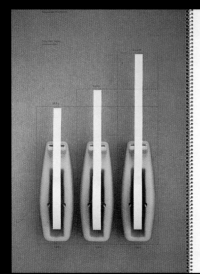

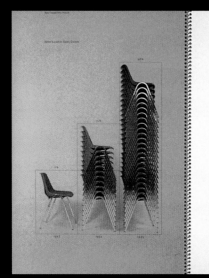

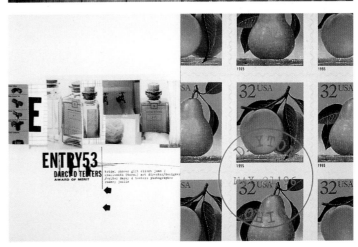

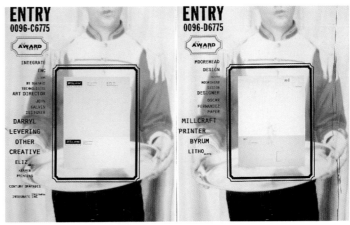

■ 288
Publication Jacor Communications, Inc. 1995 Annual Report
Creative Director Robert Petrick
Designers Robert Petrick, Laura Ress
Illustrator Mark Heckman
Photographer Paul Elledge
Issue April 1996
Category Entire Issue

■ 289
Publication CSCA Creative Best Catalog
Creative Director Charles Wilkin
Designer Charles Wilkin
Illustrator Charles Wilkin
Photographers Tracey Jolly, Chas Krider
Publisher Columbus Society of Communicating Arts
Studio Automatic Art & Design
Issue December 1996
Category Entire Issue

open
this
door

Cleveland Institute of Art

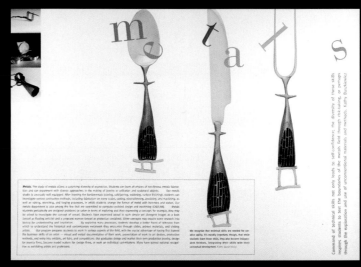

■ 290
Publication Cleveland Institute of Art Catalogue 1996-97
Creative Directors Joyce Nesnadny, Mark Schwartz
Designers Joyce Nesnadny, Brian Lavy, Michelle Moehler
Photographers Robert A. Muller, Mark Schwartz
Studio Nesnadny + Schwartz
Issue July 1996
Category Entire Issue

■ 291
Publication The Power of Suggestion:
Narrative and Notation in Contemporary Drawing
Creative Director Anna Boyiazis
Designer Anna Boyiazis
Photographer Paula Goldman
Publishers The Museum of Contemporary Art, Los Angeles
Smart Art Press, Santa Monica
Issue 1996
Category Entire Issue

■ 292
Publication The Progressive Corp.
1995 Annual Report
Creative Directors Mark Schwartz,
Joyce Nesnadny
Designers Joyce Nesnadny,
Michelle Moehler, Mark Schwartz
Studio Nesnadny + Schwartz
Issue March 1996
Category Entire Issue

ing

jump
through
hoops

step
ping
up to the
mark

■ 293
Publication The George Gund
Foundation 1995 Annual Report
Creative Director Mark Schwartz
Designer Michelle Moehler
Photographer Lee Friedlander
Studio Nesnadny + Schwartz
Issue May 1996
Category Entire Issue

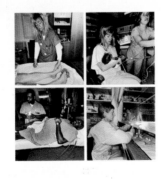

December 1996

■ 296
Publication Mark Sargent Book
Creative Director Mark Sargent
Designers Keith Ohlfs,
Mark Sargent, Scott Anguish
Publisher Nest Eggs, Inc.
Online Address
www.rubbersoul.org/Artist/MarkSargent
Issue September 21, 1996
Category Home Page

■ 297
Publication
Smithsonian Magazine On-Line
Creative Director Pilar Belhumeur
Photo Editor Edgar Rich
Photographer Ted Wood
Studio Oculus Interactive
Online Address
www.smithsonianmag.si.edu
Issue December 1996
Category Home Page

■ 294
Publication Harley-Davidson
Creative Director Dana Arnett
Designers Michael A. Peterson, Ron Spohn,
Curtis Schreiber, Ken Fox, Geoff Mark
Illustrator VSA Partners, Inc.
Photographers James Schnepf, Burke Uzzle
Studio VSA Partners, Inc.
Online Address www.harley-davidson.com
Issue July 1996
Category Home Page

■ 295
Publication Kodak Professional
Creative Director Cheryl Heller
Design Director Melanie Semerad-Radolescu
Photo Editor Steve Pollock
Photographers Ed Rusche, Frédéric Brenner
Publisher S.D. Warren
Studio Siegel & Gale
Online Address www.kodak.com
Issue October 1996
Category Entire Issue

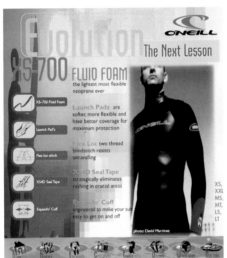

Publication O'Neill, Inc. Web Site
Creative Director Anne Endrusick
Designer Andrew Jones
Online Address
www.teamoneill.com
Issue July 1996
Category Entire Issue

SALON | ARTICLES BY SUBJECT ■ ARTICLES BY DATE ■ TABLE TALK

MOVIES

FROM GUTTER TO GALLERY

BY GLEN HELFAND

In "Basquiat," art world egotist Julian Schnabel delivers a surprisingly likeable portrait of his late friend.

"Basquiat" | Directed by Julian Schnabel

"i'll no doubt eventually look boring to the art crowd," painter Julian Schnabel said in a in a 1987 interview. Less than a decade later it appears this notoriously egotistical artist is heeding his own prediction. In the search for new fans, last year Schnabel released a musical CD that was widely panned as a bloated vanity

Publication Salon
Art Director Mignon Khargie
Designer Mignon Khargie
Online Address www.salonmagazine.com
Issue August 19, 1996
Category Feature

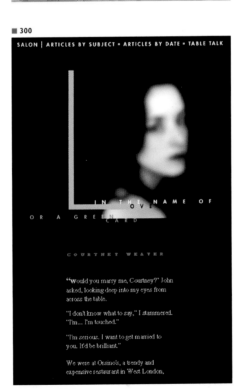

SALON | ARTICLES BY SUBJECT ■ ARTICLES BY DATE ■ TABLE TALK

IN THE NAME OF LOVE
OR A GREEN CARD

COURTNEY WEAVER

"Would you marry me, Courtney?" John asked, looking deep into my eyes from across the table.

"I don't know what to say," I stammered. "I'm... I'm touched."

"I'm serious. I want to get married to you. It'd be brilliant."

We were at Orsino's, a trendy and expensive restaurant in West London,

Publication Salon
Art Director Mignon Khargie
Designer Mignon Khargie
Illustrator Sibylla herbich
Online Address www.salonmagazine.com
Issue November 4, 1996
Category Feature

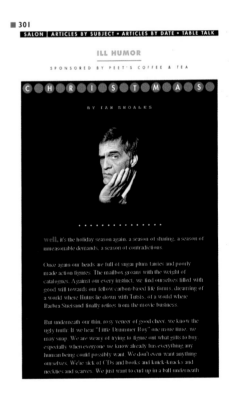

SALON | ARTICLES BY SUBJECT ■ ARTICLES BY DATE ■ TABLE TALK

ILL HUMOR

SPONSORED BY PEET'S COFFEE & TEA

CHRISTMAS

BY IAN SHOALES

well, it's the holiday season again, a season of sharing, a season of unreasonable demands, a season of contradictions.

Once again our heads are full of sugar plum fairies and poorly made action figures. The mailbox groans with the weight of catalogues. Against our every instinct, we find ourselves filled with good will towards our fellow carbon-based life forms, dreaming of a world where Hutus lie down with Tutsis, of a world where Barbra Streisand finally retires from the movie business.

But underneath our thin, rosy veneer of good cheer, we know the ugly truth: If we hear "Little Drummer Boy" one more time, we may snap. We are weary of trying to figure out what gifts to buy, especially when everyone we know already has everything; any human being could possibly want. We don't even want anything ourselves. We're sick of CDs and books and knick-knacks and neckties and scarves. We just want to curl up in a ball underneath

Publication Salon
Art Director Elizabeth Kairys
Designer Elizabeth Kairys
Illustrator Sibylla Herbrich
Online Address www.salonmagazine.com
Issue November 25, 1996
Category Feature

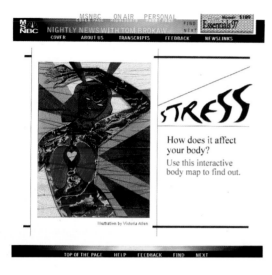

STRESS

How does it affect
your body?
Use this interactive
body map to find out.

Illustration by Victoria Allen

TOP OF THE PAGE   HELP   FEEDBACK   FIND   NEXT

TIME & AGAIN
INSIDE TIME & AGAIN   COVER STORY   THIS WEEK   TIME CAPSULE   ARCHIVE

John F. Kennedy was
the youngest man ever
elected President of
the United States. The
tragic death of this vibrant
world leader on Nov. 22,
1963 sent tremors around
the world and forever
changed the course of
history. A decorated war
hero and Pulitzer Prize-
winning author, the young
Kennedy pledged to get
America moving again. He
vowed to have a man on the
moon by the end of the
decade, championed equal
rights for all Americans and
appealed for an end to the
Cold War. All of his dreams
were realized—if not in his

Are we alone?

MSNBC
96
97

Year of the Net?
The Net gets real
Back from the dead

The new Congress' approach
to Internet and cyberspace issues.

National security and billions of dollars are
at stake in the debate over encryption.

Breaking
the
code

Business exports, national
security at stake in
encryption debate

Amy Franceschini/Special to MSNBC

By Brock N. Meeks
MSNBC Chief Washington Correspondent

■ 302
Publication MSNBC/Nightly News with Tom Brokaw
Art Director Lisa Powers
Designer Lisa Powers
Illustrator Victoria Allen
Publisher MSNBC Interactive
Online Address
www.msnbc.com/onair/nbc/nightlynews
Issue October 1996
Category Home Page

■ 303
Publication MSNBC/Time & Again
ART Director Lisa Powers
Designers Lisa Powers, Scott Irwin, Julie Threlkeld
Illustrator Victoria Allen
Publisher MSNBC Interactive
Online Address
www.msnbc.com/onair/msnbc/timeandagain
Issue November 6, 1996
Category Home Page

■ 304
Publication MSNBC Interactive
Art Director Galie Jean-Louis
Designers Paul Segner, Denise Trabona, Sofia Vecchio
Illustrators Amy Franceschini, Modem Dog, Calef Brown
Publisher MSNBC Interactive
Online Address www.msnbc.com/specials/./eoy/splash.asp
Issue December 17, 1996
Category Feature Story

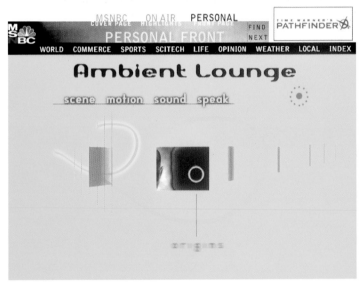

■ 306
Publication Design Mind
Art Directors Ann Donovan, Cynthia Pearce
Designer Ann Donovan
Publisher Photo Disc Inc.
Studio Photo Disc Web Group
Online Address www.photodisc.com/design
Issue Volume One, Issue Three
Category Cover

■ 307
Publication DoubleTake
Art Director Molly Renda
Designers Jennifer Cox, Ben Glenn
Photo Editor Alex Harris
Publisher Center for Documentary Studies
Online Address www.duke.edu/doubletake/
Category Home Page

■ 305
Publication MSNBC Interactive
Art Director Galie Jean-Louis
Designers Sofia Vecchio, Dave Fenigson
Photographer Larry Dailey
Publisher MSNBC Interactive
Online Address www.msnbc.com/specials/triphop/splash.asp
Issue November 15, 1996
Category Feature Story

■ 308

Publication Cosmopolitan Online
Creative Director Peter Seidler
Art Director Andreas Lindstron
Designer Kendall Thomas
Photo Editor Kris Konno
Publisher The Hearst Corporation-Magazines Division
Studio Avalanche Systems
Online Address www.cosmomag.com
Category Entire Issue

■ 309

Publication
Discovery Channel Online
Design Director John Sanford
Art Director Lisa Waltuch
Designers Britt Funderburk,
Blanca Piera, Brian Frick, David
Whitmore, Elizabeth Hare
Photo Editor Sue Klemens
Publisher
Discovery Communications Inc.
Online Address www.discovery.com
Issue December 30, 1996
Category Home Page

■ 310

Publication
Discovery Channel Online
Design Director John Sanford
Art Director Lisa Waltuch
Designers Britt Funderburk,
Blanca Piera, David Whitmore,
Brian Frick
Photo Editor Sue Klemens
Publisher
Discovery Communications Inc.
Online Address www.discovery.com
Category Department

■ 311

Publication
Discovery Channel Online
Design Director John Sanford
Art Director Lisa Waltuch
Designer Blanca Piera
Illustrator Blanca Piera
Photo Editor Sue Klemens
Publisher
Discovery Communications Inc.
Online Address www.discovery.com
Issue November 27, 1996
Category Feature

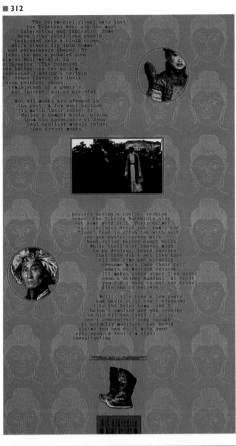

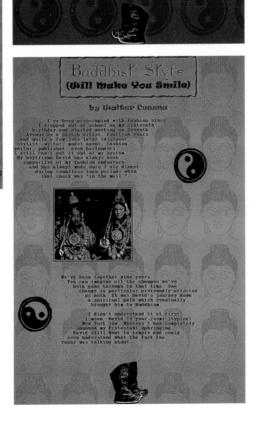

■ 312
Publication Word
Creative Director Jane Mount
Designer Kit Alderdice
Illustrator Kit Alderice
Studio Kit Alderice
Online Address
www.word.com/habit/cessna
Issue March 1996
Category Feature Story

■ 313
Publication Russian Web Girls
Art Directors Alona Makeeva, Vica Vinogradova
Illustrators Alona Makeeva, Katya Marchik
Photographer Tamara Leudy
Studio Octet Media
Online Address www.russianwebgirls.com
Issue December 15, 1996
Category Entire Issue

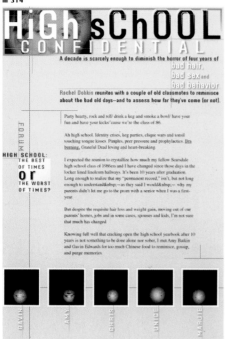

HiGh sChOOL
CONFIDENTIAL

A decade is scarcely enough to diminish the horror of four years of **bad hair, bad sex** and **bad behavior.**

Rachel Dobkin reunites with a couple of old classmates to reminisce about the bad old days—and to assess how far they've come (or not).

FORUM

HIGH SCHOOL: THE BEST OF TIMES **or** THE WORST OF TIMES?

Party hearty, rock and roll/ drink a keg and smoke a bowl/ have your fun and have your kicks/'cause we're the class of '86.

Ah high school. Identity crises, keg parties, clique wars and tonsil-touching tongue kisses. Pimples, peer pressure and prophylactics. Bra burning, Grateful Dead loving and heart-breaking.

I expected the reunion to crystallize how much my fellow Scarsdale high school class of 1986ers and I have changed since those days in the locker lined linoleum hallways. It's been 10 years after graduation. Long enough to realize that my "permanent record," isn't, but not long enough to understand —as they said I would — why my parents didn't let me go to the prom with a senior when I was a first-year.

But despite the requisite hair loss and weight gain, moving out of our parents' homes, jobs and in some cases, spouses and kids, I'm not sure that much has changed.

Knowing full well that cracking open the high school yearbook after 10 years is not something to be done alone nor sober, I met Amy Batkin and Gavin Edwards for too much Chinese food to reminisce, gossip, and purge memories.

what's YOUR problem?

TO SCREW UP IS HUMAN. LUCKILY, JANE ERR'S ADVICE IS DIVINE.

DEAR JANE ERR,

I have a close friend named Scott who got dumped two months ago. Ever since the breakup, all he wants to do is rehash the details of his lost love. I mean, let's be real. He dated this guy for all of three months! And yet he insists on going over it again and again with me. The other night he had me on the phone for nearly an hour. When I got another call, I clicked over and told the person on the other line to hold on. I'd be right back. Then, after informing Scott that I'd call him later, I switched back yet again (or so I thought). "Thank God you called," I said. "I've been listening to Scott whine about his ex-boyfriend for ever." I guess my call waiting is a reward or something, because the next thing I heard was "Hello?" It's whom Scott. I'm still here. Thanks a lot!" I tried to apologize, but he hung up on me. I want to call him, but I'm afraid he'll just start moaning about Mr. Wrong again. Please help!

PHONE JACK

DEAR PHONE JACK,

Ah, the ex-files. Haven't we all had a pal who just can't let go? "Move on." you urge. "You're better off without that demonic bum," you console. Often, as you're discovered, your kind words fall on deaf ears. And after a while, you get tired of running the Heartbreak Holiday Inn. But even if you inadvertently did Scott a favor by mistakenly voicing your annoyance with him, his anger at your cattiness is justified. Still, two months of mourning over a 90-day relationship is way excessive. Someone had to step in and end the pity party.

Scott's probably carping to his other friends right now (about his lost love and your faux pas). Or trying to, at least. My hunch is that they're sick of his complaining, too, and screening their calls to avoid him. For that very reason, you need to get him on the horn and metaphorically wipe his nose. Gently tell him that he's got to stop sniveling over yesterday's news. Of course, he'll use this call as an opportunity to indulge his suffering some more. Let him "woe is moi" a bit. Then, you need to lay some ground rules. Explain to him that he's got two more hours worth of "ex-chat" left and the meter is running. After that, the topic is forbidden. You will keep a record every time he brings up his former fling. Once Scott has chewed up his 120 minutes of talk, don't let the boy bring up his blues again. Be firm. And, next time, be sure to identify your caller before you issue such a brutal dissing.

JANE

How do you handle a friend who can't seem to get over a lost love?

ARE YOU IN HOT WATER WITH SOMEONE BECAUSE OF SOMETHING YOU DID OR DIDN'T DO?

NEED HELP GETTING OUT OF TROUBLE?

JANE ERR'S HERE TO HELP. TELL HER YOUR PROBLEM IN THE FORM BELOW.

Dear Jane Err,

SUBMIT

LIVING IN sin

EXPLOSIVE SEX. ROMANTIC, HOME-COOKED MEALS. AN IMPECCABLY DECORATED APARTMENT. A SMILING FACE TO COME HOME TO EVERY NIGHT...

YEAH, RIGHT.

text by JOSH ROTTENBERG AND SADIE VAN GELDER

photography by STEPHEN WEBSTER

We were in love, Josh's lease was due to expire, and Sadie had finally resolved to ask her roommates to move out. The stage was set for us to move into her place together. Also, we were both well aware that in the steel cage wrestling match otherwise known as the New York City real-estate market, you're usually safer if you tag in a partner. (Where else could you create a hit rock opera called Rent? Coming soon: Andrew Lloyd Webber's Utilities.) In the 15 months since then, we've combined our furniture, our friends, even our e-mail address ("sadiejosh" — yeah, we know, we might as well be "swannnyrogsample.com"). And while we're not exactly authorities on the subject of living in sin, we do know that we wouldn't be if we hadn't learned to share. So that's what we'd like to do right now — this is open our bathroom, our bedroom, and all the rest, for your perusal.

pick a room

quiz
SHOULD YOU SHACK UP?

Swoon: So, Sadie, is Josh always leaving the toilet seat in the upright and locked position?

Sadie: No, he's pretty good about it. I've never gotten up to pee in the middle of the night and had an accidental Trainspotting experience.

Josh: Actually, I've just trained myself to squat.

Swoon: Is there an open-door policy on bodily functions?

Josh: I think we're moving toward full disclosure, but it's been pretty gradual. I remember when we first started going out I'd pee toward the side of the bowl because I didn't want Sadie to hear. Now, I don't even bother closing the door — in fact, I constantly have to remind myself to close it when we have guests over. Number two is still more of a don't-ask-don't-tell sort of thing, because of the obvious olfactory considerations. We seem to be at a close-the-door-but-don't-lock-it point with that.

Sadie: But we're basically doing all the things that the women's magazines warn will take the "mystery" out of your relationship.

Swoon: Like what?

Sadie: Well, let's just say that Cosmo is never going to run a story about applying Clearasil to your lover's back zits.

Josh: "10 Ways to Put the Romance Back in Backne." Yeah, I remember before we moved in together I'd lock the door so I could groom in private. Now we're like monkeys picking bugs out of each other's fur.

Sadie: Nice.

forum
IN THE LOO: FULL DISCLOSURE OR CLOSED-DOOR POLICY?

pick a room

quiz

■ 314

Publication Swoon
Art Director Warren Corbitt
Designer Warren Corbitt
Publisher Condé Net
Online Address
www.swoon.com/c_friends/05_yearbook
Category Feature Story

■ 315

Publication Swoon
Art Director Warren Corbitt
Designer Warren Corbitt
Publisher Condé Net
Online Address
www.swoon.com/d_others/03_jane_err/jane.cgi
Category Contents Department

■ 316

Publication Swoon
Art Director Warren Corbitt
Designer Warren Corbitt
Photographer Stephen Webster
Publisher Condé Net
Online Address
www.swoon.com/b_lovers/07_cohabitation/cohab.html
Category Feature Story

■ 317

Publication Swoon
Art Director Warren Corbitt
Designer Barry Deck
Photographer Richard Burbridge
Publisher Condé Net
Online Address
www.swoon.com/j_mag_rack/01_details/details_9610
Issue December 1996
Category Home Page

■ 318

Publication Swoon
Art Director Warren Corbitt
Designer Barry Deck
Illustrator Florian Ribisch
Photographer David LaChappelle
Publisher Condé Net
Online Address
www.swoon.com/j_mag_rack/01_details/details_9610
Issue October 1996
Category Home Page

PHOTOGRAPHY

Endlich mal ein
paar neue Gesichter

Wollen Sie Ihren
Bekanntenkreis um
ein paar
Charakterköpfe
erweitern?
Dann sehen Sie sich
doch mal
zu Hause um.

PHOTOS:
FRANÇOIS UND JEAN ROBERT

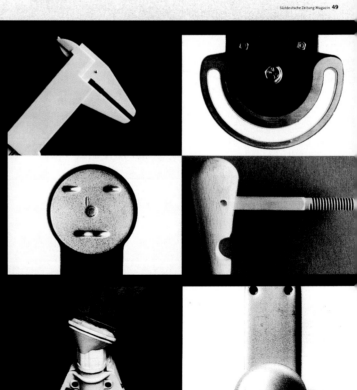

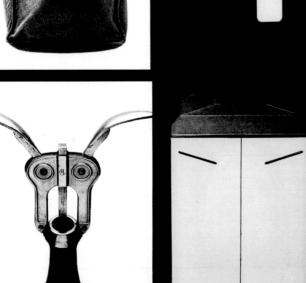

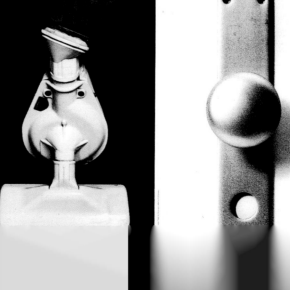

319
Publication Sueddeutsche Zeitung Magazin
Art Director Markus Rasp
Designers Anne Blaschke, Otto Dzemla, Wilhelm Raffelsberger
Photo Editors Eva Ernst, Claudia Mueller
Photographers Francois Robert, Jean Robert
Publisher Magazin Verlagsges. Sueddeutsche Zeitung mbh
Issue November 29, 1996
Category Still Life/Interiors Story

320
Publication BravoRichards
Creative Director Jurek Wajdowicz
Designers Lisa LaRochelle, Jurek Wajdowicz
Photographer Eugene Richards
Studio Emerson, Wajdowics Studios
Client Island Paper Mills/E.B. Eddy Forest Products, Ltd.
Issue September 1996
Category Photo Illustration Spread

ANIMALES SAGRADOS

Por
Francisco Umbral
FOTOGRAFÍAS DE JOSÉ AYMÁ

Show People

If you think the action is all on the runway during New York fashion week, think again. Master photographer Larry Fink captured some of the season's more surreal moments.

Alexandra von Fürstenberg and Marie-Chantal of Greece front row at the Oscar de la Renta show

Lisa Marie Presley at Vogue's party in her honor

321
Publication La Revista
Design Director Carmelo Caderot
Art Director Rodrigo Sanchez
Designers Rodrigo Sanchez, Miguel Buckenmeyer,
Maria González, Amparo Redondo
Photo Editor Chema Conesa
Photographer Jose Ayma
Publisher Unidad Editorial S.A.
Issue March 3, 1996
Category Portrait Story

322
Publication W
Creative Director Dennis Freedman
Design Director Edward Leida
Art Director Kirby Rodriguez
Designers Kirby Rodriguez, Marcella Bové
Illustrator Larry Fink
Publisher Fairchild Publications
Category Reportage/Travel Story

Skyscraper Couture

At the 1931 Beaux-Arts ball, leading architects of the day personified the New York skyline in a famous group portrait. JOSEF ASTOR commemorates that gathering with the help of such current architectural stars as I. M. Pei, Philip Johnson, and Michael Graves, while MATTHEW TYRNAUER finds that their images are bonded to the buildings they conceived

I. M. Pei

Co-founder of Pei Cobb Freed & Partners, New York, New York. Retired, as of 1991.

The world's most renowned living architect, Pei wears the structure that helped earn him that status—the glass pyramid entrance pavilion to the Louvre in Paris (1989). The pyramid was the most controversial of François Mitterrand's grands travaux; when the design was unveiled in 1984, the 71-foot-tall structure—only a small part of Pei's more than $1 billion Louvre renovation—was the object of ridicule. Today Paris is a France counts it among the capital's architectural treasures.

Philip Johnson

Principal of Philip Johnson, Ritchie & Fiore Architects, New York, New York.

Perhaps the greatest architectural figure of the day, Johnson, who turns 90 in July, is, in the words of his one-time protégé Robert A.M. Stern, "the father of us all." The edifice which he wears as his rightful crown is the PPG Building (1984), the mirrored postmodern corporate cathedral which stands along the Allegheny River in downtown Pittsburgh. Johnson—who keeps a drawer full of the Le Corbusier-style glasses he has worn for 46 years—co-curated the landmark International Style show at the Museum of Modern Art in 1932, the year after the Beaux-Arts ball photo on the following page was taken.

Costumes designed and constructed by JOSEPH HUTCHINS, Works, N.Y.

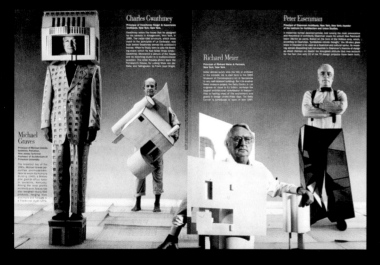

Charles Gwathmey

Richard Meier

Peter Eisenman

Michael Graves

Philippe Starck

Robert A. M. Stern

323
Publication Vanity Fair
Design Director David Harris
Art Director Gregory Mastrianni
Designers John Dixon, David Harris
Photo Editor Susan White
Photographer Josef Astor
Publisher Condé Nast Publications Inc.
Issue July 1996
Category Portrait Story

324
Publication Martha Stewart Living
Creative Director Gael Towey
Design Director Eric Pike
Designers Eric Pike, Susan Spungen, Wendy Kromer
Photo Editor Heidi Posner
Photographer Victoria Pearson
Publisher Time Inc.
Issue Winter 1996/Spring 1997
Category Still Life/Interiors Spread

325
Publication US
Art Director Richard Baker
Designer Richard Baker
Photo Editor Jennifer Crandall
Photographer Robert Paul Maxwell
Publisher US Magazine Co., L.P.
Issue October 1996
Category Portraits Spread

FROM FASHION TO FONDANT... **COUTURE**CAKES

PHOTOGRAPHS BY VICTORIA PEARSON

219

O MAR EPPS

The Brooklyn-born actor won't get a swelled head even with his debut as the new resident on ER, America's No. 1 show.

BY MICHAEL KAPLAN

Photographs by ROBERT MAXWELL

137

THE LIGHT IN THE NORTH

Style, grit, pride, prayer, sport, dreams, talk, desolation, beauty, and other aspects of Harlem life. Photographed by Dan Winters

SYLVIA'S DOORMAN DAVID CALLOWAY GREETS A PATRON.

ABOVE, THE NEON AT 125TH STREET'S LEGENDARY APOLLO THEATRE.
OPPOSITE, 10-YEAR-OLD DAVID THOMAS ON HIS WAY TO CHURCH.

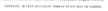

OPPOSITE, CLOUDS OVER THE OLD HOTEL THERESA, 125TH STREET AND SEVENTH AVENUE.
ABOVE, OUTSIDE THE LAGREE BAPTIST CHURCH ON THURSDAY AFTERNOON.

326
Publication New York
Design Director Robert Newman
Art Director Florian Bachleda
Photo Editor Margery Goldberg
Photographer Dan Winters
Publisher K-III Publications
Issue December 23-30, 1996
Category Reportage/Travel Story

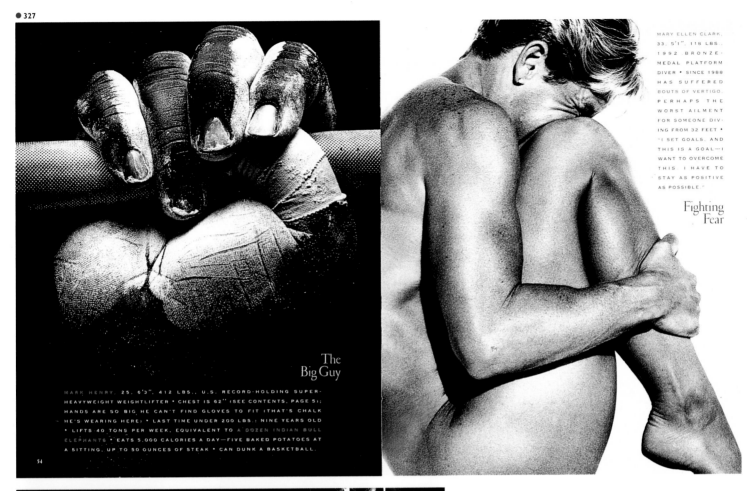

MARY ELLEN CLARK, 33, 5'1", 118 LBS. 1992 BRONZE-MEDAL PLATFORM DIVER • SINCE 1988 HAS SUFFERED BOUTS OF VERTIGO. PERHAPS THE WORST AILMENT FOR SOMEONE DIVING FROM 32 FEET • "I SET GOALS. AND THIS IS A GOAL—I WANT TO OVERCOME THIS. I HAVE TO STAY AS POSITIVE AS POSSIBLE."

Fighting
Fear

The
Big Guy

MARK HENRY, 25, 6'3", 412 LBS., U.S. RECORD-HOLDING SUPER-HEAVYWEIGHT WEIGHTLIFTER • CHEST IS 62" (SEE CONTENTS, PAGE 5); HANDS ARE SO BIG HE CAN'T FIND GLOVES TO FIT (THAT'S CHALK HE'S WEARING HERE) • LAST TIME UNDER 200 LBS.: NINE YEARS OLD • LIFTS 40 TONS PER WEEK, EQUIVALENT TO A DOZEN INDIAN BULL ELEPHANTS • EATS 5,000 CALORIES A DAY—FIVE BAKED POTATOES AT A SITTING, UP TO 50 OUNCES OF STEAK • CAN DUNK A BASKETBALL.

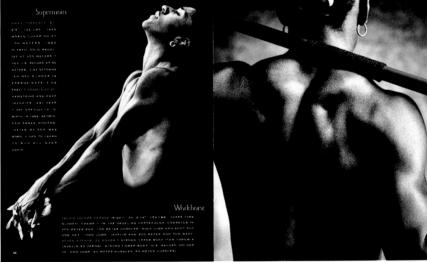

Supermom

Workhorse

Mermaids

● 327
Award Silver
Publication LIFE
Design Director Tom Bentkowski
Designer Tom Bentkowski
Photo Editor David Friend
Photographer Joe Mcnally
Publisher Time Inc.
Issue July 1996
Category Portrait Story

The Dubliners

The back streets of Dublin are the perfect environment for fall's gritty style.

Daryl K's lace-trimmed nylon tulle shell, at Daryl K, New York. Marc Jacobs Look's boiled wool skirt, at Bloomingdale's, New York; Ultimo, Chicago; and Marc Jacobs boutique, New York (opening in September). Carhartt's hooded sweatshirt jacket. Wool scarf from Petro Zillia. Shoes from Patrick Cox.

PHOTOGRAPHED BY PERRY OGDEN

On him: Nautica's charcoal wool jacket and pants, at The Nautica Store, New York. Calvin Klein's black wool twisted crepe sweater, at Louis Boston, select Marshall Field's stores and Calvin Klein, New York. On her: Martine Sitbon's purple wool and nylon sweater and brown tweed skirt, at Henri Bendel and Barneys New York. Fendi handbag.

Beauty Note:
A shimmery finish gives nude lipstick a touch of vim and vigor. From Vincent Longo, try Divine Flesh.

● 328
Publication W
Creative Director Dennis Freedman
Design Director Edward Leida
Art Director Kirby Rodriguez
Designers Edward Leida, Rosalba Sierra, Marcella Bové
Photographer Perry Ogden
Publisher Fairchild Publications
Category Fashion/Beauty Story

LOLLIPOP ALERT
Rubber slip dress $80
by Daang Goodman for Tripp,
N.Y.C. white net
zip-up go-go boots $32
available at Smylonylon.
Opposite page:
Transparent baby
windbreaker $15
available at Smylonylon,
rubber nipple skirt $60
by Daang Goodman
for Tripp, N.Y.C.
spiked choker
custom-made by
Futaba Hatashi,
sunglasses by
Ray-Ban.

PHOTOGRAPHY SILVER ●

FLY GIRLS

BUBBLEGUM CRISIS
High-tech quilted jacket $82
and high-tech leggings $94
both by Daang Goodman
for Tripp, N.Y.C.
Opposite page:
Camouflage tank top $71 by
Meme, army fatigue pant $54,
camouflage sweat belt,
wear gloves, and bullet necklace
all available at Canal Jeans
N.Y.C. spiked bracelet custom-
made by Futaba Hatashi.

● 329
Award Silver
Publication Vibe
Art Director Diddo Ramm
Designer Diddo Ramm
Illustrator Butch Belair
Photo Editor George Pitts
Publisher Time Inc.
Issue February 1996
Category Photo Illustration Story

my hands

THE LIFE THEY'VE LED, THE STORIES THEY KNOW

My hands were born breech in the winter of 1945, two hours before sunrise. Sitting with them today, 2,000 miles and more from that spot, turning each one slowly in bright sunshine, watching the incisive light raise short pale lines from old cuts, and seeing the odd cant of the left ring finger, I know they have a history, though I cannot remember where it starts. As they began, they gripped whatever might hold me upright, surely caressed and kneaded my mother's breasts, yanked at the restrictions of pajamas. And then they learned to work buttons, to tie shoelaces and lift the milk glass, to work together.

The pressure and friction of a pencil as I labored down the spelling of words right-handed raised the oldest permanent mark, a callus on the third joint of the middle finger. I remember no trying accident to either hand in these early years, though there must have been glass cuts, thorn punctures, spider bites, nails torn to the cuticle, scrapes from bicycle falls, pin blisters from kitchen grease, splinters, nails blackened from door pinches, pain lingering from having all four fingers forced backward at once, and the first true weariness, coming from work with lumber and stones, with tools made for larger hands.

It is from these first years, 5 and 6 and 7, that I am able to remember so well, or perhaps the hands themselves remember, a great range of texture — the subtle corrugation of cardboard boxes, the thickness of the oilcloth on the kitchen table, the shuddering bend of a horse's short-haired belly, the even give in warm wax, the raised oak grain in my school-desk top, the fuzziness of dead bumblebees, the coarseness of sheaves immediate to the polished silk of unhusked corn, the burnish of rake handles and bucket bails, the rigidness of the bony crest rising beneath the skin of a dog's head, the tackiness of flypaper, the sharpness of saws and ice picks.

It is impossible to determine where in any such specific memory, of course, texture gives way to heft, to shape, to temperature. The coolness of a camellia petal seems inseparable from that texture, warmth from the velvet rub of a horse's nose, heft from a brick's dry burr. And what can be said, as the hand recalls the earliest touch and exploration, of how texture changes with depth? Not alone the press of the palm on a dog's head or fingers boring to the roots of wool on a sheep's flank, but of, say, what happens with an orange. The hands work in concert to disassemble the fruit, running a thumb over the beaded surface of the skin, plying the soft white flay of the interior, the stringent of fiber clinging to the translucent skin cases, dividing the yielding grain of the flesh beneath, with its hard, wrinkled seeds. And, further, how is one to separate these textures from a memory of the burst of fragrance as the skin is torn, or from the sound of the sections being parted — to say nothing of the taste, juice dripping from the chin, or the urge to devour, then, even the astringent skin, all initiated by the curiosity of the hands?

Looking back, it's easy to see that the education of the hands (and so the person) begins like a language: a gathering of simple words, the assembly of simple sentences, all this leading eventually to the forging of instructive metaphors. Afterward nothing can truly be separated, to

By Barry Lopez

PHOTOGRAPHS BY KURT MARKUS

98

MEN'S JOURNAL, DECEMBER 1996/JANUARY 1997

the slow petting
OF THE LOVED DOG IS THE INCREASINGLY
COMPLICATED HEART SPEAKING WITH THE HAND

i marveled at the hands
OF OTHER CREATURES, AT THE ELEGANT AND
INCONTROVERTIBLE BEAUTY OF THEIR DESIGN.

Publication Men's Journal
Art Director David Armario
Designers David Armario, Tom Brown
Photographer Kurt Markus
Publisher Wenner Media
Issue December 1996/January 1997
Category Still Life/Interiors Story

SILVER PHOTOGRAPHY

Gerry Spence vs. Janet Reno

Not content with clearing Randy Weaver of the Ruby Ridge murder charge, the legendary attorney says he has one last score to settle. He wants to punish the federal agents who killed Vicki and Sammy Weaver

BY MARY A. FISCHER • PHOTOGRAPHS BY NIGEL PARRY

PHIL BORGES

The art of award-winning Seattle-based photographer Phil Borges documents and celebrates the complexity, diversity, and humanity of the world's cultures and subcultures. From an interactive documentary featuring high-risk, inner-city teenagers to the images from his latest book *Tibetan Portrait: The Power of Compassion*, he evokes the most sympathetic and tender of emotions. "Compassion," Borges says, "is the essence of Tibetan culture." These powerful images, which begin an international tour this month at the Capitol Rotunda in Washington, DC, not only capture the spirituality and caring of these remarkable people but the talent and empathy of this exceptional photographer.

the cutting edge

Anglo-grunge kings Bush take a hard look at their contemporaries and, laughing in the face of the sophomore jinx, examine their new release, *Razorblade Suitcase*.

■ 331
Publication GQ
Design Director John Korpics
Designer John Korpics
Photo Editor Karen Frank
Photographer Nigel Parry
Publisher Condé Nast Publications Inc.
Issue January 1996
Category Portraits Spread

■ 332
Publication Guitar World
Design Director Peter Yates
Designer Peter Yates
Photographer Alastair Thain
Publisher Harris Publications
Issue January 1997
Category Portraits Spread

■ 333
Publication Guardian Weekend
Art Director Mark Porter
Designer Mark Porter
Photographer Noelle Hoeppe
Publisher Guardian Media Group
Issue November 30, 1996
Category Portraits Single Page

■ 334
Publication Hemispheres
Creative Director Jaimey Easler
Designer J. Kirby Heard
Photographer Phil Borges
Publisher Pace Communications, Inc.
Client United Airlines
Issue June 1996
Category Portrait Story

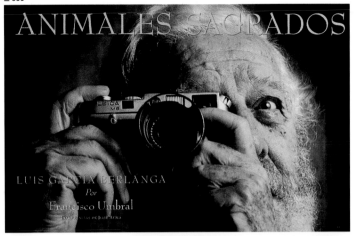

ANIMALES SAGRADOS

LUIS GARCIA BERLANGA

Por

Francisco Umbral

FOTOGRAFÍAS DE JOSÉ AYMA

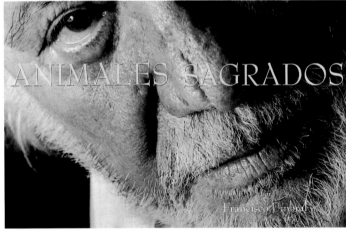

ANIMALES SAGRADOS

Francisco Umbral

ANIMALES SAGRADOS

LA VOZ O PACO RABAL

De electricista a galán, de galán a santo, un santo inocente con milana posada sobre el hombro. El tiempo y la vida le han ido dejando cicatrices, huellas como las de un torero contra las que nunca se ha revelado y así son tan suyas como la calva cultivada que le corona. Francisco Umbral, galardonado la semana pasada con el Premio Príncipe de Asturias de las Letras 1996, retrata al actor.

ANIMALES SAGRADOS

Por

Francisco Umbral

FOTOGRAFÍAS DE JOSÉ AYMA

ANIMALES SAGRADOS

LA LIBERTAD O CELA

Francisco Umbral comienza con Camilo José Cela –"un mito de adolescencia, un amigo de juventud y un maestro de madurez"– una serie mensual de retratos, de perfiles, conversaciones y recuerdos de sus "animales sagrados". Desmesurado y genial, "un hombre libre entre un millón de cadáveres", Umbral dibuja un personaje apasionante que, cinco años después de ganar el Nobel, acaba de ser galardonado con el Cervantes.

■ 335
Publication La Revista
Design Director Carmelo Caderot
Art Director Rodrigo Sanchez
Designers Rodrigo Sanchez,
Maria González, Amparo Redondo,
Miguel Buckenmeyer
Photo Editor Chema Conesa
Photographer Jose Ayma
Publisher Unidad Editorial S.A.
Issue December 1, 1996
Category Portrait Story

■ 336
Publication La Revista
Design Director Carmelo Caderot
Art Director Rodrigo Sanchez
Designers Rodrigo Sanchez, Miguel Buckenmeyer,
Maria González, Amparo Redondo
Photo Editor Chema Conesa
Photographer Jose Ayma
Publisher Unidad Editorial S.A.
Issue May 19, 1996
Category Portrait Story

■ 337
Publication La Revista
Design Director Carmelo Caderot
Art Director Rodrigo Sanchez
Designers Rodrigo Sanchez, Miguel
Buckenmeyer, Maria González,
Amparo Redondo
Photo Editor Chema Conesa
Photographer Jose Ayma
Publisher Unidad Editorial S.A.
Issue January 7, 1996
Category Portrait Story

ANIMALES SAGRADOS

Por Francisco Umbral

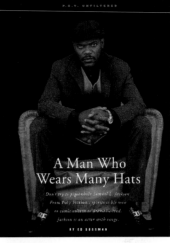

P.O.V. UNFILTERED

A Man Who Wears Many Hats

Don't try to pigeonhole Samuel L. Jackson. From Pulp Fiction's righteous hit man to comic villain to dramatic lead, Jackson is an actor with range.

BY ED GROSSMAN

■ 340
Publication P.O.V.
Design Director Lynette Cortez
Designer Lynette Cortez
Photo Editor Michael Green
Photographer Art Streiber
Publisher Byob/Freedom Ventures, Inc.
Studio Lynette Cortez Design, Inc.
Issue September 1996
Category Portrait Story

Esquire

Mister Lonely Hearts

Why would a fifty-year-old comic genius like Steve Martin want to spend the rest of his life alone? He wouldn't. Know any nice girls? BY MARTHA SHERRILL

"Just working no longer makes you happy"

"I'm not concerned about my place on the Hollywood feeding scale. That's somebody else's concern."

■ 341
Publication DoubleTake
Design Director Molly Renda
Designer Molly Renda
Photo Editor Alex Harris
Photographer Ethel Wolvovitz
Publisher Center for Documentary Studies
Issue Summer 1996
Category Portrait Spread

■ 338
Publication La Revista
Design Director Carmelo Caderot
Art Director Rodrigo Sanchez
Designers Maria González,
Miguel Buckenmeyer,
Amparo Redondo, Rodrigo Sanchez
Photo Editor Chema Conesa
Photographer Jose Ayma
Publisher Unidad Editorial S.A.
Issue September 29, 1996
Category Portrait Story

■ 339
Publication Esquire
Design Director Diana LaGuardia
Art Directors Rockwell Harwood,
Michael Mrak
Photo Editor Marianne Butler
Photographer Andrew Eccles
Publisher The Hearst Corporation-
Magazines Division
Issue April 1996
Category Portrait Story

■ 342

JOURNEY
THROUGH THE GATES OF HELL
Photographs by Giorgia Fiorio Text by Tala Skari

THE QUEST FOR DANGER

■ 343

LIFE SPECIAL
In the glittering twilight of the second Friday of this month, several million Americans will undergo a spectacular transformation, departing from the mainstream of American life. They will begin chanting beautiful ancient blessings as candles flicker in the gathering darkness of their homes. They will share loaves of sweet, amber bread and apples dipped in honey. In the morning, they will enter tabernacles where white-robed cantors sing the praises of the Lord and loud blasts are trumpeted on ram's horns. Then they will embrace one another and offer a traditional greeting: "May you be inscribed for a good year in the Book of Life." Later, many will walk to a stream or a lake and cast crusts of bread upon the water, a symbol of their wish to cleanse themselves of selfishness and sin. And then, on Monday, their ancient identities will once again recede as they reenter the American mainstream. A few of these Americans are pictured here. They are Jews.
PORTRAITS OF A PEOPLE
Frédéric Brenner
Charles Hirshberg

■ 342
Publication LIFE
Design Director Tom Bentkowski
Designer Jean Andreuzzi
Photo Editor David Friend
Photographer Giorgia Fiorio
Publisher Time Inc.
Issue March 1996
Category Portrait Story

■ 343
Publication LIFE
Design Director Tom Bentkowski
Designer Jean Andreuzzi
Photo Editor David Friend
Photographer Frédéric Brenner
Publisher Time Inc.
Issue September 1996
Category Portrait Story

■ 344

DISCOVERY
See Me, Feel Me, Touch Me, Heal Me
The mud-caked man on the facing page is Andrew Weil, a 54-year-old Harvard-trained physician who believes that a revolution is brewing in American medicine. He is only one among a rapidly growing number of M.D.s who combine traditional Western techniques with alternative therapies such as herbalism and acupuncture. "By uniting philosophies that have been separate for a long time," says Weil of the integrative medicine movement, "health care will be completely transformed."
By George Howe Colt
Photography by Joe McNally

■ 344
Publication LIFE
Design Director Tom Bentkowski
Designer Tom Bentkowski
Photo Editor Bobbi Baker Burrows
Photographer Joe McNally
Publisher Time Inc.
Issue September 1996
Category Portraits Spread

THE LIGHT OF HIS LOVE

He wanted a boy. In the summer of 1984 his wife Cathy gave birth to Sharon. It took the new father about three hours to fall hopelessly in love. But something was wrong with their beautiful baby, and the Paderborn photographer and his American wife could not get doctors to agree on a diagnosis. As years went by, they learned that Sharon has a seizure disorder, speech delay, perhaps a bit of autism. She has severely impaired vision and tests at six or so years below grade level. Still, as the following excerpts from her father's journal make heartbreakingly clear, once in love with a child in love for a lifetime.

IN HIS OWN WORDS AND PHOTOGRAPHS, LEON BORENSZTEIN ILLUMINATES HIS DAUGHTER'S JOURNEY THROUGH DARKNESS

It looks as if I'll always have more **questions** *than answers.*

I am **fearful** *and I don't know of what.*

Where is God? Somebody young, innocent and **helpless** *needs Him.*

Will my darling remember all the **good times** *we had together?*

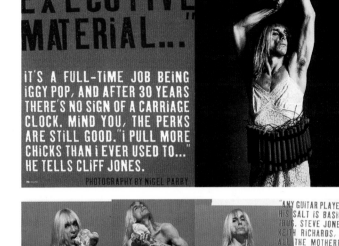

"NOT EXECUTIVE MATERIAL..."

IT'S A FULL-TIME JOB BEING IGGY POP, AND AFTER 30 YEARS THERE'S NO SIGN OF A CARRIAGE CLOCK. MIND YOU, THE PERKS ARE STILL GOOD. "I PULL MORE CHICKS THAN I EVER USED TO..." HE TELLS CLIFF JONES.

PHOTOGRAPHY BY NIGEL PARRY

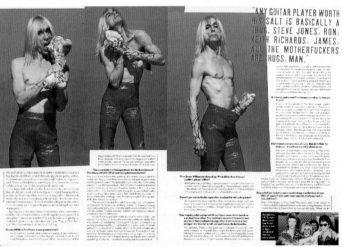

"ANY GUITAR PLAYER WORTH HIS SALT IS BASICALLY A THUG. STEVE JONES, RON, KEITH RICHARDS, JAMES, ALL THE MOTHERFUCKERS ARE THUGS, MAN."

Dick Gregory is a comic, but his 30 years of activism is no laughing matter

By Sherry L. Howard

He's No Joke

At a press conference about allegations that the CIA helped pump crack cocaine into a Los Angeles neighborhood, Dick Gregory is doing what he's always done: making folks laugh.

After weeks of radio shows, protests and arrests, Gregory and radio host Joe Madison have finally gotten the media's attention. Reporters jam the room in a Washington, D.C., hotel. The faces behind the podium are stern, the mood somber. As Gregory put it earlier, "Nothing in the history of this planet is as foul as what we are about to uncover."

■ 345
Publication LIFE
Design Director Tom Bentkowski
Designer Tom Bentkowski
Photo Editor David Friend
Photographer Leon Borensztein
Publisher Time Inc.
Issue December 1996
Category Portrait Story

■ 346
Publication Mojo
Creative Director Andy Cowles
Art Director Stephen Fawcett
Designer Stephen Fawcett
Photo Editor Susie Hudson
Photographer Nigel Parry
Publisher EMAP Metro
Issue April 1996
Category Portrait Story

■ 347
Publication Emerge
Design Director Wayne Fitzpatrick
Designers Wayne Fitzpatrick, Debra Moore
Photographer Dwight Carter
Publisher B.E.T. Publications
Issue December 1996
Category Portraits Spread

14 x 2

Fourteenth Street, Manhattan's melting pot and great divide, is also a romantic promenade. Here are ten pairs who happily show the world their love. Photographed by Christian Witkin

THE HOMELESS MESS

A squat, mean building in the Bronx is the first step for homeless families looking for shelter, as well as the center of a white-hot battle between the mayor and advocacy groups. A hard look at what goes on there, and inside the places families are sent afterward, reveals just how desperately off-track our homeless policy is.
By Peter Hellman

big

Julian Schnabel, he of the oversize paintings and the oversize ego, has always been his own best publicist. Now, with his new movie, *Basquiat*, he's written himself into an eighties legend.
By James Kaplan

Schnabel in Montauk: "Most of the artists I know are artless."
Photographed by Dan Chavkin for *New York*

ANDREW WYLIE'S GREAT INVENTION

A failure as a writer, he re-made himself as a cartoon villain of an agent: The Jackal, scourge of publishers, hijacker of other agents' writers. Is Wylie serious about the role he is playing?
By Rebecca Mead

■ 348
Publication New York
Design Director Robert Newman
Art Director Florian Bachleda
Photo Editor Margery Goldberg
Photographer Christian Witkin
Publisher K-III Publications
Issue December 23-30, 1996
Category Portrait Story

■ 349
Publication New York
Design Director Robert Newman
Photo Editors Margery Goldberg, Nakyung Han
Photographer Bastienne Schmidt
Publisher K-III Publications
Issue September 2, 1996
Category Portraits Spread

■ 350
Publication New York
Design Director Robert Newman
Designer Deanna Lowe
Photo Editors Margery Goldberg, Sabine Meyer
Photographer Dan Chavkin
Publisher K-III Publications
Issue August 12, 1996
Category Portraits Spread

■ 351
Publication New York
Design Director Robert Newman
Photo Editors Margery Goldberg, Sabine Meyer
Photographer Frank W. Ockenfels 3
Publisher K-III Publications
Issue August 5, 1996
Category Portraits Spread

THE THIRD SEX

Just as gay men and lesbians once battled against the medical establishment, "intersexuals," or hermaphrodites—many of them gay—are now fighting for their bodies. Anne-christine d'Adesky reports.

Photograph by Mary Ellen Mark

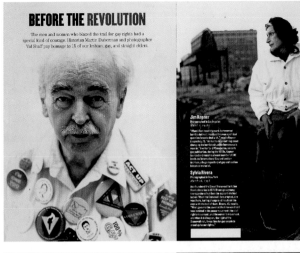

BEFORE THE REVOLUTION

The men and women who blazed the trail for gay rights had a special kind of courage. Historian Martin Duberman and photographer Val Shaff pay homage to 15 of our lesbian, gay, and straight elders.

Jim Kepner

Sylvia Rivera

Harry Hay

■ 352
Publication New York
Design Director Robert Newman
Art Director Florian Bachleda
Photo Editor Margery Goldberg
Photographer Dan Winters
Publisher K-III Publications
Issue December 23-30, 1996
Category Portraits Single Page

■ 353
Publication Out
Art Director David O'Connor
Designer David O'Connor
Photo Editor Amy Steiner
Photographer Mary Ellen Mark
Publisher Out Magazine
Issue September 1996
Category Portraits Spread

■ 354
Publication Out
Art Director David O'Connor
Designer David O'Connor
Photo Editor Amy Steiner
Photographer Val Shaff
Publisher Out Magazine
Issue July 1996
Category Portrait Story

PHOTOGRAPHY PORTRAITS ■ MERIT

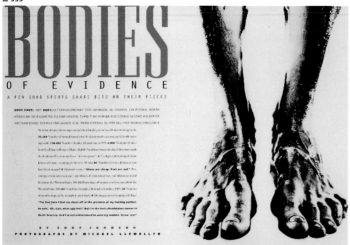

BODIES
OF EVIDENCE
A FEW GOOD SPORTS SHARE BITS ON THEIR PIECES

BY CORY JOHNSON
PHOTOGRAPHS BY MICHAEL LLEWELLYN

IN THE WAKE OF A HELI-SKIING CRASH THAT KILLED HIS WIFE AND THREE OTHERS AND SHATTERED HIS BODY, MAVERICK FILMMAKER MIKE HOOVER HAS BEEN LEFT TO REJOIN THE LIVING THE ONLY WAY HE KNOWS HOW

SURVIVOR

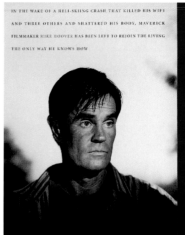

SNOW WAS FALLING HEAVILY AS TWO BELL HELICOPTERS DROPPED THE SKIERS on a powdery slope in Nevada's Ruby Range. The heli-skiing vacation was planned to be the high point of the winter, a reunion of friends with commingled roots in Hollywood and the high mountains, hosted by Frank G. Wells, president of the Walt Disney Company. Included in the party were Wells's old climbing buddy Dick Bass, owner of Utah's Snowbird Ski Resort, actor Clint Eastwood, and Mike Hoover and Beverly Johnson, a husband-and-wife team of adventure filmmakers. Hoover knew Eastwood from *The Eiger Sanction*, the 1975 action film for which Hoover had shot the climbing sequences and served as Eastwood's stunt double.

Despite the bad weather, the skiers stayed in the high country, swooping through open bowls and over rolling benches studded with limber pines. At the end of the day, two helicopters came to ferry them back to their base lodge. By the time the chopper carrying Wells, Hoover, and Johnson took off, a fierce storm had blown in, forcing them to land minutes later. They waited out the squall for

BY TRIP GABRIEL PHOTOGRAPH BY DAN WINTERS

Birds of a Feather

Whether it's joking with Christopher Reeve or reading up Barbara Bush, ROBIN WILLIAMS & NATHAN LANE the loving couple of The Birdcage share a willingness to do anything for a laugh

by BRUCE BIBBY

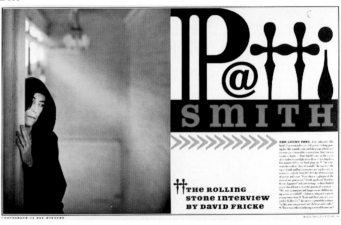

P@TTI
SMITH

>>>>>>>>>>>

†† THE ROLLING STONE INTERVIEW BY DAVID FRICKE

SEE LOOKS THIS

LEGENDS OF COUNTRY MUSIC

PORTFOLIO BY MARK SELIGER

"WOMEN ARE PROBABLY closest to God," says Me'Shell Ndegéocello, 27-year-old mother, rock & roll activist and funk philosopher. She raises an arched eyebrow and gives a confident shrug. "We make life." She's in New York, in her favorite Harlem breakfast spot, discussing "Peace Beyond Passion," her new album.

Me'Shell Ndegéocello fights

BLACK&BLUE

for your rights on "Peace Beyond Passion"

BY ANN POWERS

■ 359
Publication Rolling Stone
Creative Director Fred Woodward
Designers Fred Woodward, Gail Anderson
Photo Editor Jodi Peckman
Photographer Mark Seliger
Publisher Wenner Media
Issue December 26, 1996-Jan. 9, 1997
Category Portrait Story

■ 360
Publication Rolling Stone
Creative Director Fred Woodward
Designers Fred Woodward, Gail Anderson
Photo Editor Jodi Peckman
Photographer Albert Watson
Publisher Wenner Media
Issue October 17, 1996
Category Portraits Spread

■ 361
Publication Rolling Stone
Creative Director Fred Woodward
Designers Fred Woodward, Lee Bearson
Photo Editor Jodi Peckman
Photographer Mary Ellen Mark
Publisher Wenner Media
Issue September 19, 1996
Category Portraits Spread

■ 362
Publication Rolling Stone
Creative Director Fred Woodward
Designer Geraldine Hessler
Photo Editor Jodi Peckman
Photographer Mark Seliger
Publisher Wenner Media
Issue September 5, 1996
Category Portraits Spread

PHOTOGRAPHY PORTRAITS ■ MERIT

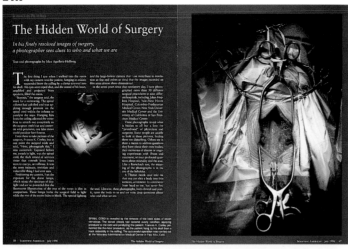

The Hidden World of Surgery

*In his finely resolved images of surgery,
a photographer sees clues to who and what we are*

Text and photographs by Max Aguilera-Hellweg

OFF TRACK

Parker Chapin might not have laid off associate Jan Sigmon just because she was a woman with a child. But her sex discrimination suit provides an object lesson for firms in how not to navigate parenting issues.

By Alison Frankel

PHOTOGRAPHS BY DOUGLAS LEVERE

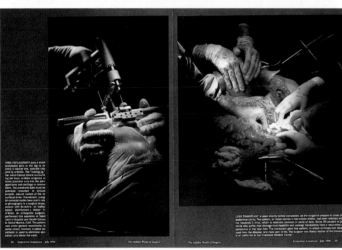

IF JAN SIGMON WASN'T THE
model associate, neither was Parker Chapin's corporate department a model workplace for women in the early 1990s. Not only did the department have no women partners—according to trial testimony, no woman associate had ever stuck it out long enough to be considered for partner.

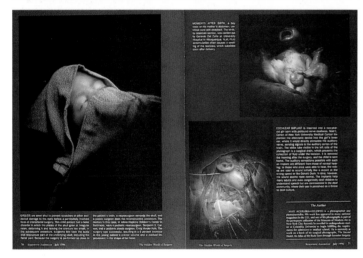

THERE'S A WEIRDNESS
about the testimony from Sigmon's trial. She and the partners seemed to have been working in different law firms. Sigmon saw everything that happened after the spring of 1991 as an attempt to drive her out; partners, meanwhile, were worried about keeping the firm alive.

■ 363
Publication Scientific American
Creative Directors Edward Bell,
Jana Brenning
Photo Editor Nisa Geller
Photographer Max Aguilera-Hellweg
Publisher Scientific American Inc.
Issue July 1996
Category Portrait Story

■ 364
Publication The American Lawyer
Art Director Caroline Bowyer
Designer Caroline Bowyer
Photo Editor Tracey Litt
Photographer Douglas Levere
Publisher American Lawyer Media
Issue December 1996
Category Portrait Story

PawPrints

Why do I love *Bones*, **Keith Carter**'s latest pet project?

What Nan Goldin Saw This Summer

On Oct. 3, the acclaimed photographer of the downtown demimonde goes uptown for her big Whitney retrospective. With the show approaching, she did what she has done for more than 25 years: documented the lives of the people she loves.

By Michael Kimmelman

THE UGLY GIRL

For Heather Matarazzo, 13, playing a loser in the movies was totally cool.

BY LAURA JAMISON

■ 365
Publication Texas Monthly
Creative Director D.J. Stout
Designers D.J. Stout, Nancy McMillen
Photo Editor D.J. Stout
Photographer Keith Carter
Publisher Texas Monthly
Issue December 1996
Category Portrait Story

■ 366
Publication
The New York Times Magazine
Art Director Janet Froelich
Photo Editor Kathy Ryan
Photographer Nan Goldin
Publisher The New York Times
Issue September 22, 1996
Category Portrait Story

■ 367
Publication
The New York Times Magazine
Art Director Janet Froelich
Designer Susan Dazzo
Photo Editor Sarah Harbutt
Photographer Gentl & Hyers
Publisher The New York Times
Issue May 26, 1996
Category Portraits Spread

■ 368

■ 369

■ 370

■ 371

■ 372

■ 373

■ 368
Publication US
Art Director Richard Baker
Designer Richard Baker
Photo Editors Jennifer Crandall,
Rachel Knepfer
Photographer Richard Burbridge
Publisher US Magazine Co., L.P.
Issue April 1996
Category Portraits Single Page

■ 369
Publication US
Art Director Richard Baker
Designer Richard Baker
Photo Editor Jennifer Crandall
Photographer Matthew Rolston
Publisher US Magazine Co., L.P.
Issue December 1996
Category Portraits Single Page

■ 370
Publication US
Art Director Richard Baker
Photo Editor Jennifer Crandall
Photographer Dana Lixenberg
Publisher US Magazine Co., L.P.
Issue June 1996
Category Portraits Single Page

■ 371
Publication US
Art Director Richard Baker
Designer Richard Baker
Photo Editor Jennifer Crandall
Photographer Max Vadukul
Publisher US Magazine Co., L.P.
Issue April 1996
Category Portraits Spread

■ 372
Publication US
Art Director Richard Baker
Designer Richard Baker
Photo Editor Jennifer Crandall
Photographer Mark Seliger
Publisher US Magazine Co., L.P.
Issue December 1996
Category Portraits Spread

■ 373
Publication US
Art Director Richard Baker
Designer Richard Baker
Photo Editor Jennifer Crandall
Photographer Mark Seliger
Publisher US Magazine Co., L.P.
Issue August 1996
Category Portraits Spread

■ 374

■ 375

■ 374
Publication US
Art Director Richard Baker
Designers Richard Baker, Dan Stark
Photo Editor Jennifer Crandall
Photographer Mark Seliger
Publisher US Magazine Co., L.P.
Issue May 1996
Category Portraits Single Page

■ 375
Publication US
Art Director Richard Baker
Photo Editors Jennifer Crandall, Rachel Knepfer
Photographer Mary Ellen Mark
Publisher US Magazine Co., L.P.
Issue October 1996
Category Portraits Single Page

■ 376

■ 378

■ 377

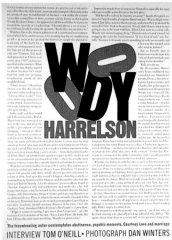

■ 379

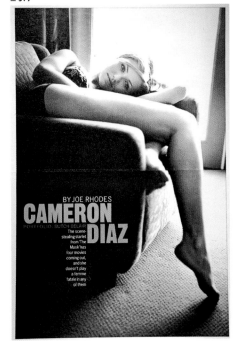

■ 376
Publication US
Art Director Richard Baker
Designer Richard Baker
Photo Editor Jennifer Crandall
Photographer Peggy Sirota
Publisher US Magazine Co., L.P.
Issue January 1996
Category Portraits Spread

■ 377
Publication US
Art Director Richard Baker
Designer Richard Baker
Photo Editors Jennifer Crandall, Rachel Knepfer
Photographer Kate Garner
Publisher US Magazine Co., L.P.
Issue October 1996
Category Portraits Single Page

■ 378
Publication US
Art Director Richard Baker
Designer Richard Baker
Photo Editor Jennifer Crandall
Photographer Dan Winters
Publisher US Magazine Co., L.P.
Issue July 1996
Category Portraits Spread

■ 379
Publication US
Art Director Richard Baker
Designer Richard Baker
Photo Editor Jennifer Crandall
Photographer Butch Belair
Publisher US Magazine Co., L.P.
Issue March 1996
Category Portraits Spread

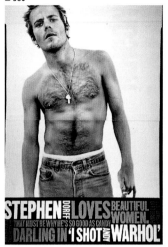

STEPHEN **DORFF** LOVES BEAUTIFUL WOMEN. THAT MUST BE WHY HE'S SO GOOD AS CANDY DARLING IN '1 SHOT AND WARHOL'

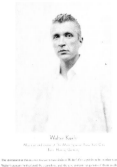

Walter Kuch

Stephen Dorff is usually a loquacious, intense, "up" kind of guy. Chances are he'd even say so himself. But the 22-year-old actor's energy is a little low tonight, as he scrunches

Philip Y. F. Lui

"IT'S A MISTAKE TO PUT HIM IN DUDE ROLES!" SAYS DIRECTOR MARY HARRON "HE HAS AN INSTINCT FOR TRAGEDY AND COMPLEXITY"

Hally Thacher

■ 380
Publication US
Art Director Richard Baker
Designers Richard Baker, Dan Stark
Photo Editor Jennifer Crandall
Photographer Mark Seliger
Publisher US Magazine Co., L.P.
Issue May 1996
Category Portrait Story

■ 382
Publication Utne Reader
Art Director Lynn Phelps
Designer Lynn Phelps
Photographer Andrew French
Publisher Lens Publishing Company, Inc
Issue December 24, 1996
Category Portrait Story

■ 381
Publication US
Art Director Richard Baker
Designer Richard Baker
Photo Editors Jennifer Crandall, Rachel Knepfer
Photographer Mary Ellen Mark
Publisher US Magazine Co., L.P.
Issue October 1996
Category Portraits Single Page

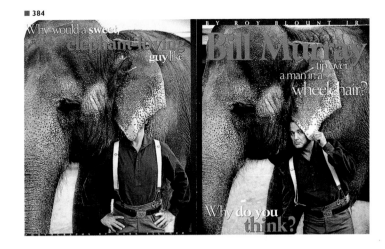

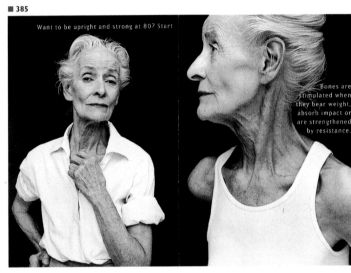

PHOTOGRAPHY PORTRAITS ■ MERIT

Publication Men's Journal
Art Director David Armario
Designer David Armario
Photo Editor Deborah Needleman
Photographer John Huet
Publisher Wenner Media
Issue April 1996
Category Portrait Story

Publication Men's Journal
Art Director David Armario
Designers Dirk Barnett,
David Armario, Tom Brown
Photo Editor Denise Sfraga
Photographer Mark Seliger
Publisher Wenner Media
Issue August 1996
Category Portraits Spread

Publication Living Fit
Art Director John Miller
Designer John Miller
Photo Editor Beth Katz
Photographer Robert Paul Maxwell
Publisher Weider Publications
Issue January/February 1996
Category Portraits Spread

VANITY FAIR
NOVEMBER 1996

MADONNA'S PRIVATE DIARIES

THIS IS A DIARY OF SORTS, a sketchbook of feelings, ideas, and dreams, all relating to one subject—the making of *Evita*. By the time this movie comes out, I will have been living vicariously through her for two years. I remember sitting down during Christmas of '94 and writing an impassioned letter to the director, Alan Parker, listing the reasons why I was the only one who could portray her, explaining that only I could understand her passion and her pain. I can honestly say that I did not write this letter of my own free will. It was as if some other force drove my hand across the page.

Soon afterward I heard from Alan and following several nerve-racking meetings the part was mine. This was only the beginning of what turned out to be a great adventure. I could kick myself for not starting my journal then, but there was so little time. I had to learn the score, train my voice, and master the tango before flying to London to record the sound track. Throughout the year I had the most extraordinary experiences, and we hadn't even begun filming, so the month before shooting began I made a promise to myself that I would write everything down that happened to me. I had butterflies in my stomach and I knew I was in for the ride of my life. I wanted to remember every detail. And so I began ...

Photographs by MARIO TESTINO • Styled by LORI GOLDSTEIN

"They're going to ask me if I am a Catholic and if I wear underwear and if I'm a lonely person."

"I believe that divorce is more socially acceptable than single motherhood or being honest about your future."

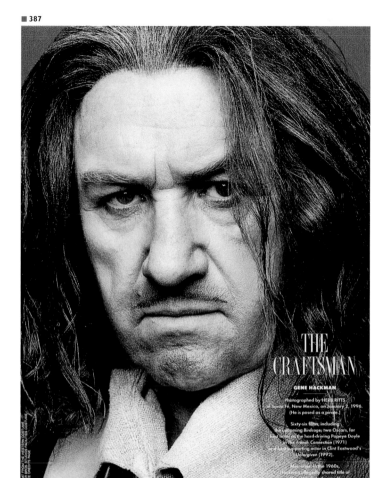

THE CRAFTSMAN

GENE HACKMAN.

Photographed by HERB RITTS in Santa Fe, New Mexico, on January 2, 1996. (He is posed as a pirate.)

Sixty-six films, including the upcoming *Birdcage*; two Oscars, for best actor as the hard-driving Popeye Doyle in *The French Connection* (1971) and best supporting actor in Clint Eastwood's *Unforgiven* (1992).

Moreover: In the 1960s, Hackman allegedly shared title of Least Likely to Succeed with friend and Pasadena Playhouse comrade Dustin Hoffman (opposite). Hackman was fired from the role of Mr. Robinson in *The Graduate* (1967) by Mike Nichols for having "so much juice and vitality."

■ 387
Publication Vanity Fair
Design Director David Harris
Art Director Gregory Mastrianni
Photographer Herb Ritts
Publisher Condé Nast Publications Inc.
Issue April 1996
Category Portraits Single Page

■ 386
Publication Vanity Fair
Design Director David Harris
Art Director Gregory Mastrianni
Designers David Harris, Gregory Mastrianni
Photo Editor Susan White
Photographer Mario Testino
Publisher Condé Nast Publications Inc.
Issue November 1996
Category Portrait Story

LET THE GAMES BEGIN...

ANNIE LEIBOVITZ photographs 61 of America's most promising athletes as they vie for a chance to compete at the 1996 Summer Olympic Games in Atlanta

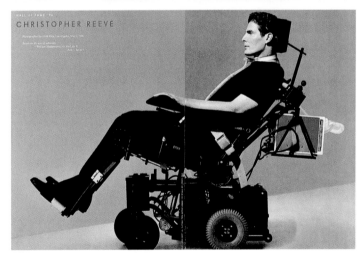

■ 388
Publication Vanity Fair
Design Director David Harris
Art Directors Annie Leibovitz, Raul Martinez
Photo Editor Susan White
Photographer Annie Leibovitz
Publisher Condé Nast Publications Inc.
Issue May 1996
Category Portrait Story

■ 389
Publication Vanity Fair
Design Director David Harris
Art Director Gregory Mastrianni
Photo Editor Susan White
Photographers Annie Leibovitz, Herb Ritts
Publisher Condé Nast Publications Inc.
Issue December 1996
Category Portrait Story

J. ORVILLE WOOD
WAS LAID TO REST ON A
BITTERLY COLD AND BLUSTERY
MORNING IN CHATTANOOGA, TENNESSEE.

PROMISES
TO KEEP

New Year's resolutions are hard to follow through on, but some of America's best financial planners have come up with ten that are well worth the willpower

1
INVESTOR,
KNOW THYSELF

BY PAUL DAVIES

WORLD
TOUR
'97

The international markets are now balanced uneasily between sluggish growth and rising stock prices. This year, that may well change.

BY TODD G. BUCHHOLZ

STRONG

suits

A celebrity-heavy crowd showed up when Joe and Gene Silverberg defied the odds and opened their new **Bigsby & Kruthers** store on Michigan Avenue. Within days, though, it was their giant portrait of His Hairness Dennis Rodman that was stopping traffic. A look at the brothers leading the war on casual days

PHOTOGRAPHY BY MARC HAUSER

It's no easy task finding solid opportunities in today's volatile market. Here's what the experts are buying for 1997.

BY JOHN FRIED

TOP PICKS
FOR 1997

■ 392
Publication Worth
Art Director Philip Bratter
Designers Philip Bratter, Cynthia Eddy, Jennifer Kapps, Lynette Cortez
Photo Editor Jennifer Graylock
Photographer Geof Kern
Publisher Capital Publishing
Issue November 30, 1996
Category Portraits Spread

■ 393
Publication Worth
Art Director Philip Bratter
Designers Philip Bratter, Cynthia Eddy, Jennifer Kapps, Lynette Cortez
Photo Editor Jennifer Graylock
Photographer Geof Kern
Publisher Capital Publishing
Issue November 30, 1996
Category Portraits Spread

■ 394
Publication Chicago
Art Director Kerry Robertson
Designer Kerry Robertson
Photographer Marc Hauser
Publisher K-III Publications
Issue February/March 1996
Category Portraits Spread

■ 390
Publication Worth
Art Director Philip Bratter
Designer Philip Bratter
Photo Editor Jennifer Graylock
Photographer Jeffery Newbury
Publisher Capital Publishing
Issue May 1996
Category Portraits Spread

■ 391
Publication Worth
Art Director Philip Bratter
Designers Philip Bratter, Cynthia Eddy, Jennifer Kapps, Lynette Cortez
Photo Editor Jennifer Graylock
Photographer Geof Kern
Publisher Capital Publishing
Issue November 30, 1996
Category Portraits Spread

THE FUNDAMENTALS

FILM NOIR

BADMODET

■ 395

Publication Vibe
Art Director Lee Ellen Fanning
Designer Lee Ellen Fanning
Photo Editor George Pitts
Photographer Robert Paul Maxwell
Publisher Time Inc.
Issue November 1996
Category Fashion/Beauty Spread

■ 396

Publication Vibe
Art Director Lee Ellen Fanning
Designer Lee Ellen Fanning
Photo Editor George Pitts
Photographer Guy Aroch
Publisher Time Inc.
Issue Summer 1996
Category Fashion/Beauty Story

■ 397

Publication
Dagens Nyheters Manadsmagasin
Art Directors Peter Alenas,
Pompe Hedengren
Photo Editor Hakan Lindgren
Photographer Lars Tunbjork
Publisher Dagens Nyheter
Issue June 29, 1996
Category Fashion/Beauty Story

PHOTOGRAPHY FASHION & BEAUTY ■ MERIT

Hunger Pains

By Joyce Ross

A rare look inside an eating-disorder clinic reveals the hard-fought recovery of women who've spent their lives battling anorexia and bulimia.

Big

Women and men of a certain avoirdupois come together for support and gripe sessions. Not to mention the sex.

By Judith Newman

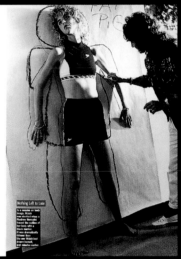

To paraphrase a slogan: We're here, we're wide, get used to it.

Fat Fiction

A Thin Line

■ 398

Publication Allure
Design Director Shawn Young
Designer Shawn Young
Photo Editor Michelle Fuertes
Photographer Mary Ellen Mark
Publisher Condé Nast Publications Inc.
Issue June 1996
Category Fashion/Beauty Story

■ 399

Publication Allure
Design Director Shawn Young
Designer Shawn Young
Photo Editor Michelle Fuertes
Photographer Mary Ellen Mark
Publisher Condé Nast Publications Inc.
Issue March 1996
Category Fashion/Beauty Story

The acid test

From bilious green to Windex blue, the   new pastels are cool and off-color

MAXiMUM ExPOSURE

In the multitudinous
Maldives, Mark Connolly
dresses up a few good islands
while Dana Dickey muses
on taking it all off

PHOTOGRAPHS BY DAVID LACHAPELLE

PHOTOGRAPHY FASHION & BEAUTY ■ MERIT

■ 400
Publication Allure
Design Director Shawn Young
Designer Shawn Young
Photo Editor Michelle Fuertes
Photographer Glen Luchford
Publisher Condé Nast Publications Inc.
Issue January 1996
Category Fashion/Beauty Story

■ 401
Publication Condé Nast Traveler
Design Director Robert Best
Photo Editor Kathleen Klech
Photographer David LaChapelle
Publisher Condé Nast Publications Inc.
Issue July 1996
Category Fashion/Beauty Story

leather bound

By Peter Webster. Styled by Robert E. Beauchamp. Photographs by Rodney Smith.

The E420 shifts fashion into highgear **Power dressing**

Photo by Norman Jean Roy

"A great-looking car is always a good accessory for one of my suits." —Paul Smith

"A man in a suit commands authority and power." —Andrew Fezza

■ 402
Publication Departures
Art Director Bernard Scharf
Designer Marc Kehoe
Photo Editor Amy Koblenzer
Photographer Rodney Smith
Publisher American Express Publishing
Issue November/December 1996
Category Fashion/Beauty Story

■ 403
Publication Mercedes Momentum
Creative Director Robb Allen
Designers Jamie Ferrand, Eugene Wang
Photo Editor Andrea Jackson
Photographer Norman Jean Roy
Publisher Hachette Filipacchi Magazines, Inc.
Client Mercedes
Issue January/February 1996
Category Fashion/Beauty Story

How to Succeed in Business...

*without really trying to look too corporate. Check out our guy, who gets to the top in a **disarmingly casual style***

Photographs by
PEGGY SIROTA

If you can't get to the top in a green coat, you won't get there sooner in a blue one.

Punctuality is the soul of business.

GQ recommends
the Flat-Front Khaki

Photographs by
Max Vadukul

IT'S HIP TO BE SQUARE...

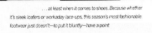

...at least when it comes to shoes. Because whether it's sleek loafers or workaday lace-ups, this season's most fashionable footwear just doesn't—to put it bluntly—have a point

To recap: For business or the weekend, the square-toed shoe and all that's cool about it is best captured by a bad pun—style that's outstanding in the field.

■ 404
Publication GQ
Design Director John Korpics
Designer Rina Migliaccio
Photo Editor Karen Frank
Photographer Peggy Sirota
Publisher Condé Nast Publications Inc.
Issue January 1996
Category Fashion/Beauty Story

■ 405
Publication GQ
Design Director John Korpics
Designer John Korpics
Photo Editor Karen Frank
Photographer Peggy Sirota
Publisher Condé Nast Publications Inc.
Issue May 1996
Category Fashion/Beauty Story

■ 406
Publication GQ
Design Director John Korpics
Designer John Korpics
Photo Editor Karen Frank
Photographer Patricia McDonough
Publisher Condé Nast Publications Inc.
Issue January 1996
Category Fashion/Beauty Spread

■ 407
Publication GQ
Design Director John Korpics
Designer Susan Dazzo
Photo Editor Karen Frank
Photographer Max Vadukal
Publisher Condé Nast Publications Inc.
Issue April 1996
Category Fashion/Beauty Story

PHOTOGRAPHY FASHION & BEAUTY ■ MERIT

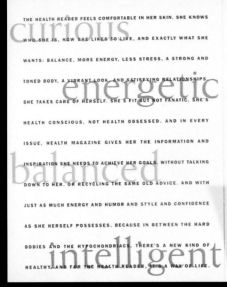

THE HEALTH READER FEELS COMFORTABLE IN HER SKIN. SHE KNOWS
WHO SHE IS, HOW SHE LIKES TO LIVE, AND EXACTLY WHAT SHE
WANTS: BALANCE, MORE ENERGY, LESS STRESS, A STRONG AND
TONED BODY, A VIBRANT LOOK, AND SATISFYING RELATIONSHIPS
SHE TAKES CARE OF HERSELF. SHE'S FIT BUT NOT FANATIC. SHE'S
HEALTH CONSCIOUS, NOT HEALTH OBSESSED. AND IN EVERY
ISSUE, HEALTH MAGAZINE GIVES HER THE INFORMATION AND
INSPIRATION SHE NEEDS TO ACHIEVE HER GOALS. WITHOUT TALKING
DOWN TO HER. OR RECYCLING THE SAME OLD ADVICE. AND WITH
JUST AS MUCH ENERGY AND HUMOR AND STYLE AND CONFIDENCE
AS SHE HERSELF POSSESSES. BECAUSE IN BETWEEN THE HARD
BODIES AND THE HYPOCHONDRIACS, THERE'S A NEW KIND OF
HEALTHY. AND FOR THE HEALTH READER, IT'S A WAY OF LIFE.

curious energetic balanced intelligent

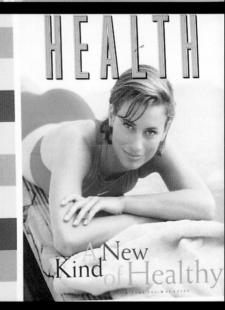

The Haircut

By Mary Roach

Photographs by Kenji Toma

Who's the Healthiest of Them All? *By Laura Fraser*

SHE IS, SAY TOP OBESITY EXPERTS.

HOGWASH, SAYS EXERCISE SCIENTIST STEVEN BLAIR. **THIS WOMAN IS** 20 POUNDS HEAVIER, BUT SHE'S IN BETTER SHAPE.

■ 408
Publication Health
Art Director Jane Palecek
Designer Dorothy Marchall
Photographers Michael Tighe, Maria Robledo, Michael Johnson, Robert Schlatter, Jonelle Weaver, Kenji Toma, Paul Franz-Moore, David Martinez, Dana Gallagher, Michael Haber, Amy Neunsinger
Publisher Time Inc.
Issue September 1996
Category Fashion/Beauty Story

■ 409
Publication Health
Art Director Jane Palecek
Designer Jane Palecek
Photographer Kenji Toma
Publisher Time Inc.
Issue January/February 1996
Category Fashion/Beauty Spread

■ 410
Publication Health
Art Director Jane Palecek
Designer Jane Palecek
Photographer David Martinez
Publisher Time Inc.
Issue May/June 1996
Category Fashion/Beauty Spread

STORMY
LEATHER

SUITS ME

You may own a sharp coat-and-pants combo or an extra-smart suit,
but that doesn't mean you know how to wear it. BY CARLOS A. ROSAS

PHOTOGRAPHS BY
JEFF BARK

FASHION EDITOR
JOSEPH OPPEDISANO

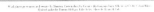

■ 411
Publication Marie Claire
Art Director Anthony Jazzar
Designer Anthony Jazzar
Photo Editor Monica Dolfini
Photographer Patrick Demarchelier
Publisher The Hearst Corporation-
Magazines Division
Issue November 1996
Category Fashion/Beauty Story

■ 412
Publication P.O.V.
Design Director Lynette Cortez
Designer Lynette Cortez
Photo Editor Michael Green
Photographer Jeff Bark
Publisher Byob/Freedom Ventures, Inc.
Studio Lynette Cortez Design, Inc.
Issue November 1996
Category Fashion/Beauty Story

the Beats go On. Spring style evokes the New York days of Kerouac and Ginsberg. Fashion by Vincent Boucher. Photographs by Stewart Shining.

THE RIPPLE EFFECT

Top hairdressers know a thing or two about making waves. In this Salon News portfolio, Didier Malige showcases the crimping and other hot-iron techniques that touched off the styling trend of the new hair season.

PHOTOGRAPHED BY DIEGO UCHITEL

■ 413
Publication Out
Art Director David O'Connor
Designer David O'Connor
Photo Editor Amy Steiner
Photographer Stewart Shining
Publisher Out Magazine
Issue May 1996
Category Fashion/Beauty Story

■ 414
Publication Salon News
Creative Director Victoria Maddocks
Design Director Jean Griffin
Designer Victoria Maddocks
Photographer Diego Uchitel
Publisher Fairchild Publications
Issue August 1996
Category Fashion/Beauty Story

um mar de lama

Há muito tempo o **Mar Morto** tem sido celebrado como um dos milagres naturais – um tesouro de minerais **vitais** para a saúde e a beleza.

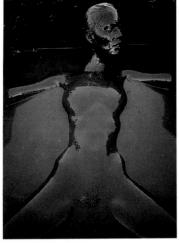

tudo nada

PEDAÇO DE AZUL QUEBRA A MONOTONIA DOS BEIGES.

NO MAR MORTO TUDO FLUTUA

E O SAL LEVA VOCÊ ÀS NUVENS.

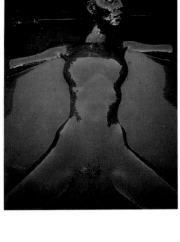

415
Publication Vogue Brazil
Creative Director Mariana Ochs
Art Director Graziela Peres
Photographer Kenneth Willardt
Publisher Carta Editorial Ltd.
Studio Mariana Ochs Design
Issue October 1996
Category Fashion/Beauty Spread

416
Publication Vogue Brazil
Creative Director Mariana Ochs
Art Director Graziela Peres
Photographer Kenneth Willardt
Publisher Carta Editorial Ltd.
Studio Mariana Ochs Design
Issue October 1996
Category Fashion/Beauty Spread

Outsmart the season

Who says winter has to send you into the depths of despair? Here are 45 health, fitness, clothing and nutrition tips that will help you stay fit in the coming season of discontent. BY JOE KITA

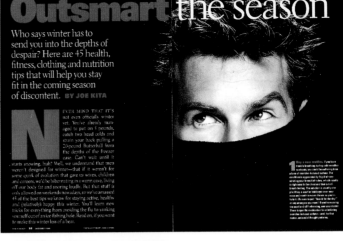

EVER MIND THAT IT'S not even officially winter yet. You've already managed to put on 5 pounds, catch two head colds and strain your back pulling a 20-pound Butterball from the depths of the freezer case. Can't wait until it starts snowing, huh? Well, we understand that men weren't designed for winter—that if it weren't for some quirk of evolution that gave us wives, children and careers, we'd be hibernating in a warm cave, living off our body fat and snoring loudly. But that stuff is only allowed on weekends nowadays, so we've amassed 45 of the best tips we know for staying active, healthy and (relatively) happy this winter. You'll learn new tricks for everything from avoiding the flu to yanking yourself out of an ice-fishing hole. Read on, if you want to make this winter less of a bear.

Clear a stuffy nose with chicken soup."

"Keep your lips sealed with petroleum jelly.

"Ask your mate to apply the moisturizer."

417
Publication Men's Health
Creative Directors Roger Black, Mary Jane Fahey
Designers Mary Jane Fahey, Michael Jones
Illustrator Ariel Capeda
Photo Editor Susan Isaak
Photographer James White
Publisher Rodale Press
Studio Roger Black Partners Inc.
Issue December 1996
Category Fashion/Beauty Story

PHOTOGRAPHY FASHION & BEAUTY ■ MERIT

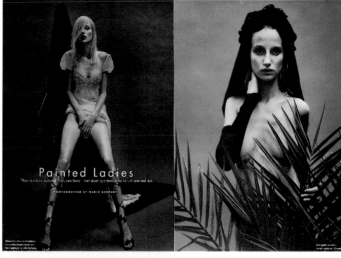

■ 418
Publication W
Creative Director Dennis Freedman
Design Director Edward Leida
Art Director Kirby Rodriguez
Designers Edward Leida, Rosalba Sierra
Photographer Nathaniel Goldberg
Publisher Fairchild Publications
Category Fashion/Beauty Story

■ 419
Publication W
Creative Director Dennis Freedman
Design Director Edward Leida
Art Director Kirby Rodriguez
Designer Rosalba Sierra
Photographer Mario Sorrenti
Publisher Fairchild Publications
Category Fashion/Beauty Story

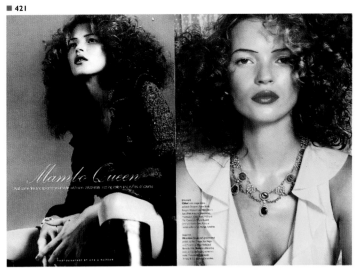

■ 420
Publication W
Creative Director Dennis Freedman
Design Director Edward Leida
Art Director Kirby Rodriguez
Designers Edward Leida, Rosalba Sierra
Photographer Mario Testino
Publisher Fairchild Publications
Category Fashion/Beauty Story

■ 421
Publication W
Creative Director Dennis Freedman
Design Director Edward Leida
Art Director Kirby Rodriguez
Designers Kirby Rodriguez, Marcella Bové
Photographer Craig McDean
Publisher Fairchild Publications
Category Fashion/Beauty Story

PHOTOGRAPHY FASHION & BEAUTY ■ MERIT

Amazing Grace

It's a stunning combination: Naomi Campbell's raw beauty and fall's sumptuous textures.

Falling in Place
Geometrics and glitter evoke the Seventies, when glamour and rock 'n' roll collided.

422
Publication W
Creative Director Dennis Freedman
Design Director Edward Leida
Art Director Kirby Rodriguez

423
Publication W
Creative Director Dennis Freedman
Design Director Edward Leida
Art Director Kirby Rodriguez

a SENSE *of* PLACE

■ 424
Publication The New York Times Magazine
Art Director Janet Froelich
Designer Joel Cuyler
Stylist Elizabeth Stewart
Photographer David LaChapelle
Publisher The New York Times
Issue August 4, 1996
Category Fashion/Beauty Story

■ 425
Publication Country Home
Art Director Paul Zimmerman
Designer Paul Zimmerman
Photographer Bryan Whitney
Publisher Meredith Corporation
Issue August 1996
Category Still Life/Interiors Story

426
Publication Bride's
Art Director Phyllis Cox
Designer Claire de Villiers
Photographer Jim Cooper
Publisher Condé Nast Publications Inc.
Issue October/November 1996
Category Still Life/Interiors Story

427
Publication Bride's
Art Director Phyllis Cox
Designer Phyllis Cox
Photographer Christopher Micaud
Publisher Condé Nast Publications Inc.
Issue December 1996/January 1997
Category Still Life/Interiors Story

428
Publication Bride's
Art Director Phyllis Cox
Designer Robin Whitney
Photographer Bob Hiemstra
Publisher Condé Nast Publications Inc.
Issue December 1996/January 1997
Category Still Life/Interiors Story

THIS IS GARDEN STYLE

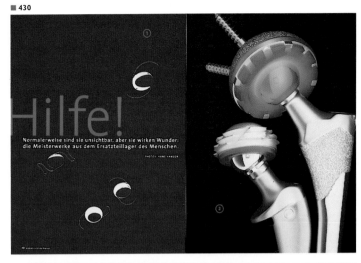

Hilfe!

Normalerweise sind sie unsichtbar, aber sie wirken Wunder: die Meisterwerke aus dem Ersatzteillager des Menschen.

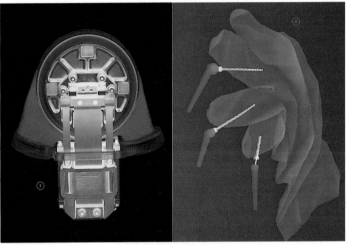

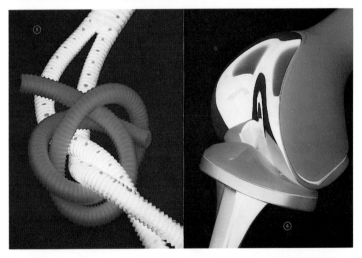

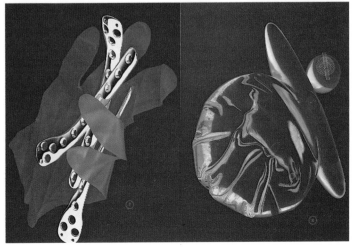

■ 429
Publication Garden Design
Creative Director Michael Grossman
Art Director Christin Gangi
Designer Christin Gangi
Photo Editor Susan Goldberger
Photographer Christopher Hirsheimer
Publisher Meigher Communications
Issue April/May 1996
Category Still Life/Interiors Story

■ 430
Publication Sueddeutsche Zeitung Magazin
Art Director Markus Rasp
Designers Anne Blaschke, Otto Dzemla, Wilhelm Raffelsberger
Photo Editors Eva Ernst, Claudia Mueller
Photographer Hans Hansen
Publisher Magazin Verlagsges. Sueddeutsche Zeitung mbh
Issue September 27, 1996
Category Still Life/Interiors Story

PHOTOGRAPHY STILL LIFES & INTERIORS ■ MERIT

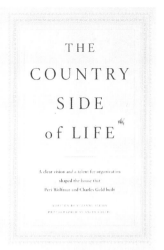

THE
COUNTRY
SIDE
of LIFE

A clear vision and a talent for organization
shaped the house that
Peri Wolfman and Charles Gold built

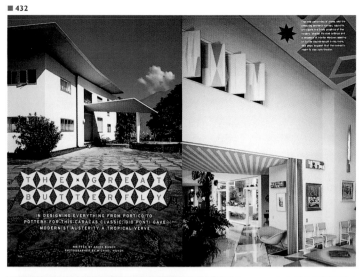

THE ONLY permissible red touch in the Wolfman-Gold universe is the red barn, a local landmark that is the focal point of the nearly surreal view of the Kansas-like open sky, and a landscape that stretches to the horizon

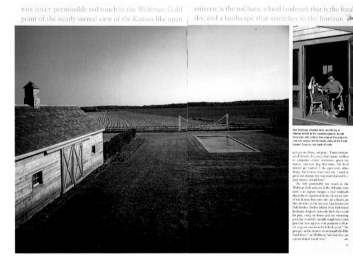

■ 431
Publication Condé Nast House & Garden
Art Director Robert Priest
Designer Debra Bishop
Photo Editor Deborah Needleman
Photographer Anita Calero
Publisher Condé Nast Publications Inc.
Issue September 1996
Category Still Life/Interiors Story

■ 432
Publication Condé Nast House & Garden
Art Director Robert Priest
Designer Robert Priest
Photo Editor Deborah Needleman
Photographer Michael Mundy
Publisher Condé Nast Publications Inc.
Issue December 1996
Category Still Life/Interiors Story

PERSIST
AND
PREVAIL

TWO MANHATTAN
CONNOISSEURS
HAVE A MOTTO
THAT PERFECTLY
DESCRIBES THEIR
LIVES AND SENSE
OF STYLE

WRITTEN BY JAMES REGINATO
PHOTOGRAPHED BY ANITA CALERO

ESSENTIAL GESTURES

PRODUCED BY JEFFREY W. MILLER   PHOTOGRAPHED BY ILAN RUBIN

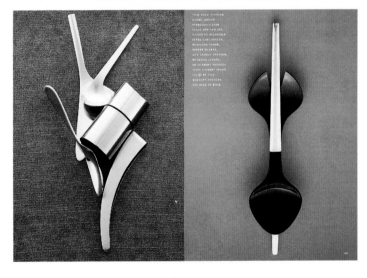

■ **433**
Publication Condé Nast House & Garden
Art Director Robert Priest
Designer Debra Bishop
Photo Editor Deborah Needleman
Photographer Anita Calero
Publisher Condé Nast Publications Inc.
Issue November 1996
Category Still Life/Interiors Story

■ **434**
Publication Condé Nast House & Garden
Art Director Robert Priest
Designer Debra Bishop
Photo Editor Deborah Needleman
Photographer Ilan Rubin
Publisher Condé Nast Publications Inc.
Issue October 1996
Category Still Life/Interiors Story

PEAS PLEASE

WE'RE ALL POD PEOPLE WHEN IT COMES TO
THESE BRIGHT GREEN JEWELS OF SPRING

BY CHINA AMUNI · PHOTOGRAPHS BY ANITA CALERO

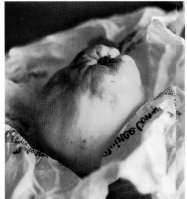

If it was a quince that tempted Eve, we know why

ENJOYING THE FORBIDDEN FRUIT

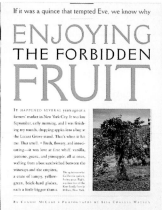

BY CONNIE McCABE · PHOTOGRAPHS BY LISA CHARLES WATSON

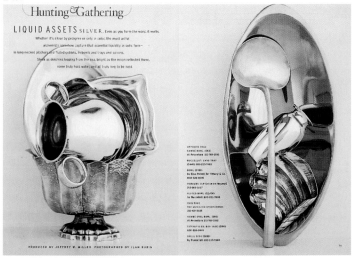

Hunting & Gathering

LIQUID ASSETS SILVER. Even as you form the word, it melts.

PRODUCED BY JEFFREY W. MILLER · PHOTOGRAPHED BY ILAN RUBIN

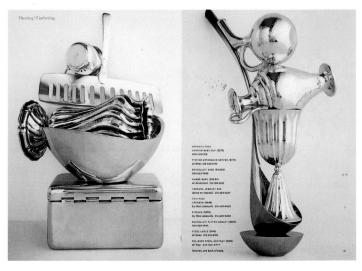

Hunting & Gathering

■ 435
Publication Saveur
Creative Director Michael Grossman
Art Director Jill Armus
Designer Jill Armus
Photo Editor Susan Goldberger
Photographer Anita Calero
Publisher Meigher Communications
Issue March/April 1996
Category Still Life/Interiors Story
　　■ **A** Still Life/Interiors Spread

■ 436
Publication Saveur
Creative Director Michael Grossman
Art Director Jill Armus
Designer Toby Fox
Photo Editor Susan Goldberger
Photographers Lisa Charles Watson,
Guy Kloppenberg
Publisher Meigher Communications
Issue November/December 1996
Category Still Life/Interiors Spread

■ 437
Publication Condé Nast Traveler
Art Director Robert Priest
Designer Laura Harrigan
Photo Editor Deborah Needleman
Photographer Ilan Rubin
Publisher Condé Nast Publications Inc.
Issue December 1996
Category Still Life/Interiors Story

MOOD INDIGO

IN WHITE-HOT MARRAKECH,
ONE HOUSE RADIATES COLORFUL COOL

PHOTOGRAPHED BY NADIR. WRITTEN BY KATRINE AMES

Desert swank

1960s Palm Springs was an inviting landscape for enthusiasts of the Modern. Three houses from that decade prove that a sleek domestic envelope can still wear a personal style.

"I realized we had a better setting for a glass house than Philip Johnson did. He was in the middle of a field in Connecticut. But we were on a mountain without any neighbors, and with spectacular views"

NADU AND LIPPINI WANTED THEIR HOUSE TO BE A COMPROMISE BETWEEN AFRICAN, MOROCCAN, AND ITALIAN—WITH A HINT OF MEXICAN

THE MOST STRIKING FEATURE OF THE HOUSE IS ITS VARIED, VIBRANT PALETTE. EACH ROOM IS A DIFFERENT COLOR, IN SHADES THAT MANAGE TO BE SUBTLE AND INTENSE

Desert sage

■ 438
Publication Condé Nast Traveler
Art Director Robert Priest
Designer Robert Priest
Photo Editor Deborah Needleman
Photographer Nadir
Publisher Condé Nast Publications Inc.
Issue December 1996
Category Still Life/Interiors Story

■ 439
Publication Condé Nast Traveler
Art Director Robert Priest
Designer Debra Bishop
Photo Editor Deborah Needleman
Photographer Dewey Nicks
Publisher Condé Nast Publications Inc.
Issue September 1996
Category Still Life/Interiors Story

PHOTOGRAPHY STILL LIFES & INTERIORS ■ MERIT

■ 440

■ 441

■ 442

■ 443

■ 440
Publication Martha Stewart Living
Creative Director Gael Towey
Design Director Eric Pike
Designers Eric Pike, Robert Fisher, Susan Spungen
Photo Editor Heidi Posner
Photographer Victoria Pearson
Publisher Time Inc.
Issue December 1996/January 1997
Category Still Life/Interiors Story

■ 441
Publication Martha Stewart Living
Creative Director Gael Towey
Design Director Eric Pike
Designers Eric Pike, Frances Boswell
Photo Editor Heidi Posner
Photographer Anita Calero
Publisher Time Inc.
Issue July/August 1996
Category Still Life/Interiors Spread

■ 442
Publication Martha Stewart Living
Creative Director Gael Towey
Design Director Eric Pike
Art Director Claudia Bruno
Designers Claudia Bruno,
Margaret Roach
Photo Editor Heidi Posner
Photographer Christopher Baker
Publisher Time Inc.
Issue June 1996
Category Still Life/Interiors Spread

■ 443
Publication Martha Stewart Living
Creative Director Gael Towey
Designer Gael Towey
Photo Editor Heidi Posner
Photographer Christopher Baker
Publisher Time Inc.
Issue March 1996
Category Still Life/Interiors Spread

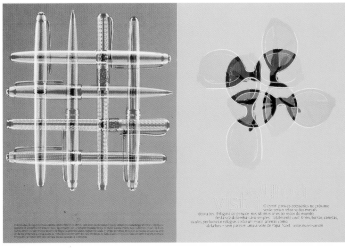

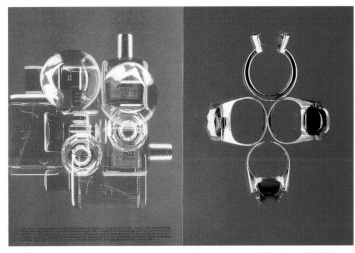

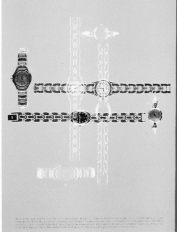

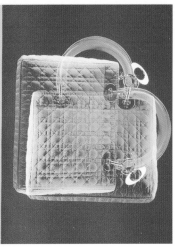

■ 444
Publication Martha Stewart Living
Creative Director Gael Towey
Design Director Eric Pike
Designers Eric Pike, Susan Spungen
Photo Editor Heidi Posner
Photographer Victoria Pearson
Publisher Time Inc.
Issue June 1996
Category Still Life/Interiors Story

■ 445
Publication Martha Stewart Living
Creative Director Gael Towey
Design Director Eric Pike
Art Director Anne Johnson
Designers Anne Johnson,
Stephana Bottom
Photo Editor Heidi Posner
Photographer Victor Schrager
Publisher Time Inc.
Issue February 1996
Category Still Life/Interiors Spread

■ 446
Publication Vogue Brazil
Creative Director Mariana Ochs
Art Director Graziela Peres
Photographer Paulo Vainer
Publisher Carta Editorial Ltd.
Studio Mariana Ochs Design
Issue August 1996
Category Still Life/Interiors Story

PHOTOGRAPHY STILL LIFES & INTERIORS ■ MERIT

living colors

BY PETCH JANEY

Photography by
VICTOR SCHRAGER

Red

Orange

Yellow

Green

Blue Purple

Juices
The Smartest Way to Get Plenty of Fruits and Vegetables

By David Sharp

PHOTOGRAPHS by MARIA ROBLEDO

Apple   Cranberry   Orange   Tomato   Wheat Grass   Carrot

AN ANCIENT TRADITION OFFERS
POWERFUL HEALTH BENEFITS
FOR MODERN TIMES.

JAPANESE
TEA
CEREMONY

BY LIZ BRODY

OUTSIDE, the sounds of Los Angeles street life scratch at the walls as if trying to get in — a woman screaming, "You stay away from here!" in Spanish, clanging pots and boom-box rap, the general scuffle of hubris. But inside a wood and paper room, where the windows have bamboo eyeblinds and the floors are hushed with mats of straw, no one notices. Once Sosei Matsumoto's class has begun, there is only tea.

THREE KINDS OF TEA

CHANOYU 101

FOR ALL THE TEA IN AMERICA

■ 447
Publication Health
Art Director Jane Palecek
Designer Jane Palecek
Photographer Victor Schrager
Publisher Time Inc.
Issue March/April 1996
Category Still Life/Interiors Story

■ 448
Publication Health
Art Director Jane Palecek
Designer Jane Palecek
Photographer Maria Robledo
Publisher Time Inc.
Issue July/August 1996
Category Still Life/Interiors Story

■ 449
Publication Shape
Creative Director Kathy Nenneker
Design Director Stephanie K. Birdsong
Art Director Yvonne Duran
Designer Yvonne Duran
Photo Editor Melissa O'Brien
Photographers Melissa Robledo,
Gregg Segal
Publisher Weider Publications
Issue April 1996
Category Still Life/Interiors Story

GRAB A POPSICLE FROM THE FREEZER AND TAKE A LOAD OFF—
we've already scouted out the season's best toys
for grownups: 25 primary goodies for sunning,
sipping, splashing, lounging, toting, grilling,
and even one for working. Because nothing
brings out our inner child like a warm breeze

THE
SHADES
of
SUMMER

PHOTOGRAPHY BY OMAN

wave washed

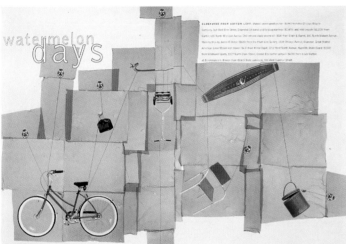

watermelon
days

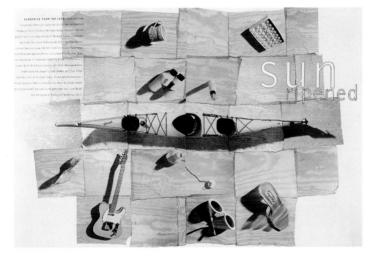

sun ripened

Ritz and Famous

Toutes Suites

■ 450
Publication Chicago
Art Director Kerry Robertson
Designer Kerry Robertson
Photographer Oman
Publisher K-III Publications
Issue June 1996
Category Still Life/Interiors Story

■ 451
Publication Town & Country
Creative Director Mary Shanahan
Art Director Margot Frankel
Designer Alice Kang
Photo Editor Miguel Flores-Vianna
Photographer Pascal Chevalier
Publisher The Hearst Corporation-Magazines Division
Issue December 1996
Category Reportage/Travel Story

SURVIVAL
of the
COLDEST

ADELIE

Text by Jeff Rubin
Photographs by Wolfgang Kaehler

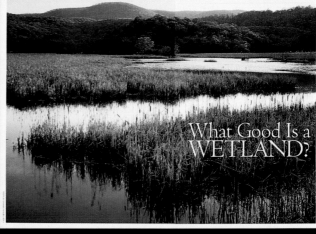

What Good Is a WETLAND?
BY TED WILLIAMS

CHINSTRAP

GENTOO AND ROCKHOPPER

EMPEROR

452
Publication Audubon
Photo Editor Peter Howe
Photographer Wolfgang Kaehler
Issue November/December 1996
Category Reportage/Travel Story

453
Publication Audubon
Photo Editor Peter Howe
Photographers Carr Clifton,
David Muench, Larry Ulrich,
Jim Brandenburg, Stephen Kirkpatrick,
David Harp, Wendy Shattil,
Bob Rozinski, Thomas Styczynski,
Charles Gurche
Issue November/December 1996
Category Reportage/Travel Story

INVISIBLE BROOKLYN

Stanley Greenberg's
photographs explore the
hidden interiors of
the city's grand landmarks
and industrial remains.

Sticks & Stones
Mickey for Mayor?
Disney's new town may be so perfect
it's a nightmare. BY MICHAEL POLLAN

PHOTOGRAPHS BY TODD EBERLE

Odyssey
That Mighty Sculptor, Time
The twelfth-century stone temples
of Angkor are reshaped by the
embrace of the centuries

PHOTOGRAPH BY KENRO IZU

IN CAMBODIA all things flow, and
nothing is permanent. Wedged
between Thailand, Vietnam, and Laos,
pierced by a long history of coloniza-
tion and internal upheaval, the country
is a place of permanent mutability.
Even Angkor Thom, one of the
world's greatest architectural monuments, has not been immune. Built in
the twelfth and thirteenth centuries
as the royal capital of the Khmer
empire, it was abandoned in the fif-
teenth century. Since then its ruins
have been continuously reshaped by
the successive invasions of banyan
trees that cascade like water over the
ancient temple stones. And yet, the
changes wrought upon Angkor Thom
and nearby Angkor Wat have made
these planes peaceful, even
inspiring—mysteriously beautiful
joinings of nature's work to man's.
Moved by the spiritual tranquility
at the heart of these trees and stones,
Kenro Izu began photographing the
ruins in 1992. As he did, he sensed a
tragic distance between these silent
monuments and the violence of the
surrounding countryside, where both
adults and children lose their legs and
sometimes their lives stepping on the
land mines that are another of
Cambodia's legacies. And so, while
Izu's photographs inspire our awe for
manifestations of accidental beauty,
the profits from them go to Friends
Without A Border, an organization
dedicated to raising money for the
Angkor Clinic for Children.

■ 454

Publication Brooklyn Bridge
Art Director Wendy Palitz
Designer Wendy Palitz
Photographer Stanley Greenberg
Publisher Brooklyn Bridge
Issue March 1996
Category Reportage/Travel Story

■ 455

Publication Condé Nast House & Garden
Art Director Robert Priest
Designers Ruth Diener, Debra Bishop
Photo Editor Deborah Needleman
Photographer Todd Eberle
Publisher Condé Nast Publications Inc.
Issue October 1996
Category Reportage/Travel Story

■ 456

Publication Condé Nast House & Garden
Art Director Robert Priest
Designers Ruth Diener, Debra Bishop
Photo Editor Deborah Needleman
Photographer Kenro Izu
Publisher Condé Nast Publications Inc.
Issue October 1996
Category Reportage/Travel Spread

Above and Beyond

Marilyn Bridges showcases America from the air.

F OR D. H. LAWRENCE, AMERICA was not the youngest country in the world, but the oldest. He came here in search of the atavistic, the aboriginal, fragments from a preindustrial world: and, carefully avoiding places like Manhattan and Los Angeles, cathedrals of the new, he sought in the Southwest, among Hopi dances and sandstone pueblos, echoes of a primeval order, runic signs from some indigenous spirits. For Lawrence, as Peter Conrad writes, America was "a continent much older than Europe," and its exploration "must proceed vertically not horizontally."

That is what I think of when I gaze at Marilyn Bridges's photographs, since, for all their varied subject matter, all of them take us back to something ancient and mysterious. Hers is an America

■ 457
Publication Condé Nast Traveler
Design Director Robert Best
Photo Editor Kathleen Klech
Photographer Marilyn Bridges
Publisher Condé Nast Publications Inc.
Issue September 1996
Category Reportage/Travel Story

DILEMMA ON THE IRRAWADDY

Burma—a.k.a. Myanmar. As a travel destination, it's virtually unparalleled —golden pagodas, misty lakes, ethereal Buddhism. But if you go—and 1996 has been proclaimed Visit Myanmar Year—there's a thing or two you should know, argues ANDREW COCKBURN, about this country where all is not as it appears

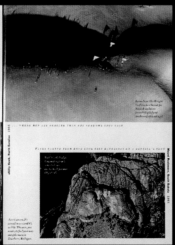

THE SLAVES

THE ASTROLOGER

■ 458
Publication Condé Nast Traveler
Design Director Robert Best
Photo Editor Kathleen Klech
Photographer Brigitte Lacombe
Publisher Condé Nast Publications Inc.
Issue June 1996
Category Reportage/Travel Story

A Giant Awakes

The past is hoarded like treasure in Beijing, but China is a nation in training, flexing its muscles and banking on its cities. John Krich went back and found the old capital bristling with construction cranes and ever-wider ring roads. Welcome to the once and future Beijing

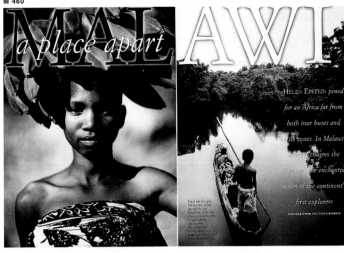

MALAWI
a place apart

HELEN EPSTEIN pined for an Africa far from both tour buses and battle zones. In Malawi's fiercest charms she discovered the enchanted realm of the continent's first explorers

PHOTOGRAPHS BY GIAN PAOLO BARBIERI

I picked up a couple and their **chicken**, two little kids, three women with babies

---

■ 459
Publication Condé Nast Traveler
Design Director Robert Best
Photo Editor Kathleen Klech
Photographer Antonin Kratochvil
Publisher Condé Nast Publications Inc.
Issue November 1996
Category Reportage/Travel Story

■ 460
Publication Condé Nast Traveler
Design Director Robert Best
Photo Editor Kathleen Klech
Photographer Gian Paolo Barbieri
Publisher Condé Nast Publications Inc.
Issue April 1996
Category Reportage/Travel Story

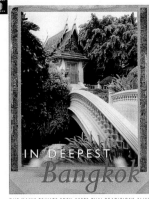

IN DEEPEST
Bangkok

ONE MAN'S PRIVATE EDEN KEEPS THAI TRADITIONS ALIVE

BY JAMIE JAMES ● PHOTOGRAPHS BY LIZZIE HIMMEL

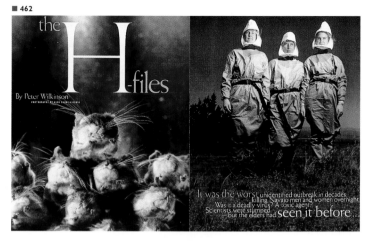

the
H-files

By Peter Wilkinson

It was the worst unidentified outbreak in decades, killing Navajo men and women overnight. Was it a deadly virus? A toxic agent? Scientists were stumped — but the elders had seen it before...

Bangkok, which the Thai call the City of Angels, has to come as an international eye-opener to great...

Prasart travels the kingdom, looking for eccentric trees to transplant

THE
BiG
STICK

Silently stalking the seas, America's boomer subs are the ultimate necessary evil. And one hell of a ride.

By Fred Schruers

PHOTOGRAPHS BY
ANTONIN KRATOCHVIL

Bricks were made with the imprint of palm leaves pressed into wet clay

THE GARDEN TRAVELER

IN AND AROUND BANGKOK

■ 461
Publication Garden Design
Creative Director Michael Grossman
Art Director Christin Gangi
Designer Christin Gangi
Photo Editor Susan Goldberger
Photographer Lizzie Himmel
Publisher Meigher Communications
Issue October/November 1996
Category Reportage/Travel Story

■ 462
Publication Men's Journal
Art Director David Armario
Designers Dirk Barnett,
Anton Klusener
Photo Editor Deborah Needleman
Photographer Nick Cardillichio
Publisher Wenner Media
Issue May 1996
Category Reportage/Travel Spread

■ 463
Publication Men's Journal
Art Director David Armario
Designers Tom Brown, David Armario
Photo Editor Denise Sfraga
Photographer Antonin Kratochvil
Publisher Wenner Media
Issue October 1996
Category Reportage/Travel Spread

When the Shooting Stops

What is the cost of war? For millions uprooted by the decade's armed conflicts—and for one photographer who traveled the world to capture these panoramas of devastation—it is too high. PHOTOGRAPHY BY JOE McNALLY

■ 464

Publication LIFE
Design Director Tom Bentkowski
Designer Marti Golon
Photo Editor David Friend
Photographer Joe McNally
Publisher Time Inc.
Issue January 1997
Category Reportage/Travel Story

■ 465

Publication LIFE
Design Director Tom Bentkowski
Designer Marti Golon
Photo Editor Bobbi Baker Burrows
Photographer Tom Stoddart
Publisher Time Inc.
Issue January 1996
Category Reportage/Travel Spread

■ 466

Publication LIFE
Design Director Tom Bentkowski
Designer Jean Andreuzzi
Photo Editor Lee Dudley
Photographer Jane Evelyn Atwood
Publisher Time Inc.
Issue June 1996
Category Reportage/Travel Story

■ 465

Back from the Abyss
BY DAVID FRIEND

■ 466

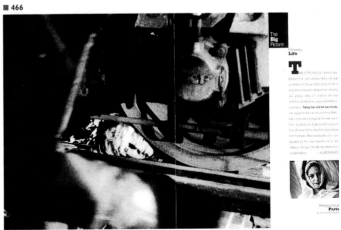

THE WAY WE LIVE

Photography by
Tony O'Brien
Text by
Claudia Glenn Dowling

A
LIGHT
IN THE
DESERT

DISCOVERY
Life and
Death
on the
Serengeti
A BREATHTAKING, INTIMATE LOOK AT THE
BRUTAL AND DANGEROUS WORLD OF THE
SAVANNA'S MOST FRIGHTENING CARNIVORE

Photography by **Mitsuaki Iwago** Text by **George Howe Colt**

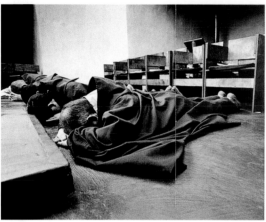

WHEN THEY CAN EAT NO MORE, THE LIONS FALL TO THE GROUND   AND SLEEP WITHIN THREE DAYS, THEY WILL BEGIN TO HUNT AGAIN

■ 467
Publication LIFE
Design Director Tom Bentkowski
Designer Tom Bentkowski
Photo Editor David Friend
Photographer Tony O'Brien
Publisher Time Inc.
Issue June 1996
Category Reportage/Travel Story

■ 468
Publication LIFE
Design Director Tom Bentkowski
Designer Marti Golon
Photo Editor Vivette Porges
Photographer Mitsuaki Iwago
Publisher Time Inc.
Issue May 1996
Category Reportage/Travel Story

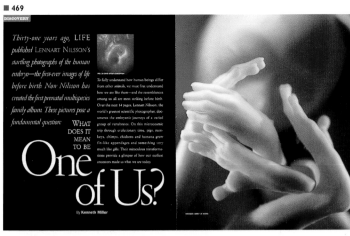

DISCOVERY

Thirty-one years ago, LIFE published LENNART NILSSON'S startling photographs of the human embryo—the first-ever images of life before birth. Now Nilsson has created the first prenatal multispecies family album. These pictures pose a fundamental question:

WHAT DOES IT MEAN TO BE

One of Us?

By Kenneth Miller

To fully understand how human beings differ from other animals, we must first understand how we are like them—and the resemblances among us all are most striking before birth. Over the next 14 pages, Lennart Nilsson, the world's greatest scientific photographer, documents the embryonic journeys of a varied group of vertebrates. On this microcosmic trip through evolutionary time, pigs, monkeys, chimps, chickens and humans grow fin-like appendages and something very much like gills. Their miraculous transformations provide a glimpse of how our earliest ancestors made us what we are today.

LIFE SPECIAL

One crumbles crackers in her soup, the other says "Yecch!" One wants to be a pilot, the other a dentist. But the Hensel twins share so much—a body, a life, an abiding love.

Together Forever

Photography by **Steve Wewerka** Text by **Kenneth Miller** Reporting by **Jen M.R. Doman**

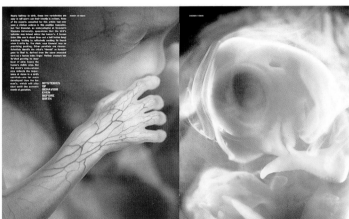

MYSTERIES OF BEHAVIOR EVEN BEFORE BIRTH

A For Patty and Mike, the initial shock was followed by acceptance— and then absolute devotion.

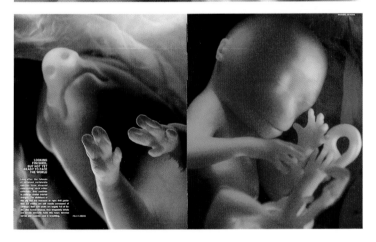

LOOKING FINISHED, BUT NOT YET READY TO FACE THE WORLD

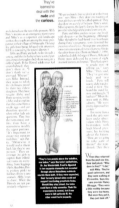

They've learned to deal with the rude and the curious.

■ 469
Publication LIFE
Design Director Tom Bentkowski
Designer Tom Bentkowski
Photo Editor Bobbi Baker Burrows
Photographer Lennart Nilsson
Publisher Time Inc.
Issue November 1996
Category Reportage/Travel Story

■ 470
Publication LIFE
Design Director Tom Bentkowski
Designer Tom Bentkowski
Photo Editor Marie Schumann
Photographer Steve Wewerka
Publisher Time Inc.
Issue April 1996
Category Reportage/Travel Story

PHOTOGRAPHY REPORTAGE & TRAVEL ■ MERIT

The city is considering spending serious money (finally) on New York's appallingly decayed public schools. Here are a few places to start.

All Fall Down

Text by Michael Tomasky
Photographs by Tomas Muscionico

FOREVER ELAINE'S

Elaine's is New York's longest-running THEATER OF CELEBRITY, where BOLD-FACE NAMES from Mailer and Woody to Bill Bratton and the Weinstein brothers have gone to improvise a blustering, swaggering, self-important GOOD TIME. But if Elaine's is still hot, what can hot possibly mean? By James Kaplan

471
Publication New York
Art Director Syndi Becker
Photo Editor Margery Goldberg
Photographer Thomas Muscionico
Publisher K-III Publications
Issue February 12, 1996
Category Reportage/Travel Story

472
Publication New York
Design Director Robert Newman
Designer Florian Bachleda
Photo Editor Margery Goldberg
Photographer Larry Fink
Publisher K-III Publications
Issue July 8, 1996
Category Reportage/Travel Story

THAT OTHER ISLAND

Instead of brownstones, clapboards;
instead of Ed Koch, Guy Molinari:
Staten Island is Manhattan's antipode.
Photographed by Dana Lixenberg

LEFT: DONNA IN FRONT OF HER HOUSE ON SATURN LANE
ABOVE: CELEBRANTS AT THE EXCELSIOR GRAND

ABOVE: FATHER AND SON AT WHITE CASTLE
RIGHT: WAITING FOR THE KIDS OUTSIDE A DANCE STUDIO
OPPOSITE: A CHURCH-LIKE HOUSE ON STEGMAN STREET

LEFT: A HUNTER SHOWS OFF HIS PRIZE
ABOVE: MAN, WOMAN, AND DOG ON MIDDLE BEACH
BELOW: A HOOTERS WAITRESS ON BREAK

The Republican revolution has degenerated into an orgy of self-aggrandizement.

Photographs by Larry Fink • Essay by William Saletan

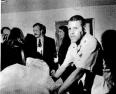

If the revolutionaries failed to use the electoral process to help others, they've succeeded in using it to help themselves.

Political gamesmanship may help win elections for the Republican Party, but it has undone core conservative principles as well as the public good.

■ 473
Publication New York
Design Director Robert Newman
Art Director Florian Bachleda
Photo Editor Margery Goldberg
Photographer Dana Lixenberg
Publisher K-III Publications
Issue December 23-30, 1996
Category Reportage/Travel Story

■ 474
Publication Mother Jones
Creative Director Kerry Tremain
Design Director Barsha Sessa
Designer Marsha Sessa
Photographer Larry Fink
Publisher Foundation for National Progress
Issue July/August 1996
Category Reportage/Travel Story

THE MARTINI* • DAVID STRICK

WIG ADJUSTMENT DURING FIGHT SCENE, *BEVERLY HILLS NINJA*, MAY 3, 1996

* *"The Martini" is Hollywood lingo for the last shot of the day.*

Paramount (ISSN 8494-3255) (GST 120082395) Sales Agreement 0816531, the American edition is published monthly by Paramount Publishing Company, LLC, a joint venture owned by Hachette Filipacchi USA, Inc., and New World Communications Group, Inc. and managed by Hachette Filipacchi Magazines, II, Inc. 1633 Broadway, New York, NY 10019. Paramount is a registered trademark of Hachette Filipacchi Presse. Canadian Patent Corden. Patent. Periodicals postage paid at New York, NY, and at additional mailing offices. One-year subscription rate (12 issues) for U.S. and possessions $19.94. Canada, $29.34. Authorized as periodicals postage by the Post Office Department, Ottawa, Canada, and for payment in cash. One-year subscription rate for all other countries, $27.94. Cash orders only, payable in U.S. currency. Bulk orders: Send check or money order for $7.99 cash ($9.25 Canada; $14.25 other foreign) to ISI Paramount, 10 Montgomery St., Jersey City, NJ 07302, or call (201) 451-9420. Postmaster: Send address changes to Paramount, P.O. Box 55393, Boulder, CO 80322-5393, 800-289-2489. Copyright 1996, Paramount Publishing Company, LLC. All rights reserved. Printed in the U.S.A.

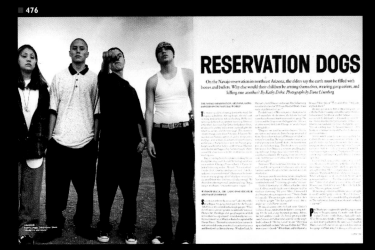

RESERVATION DOGS

On the Navajo reservation in northeast Arizona, the elders say the earth must be filled with bones and bullets. Why else would their children be tattooing themselves, wearing gang colors, and killing one another? *By Kathy Dobie. Photographs by Dana Lixenberg*

W/Society **Summer Camp**

The New York Social Circus doesn't close down for the summer—it just hits the road. One hundred miles to the east, in the Hamptons, the living is easy, the pace is fast and photo ops are plentiful.

PHOTOGRAPHED BY LARRY FINK

Summer Camp

Summer Camp

BOMBAY
Photographs by SEBASTIÃO SALGADO

{ Despite crushing poverty and overpopulation, a mighty middle-class economy has turned Bombay into a city of hope }

Text by ISMAIL MERCHANT

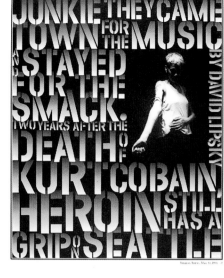

JUNKIE TOWN. THEY CAME FOR THE MUSIC & STAYED FOR THE SMACK. TWO YEARS AFTER THE DEATH OF KURT COBAIN, HEROIN STILL HAS A GRIP ON SEATTLE BY DAVID LIPSKY

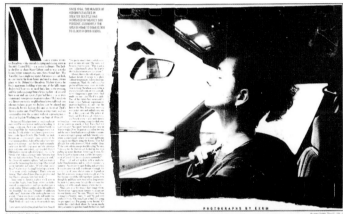

PHOTOGRAPHS BY EXUM

■ 478
Publication Rolling Stone
Creative Director Fred Woodward
Designers Fred Woodward, Gail Anderson
Photo Editor Jodi Peckman
Photographer Sebastião Salgado
Publisher Wenner Media
Issue July 11–25, 1996
Category Reportage/Travel Story

■ 479
Publication Rolling Stone
Creative Director Fred Woodward
Designer Gail Anderson
Photo Editor Jodi Peckman
Photographer Exum
Publisher Wenner Media
Issue May 30, 1996
Category Reportage/Travel Story

PHOTOGRAPHY REPORTAGE & TRAVEL ■ MERIT

WHERE THE
WILD THINGS
ARE

Vernon Bates and Weecho Sannas have been dragging their nets in Matagorda Bay for decades. But these days they're tangling with state regulators and watching profits plunge, which is why their way of life could soon be dead in the water.

A Shrimp Tale

by Robert Draper

A Night Cage

Lion Habitat

One-Day-Old Cheetah

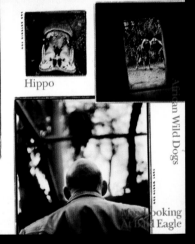

Hippo

African Wild Dogs

Keeper

Floating

Monkey-looking
Actual Eagle

Ringtail
Lemur

Elephant

Oldest Giraffe in Captivity

Rhinos

▣ 480
Publication Texas Monthly
Creative Director D.J. Stout
Designers D.J. Stout, Nancy McMillen
Photo Editor D.J. Stout
Photographer Keith Carter
Publisher Texas Monthly
Issue March 1996
Category Reportage/Travel Story

▣ 481
Publication Texas Monthly
Creative Director D.J. Stout
Designers D.J. Stout, Nancy McMiller
Photo Editor D.J. Stout
Photographer Raymond Meeks
Publisher Texas Monthly
Issue October 1996
Category Reportage/Travel Story

Southern Exposures

Arresting images of bodies in motion surfaced at
far-flung venues during the first half of the '96 Games

Up, Up
And
Away

LIKE NADIA COMANECI
20 YEARS BEFORE
THEM, THE DIVAS OF
DEVA DWELL IN THEIR
SPORT'S RAREST AIR

■ 482

Publication Sports Illustrated
Design Director Steven Hoffman
Art Director Katharine Van Itallie
Photographer Lynn Johnson
Publisher Time Inc.
Issue August 5, 1996
Category Reportage/Travel Story

■ 483

Publication Sports Illustrated
Design Director Steven Hoffman
Art Director Katharine Van Itallie
Designer Karen Meneghin
Photographer Lynn Johnson
Publisher Time Inc.
Issue July 22, 1996
Category Reportage/Travel Story

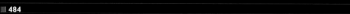

Witness To Mao's Crimes

A photographer's evidence of Cultural Revolution brutality has come to light.

Photographs by
LI ZHEN SHENG

Text by
EDWARD A. GARGAN

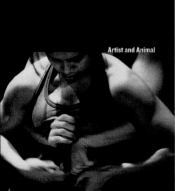

The China Left Behind

A photographer returns to his ancestral village and finds that his family wasn't the only one that moved on.

Photographs by MARK LEONG

NO REASON TO STAY

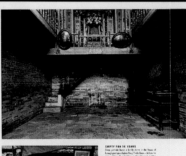

THE LONG WAIT

EMPTY FOR 50 YEARS

WISH YOU WERE HERE

Artist and Animal

Female wrestlers, coming on strong.

Photographs by Kurt Markus Text by Mary Nuttle

■ 484

Publication The New York Times Magazine
Art Director Janet Froelich
Designer John Walker
Photo Editor Kathy Ryan
Photographer Li Zhen Sheng
Publisher The New York Times
Issue June 30, 1996
Category Reportage/Travel Story

■ 485

Publication The New York Times Magazine
Art Director Janet Froelich
Designer Joel Cuyler
Photo Editor Kathy Ryan
Photographer Kurt Markus
Publisher The New York Times
Issue March 3, 1996
Category Reportage/Travel Story

■ 486

Publication The New York Times Magazine
Art Director Janet Froelich
Designer Lou DiLorenzo
Photo Editor Kathy Ryan
Photographer Mark Leong
Publisher The New York Times
Issue November 17, 1996
Category Reportage/Travel Story

In the fashion world of the 90's, teen-age models
simulate an adulthood they've yet to experience for women who
crave a youthful beauty they'll never achieve. Sweet 16 it's not.
By Jennifer Egan   Photographs by Nan Goldin

James
is a girl

MODEL LIFE

James met Michael Flutie,
founder and owner of
the Company Management
modeling agency, when
she was 14. "I wanted to go
somewhere with my
life and I wanted it now,"
she recalls.

At Richard Tyler, one
of James's biggest fall shows
at Bryant Park, she wore
three outfits that had
in common transparency from the
waist up, so that her breasts
were fully visible.

MODEL LIFE

MODEL LIFE

"I remember the
times when I was bawling
and howling, thinking,
God, I'm never going to be a
kid," James says. "But
looking back, you know
what? It made me nothing
but stronger."

MODEL LIFE

Savage Spite

Photographs by
Gilles Peress

Text by Kit R. Roane

■ 487

Publication The New York Times Magazine
Art Director Janet Froelich
Designers Joel Cuyler, Lisa Naftolin
Photo Editor Kathy Ryan
Photographer Nan Goldin
Publisher The New York Times
Issue February 4, 1996
Category Reportage/Travel Story

■ 488

Publication The New York Times Magazine
Art Director Janet Froelich
Designer Joel Cuyler
Photo Editor Kathy Ryan
Photographer Gilles Peress
Publisher The New York Times
Issue April 28, 1996
Category Reportage/Travel Story

johnny blacksmith

A romance with fire and metal

BY JEANNE HUBER   PHOTOGRAPHS BY J. MICHAEL MYERS

f e n c e s

Our futile but fascinating bid to **replace nature's boundaries** with our own.

BY STEPHEN HARRIGAN

'We're called blacksmiths because iron was the black metal.'

'All the alchemy is in the fire.'

Every leaf has veins, every feather has barbs.

■ 489
Publication This Old House
Design Director Matthew Drace
Art Director Timothy Jones
Photographer J. Michael Myers
Publisher Time Inc.
Issue July/August 1996
Category Reportage/Travel Story

■ 490
Publication This Old House
Design Director Matthew Drace
Art Director Timothy Jones
Photographers Andrea Gentl, Simon Watson, William Abranowicz, Melanie Acevedo, Eric Rank, Brian Smith, Kent Baker
Publisher Time Inc.
Issue May/June 1996
Category Reportage/Travel Story

The Washington Post

MARCH 10, 1996

Magazine

Separate but Unequal?
Women and Men and VMI

Photographs by Nancy Andrews
Text by Liza Mundy

'It Couldn't Be the Same Thing as VMI'

On the front lines of Virginia's gender war

■ 491
Publication The Washington Post Magazine
Art Director Kelly Doe
Designer Kelly Doe
Photo Editor Karen Tanaka
Photographer Nancy Andrews
Publisher The Washington Post Co.
Issue March 10, 1996
Category Reportage/Travel Story

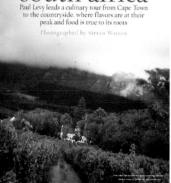

a taste of the new
south africa

Paul Levy leads a culinary tour from Cape Town to the countryside, where flavors are at their peak and food is true to its roots

Photographed by Simon Watson

Tango
Argentino

Listening to the rhythms of Buenos Aires, a city of opera and soccer, psychotherapy and the occult, Borges and Eva Perón • By Gabriella De Ferrari
Photographed by Daniela Stallinger

You may find yourself wondering just where you are at times. We encountered only a single restaurant that left no question we were in Africa

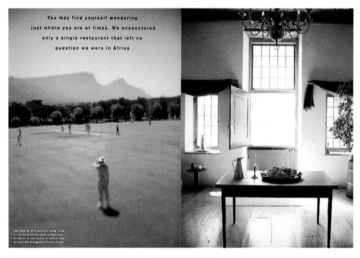

south africa's best wines

■ 492

Publication Travel & Leisure
Design Director Pamela Berry
Designer Pamela Berry
Photo Editor Jim Franco
Photographer Simon Watson
Publisher American Express Publishing
Issue August 1996
Category Reportage/Travel Story

■ 493

Publication Travel & Leisure
Design Director Pamela Berry
Designer Pamela Berry
Photo Editor Jim Franco
Photographer Daniela Stallinger
Publisher American Express Publishing
Issue December 1996
Category Reportage/Travel Story

INDIAN SUMMER

KERALA IS INDIA'S WARM AND EASY OASIS: AS
SIMPLE AS A SOUTH SEAS ISLAND, AS LUSH AS A
FIELD OF TEA, AS CALMING AS AN EVENING STROLL.
BY CALVIN TRILLIN · PHOTOGRAPHED BY RUVEN AFANADOR

Melbourne's Big Splash

The wave is beginning to crest: you can see it in the
chic shops, the state-of-the-art hotels, the bold
new restaurants. Is this the hippest city in the
Southern Hemisphere? By Richard Alleman
Photographed by Victoria Pearson

Could this be a trip to India?
Where's the punishing itinerary? Where's
the monumental payoff?

The cultural attractions of Kerala are short on imposing
buildings and long on exotic customs, such as temple festivals
and snake-boat races and ritual dance performances

■ 494
Publication Travel & Leisure
Design Director Pamela Berry
Designer Pamela Berry
Photo Editor Jim Franco
Photographer Ruven Afanador
Publisher American Express Publishing
Issue January 1997
Category Reportage/Travel Story

■ 495
Publication Travel & Leisure
Design Director Pamela Berry
Designer Pamela Berry
Photo Editor Jim Franco
Photographer Victoria Pearson
Publisher American Express Publishing
Issue July 1996
Category Reportage/Travel Story

the sea's own secret

saba is nothing
but a tiny caribbean island
should be... and that's
exactly why the faithful few
keep coming back

By Frank Conroy
Photographed by Stewart Shining

From the foothills of the Pyrenees
through the vineyards of the Rioja
to the mystical city of Santiago
de Compostela, hikers and
worshipers alike still walk Spain's
pilgrimage trail by Nicholas Shrady
Photographed by Alen MacWeeney

SPANISH
STEPS

i watched a cloud approach below. soon i was sitting on a very small island looking down at the top of the cloud as it drifted past

The remains of the apostle himself are stored in a silver chest in the cathedral crypt. The pious line up, often for hours, to catch a glimpse

since saba has no water supply except rain. the pool—at 20 by 40 feet, the island's largest—is an extravagance

The Top 10 Pilgrimage Sites

fifty years hence. saba will doubtless look and feel much as it does now

■ 496
Publication Travel & Leisure
Design Director Pamela Berry
Designer Pamela Berry
Photo Editor Jim Franco
Photographer Stewart Shining
Publisher American Express Publishing
Issue March 1996
Category Reportage/Travel Story

■ 497
Publication Travel & Leisure
Design Director Pamela Berry
Designer Gaemer Gutierrez
Photo Editor Jim Franco
Photographer Alen MacWeeney
Publisher American Express Publishing
Issue March 1996
Category Reportage/Travel Story

A Week in Sweden

The ideal itinerary—Stockholm, the lake district, and more, from spas and design shops to a floating hotel and a great country drive By Heather Smith MacIsaac
Photographed by Denise Grünstein

THE ART OF
EATING WELL IN VENICE

FORGET WHAT THEY TOLD YOU

A SUPERB MEAL CAN BE HAD, AND YOU DON'T HAVE TO SPEND A FORTUNE

YOU JUST HAVE TO KNOW WHERE

BY PAUL LIVY · PHOTOGRAPHED BY SIMON WATSON

> Swedes share a passion for the wildness and subtlety of nature. Their law guarantees public access to private land, even allowing visitors to pick berries, mushrooms, and flowers but not to break branches

In typically Swedish fashion, the grandeur of Hagaparken is subdued, even modest for royal grounds. Gustav III, the Midnight Sun King, let loose in a dramatic gesture, though, when he commissioned sweeping copper tents for his stables

AFTER A VISIT TO THE ACCADEMIA AND A CANAL-SIDE LUNCH AT RISTORANTE RIVIERA, STROLL OVER TO NICO'S FOR THE FINEST GELATI IN TOWN—THEN CROSS THE CANAL AND LINGER UNTIL TWILIGHT AT ONE OF PIAZZA SAN MARCO'S CAFES

> Behind the noble buildings of the Old Town wind pedestrian streets, ranging in width from narrow to narrower. Just as the walls seem to close in, you'll emerge in a little square where horse carts used to turn around

■ 498
Publication Travel & Leisure
Design Director Pamela Berry
Designer Pamela Berry
Photo Editor Jim Franco
Photographer Denise Grunstein
Publisher American Express Publishing
Issue May 1996
Category Reportage/Travel Story

■ 499
Publication Travel & Leisure
Design Director Pamela Berry
Designer Pamela Berry
Photo Editor Jim Franco
Photographer Simon Watson
Publisher American Express Publishing
Issue May 1996
Category Reportage/Travel Story

PHOTOGRAPHY REPORTAGE & TRAVEL ■ MERIT

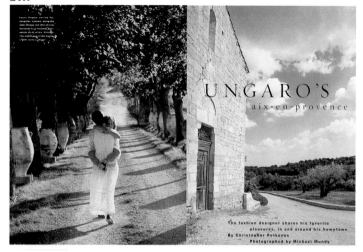

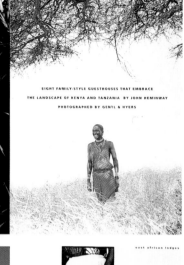

UNGARO'S
aix-en-provence

The fashion designer shares his favorite
pleasures, in and around his hometown
By Christopher Petkanas
Photographed by Michael Mundy

e a s i n g

into east

africa

EIGHT FAMILY-STYLE GUESTHOUSES THAT EMBRACE
THE LANDSCAPE OF KENYA AND TANZANIA BY JOHN HEMINWAY
PHOTOGRAPHED BY GENTL & HYERS

A

'The gaiety and insouciance
you feel in Aix is Italian,' says Ungaro.
'The restraint, the discretion, the
control—that's French'

kenya

WALKING IN AFRICA IS AN INTRODUCTION TO
SUBTLETIES OVERLOOKED IN TRAVEL BY VEHICLE. OUR FIVE
HOURS AFOOT IN THE MORNING FEEL LIKE TWO, AND THE
LIONESS WE ENCOUNTER KEEPS HER DISTANCE

HOTELS

A Place in the Country

■ 500
Publication Travel & Leisure
Design Director Pamela Berry
Designer Pamela Berry
Photo Editor Jim Franco
Photographer Michael Mundy
Publisher American Express Publishing
Issue May 1996
Category Reportage/Travel Story

■ 501
Publication Travel & Leisure
Design Director Pamela Berry
Designer Daniel Josephs
Photo Editor Jim Franco
Photographer Gentl & Hyers
Publisher American Express Publishing
Issue November 1996
Category Reportage/Travel Story

next great
neighborhoods

The insider's take on streets worth a look in NEW YORK, LONDON, PARIS, L.A. and TOKYO

Photographed by Daniela Stallinger

NEW YORK

LONDON

PARIS

Gini Alhadeff finds healers, seekers, and stargazers in New Mexico's
LAND OF THE SPIRITS
PHOTOGRAPHED BY KURT MARKUS

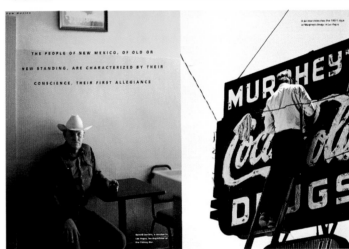

THE PEOPLE OF NEW MEXICO, OF OLD OR
NEW STANDING, ARE CHARACTERIZED BY THEIR
CONSCIENCE, THEIR FIRST ALLEGIANCE

THERE IS NO SUCH THING
AS SILENCE IN A SILENT PLACE: BENDING
AN ARM TO REMOVE A HANDKERCHIEF
FROM A POCKET BECAME A COMPLEX
SEQUENCE OF SOUNDS

■ 502
Publication Travel & Leisure
Design Director Pamela Berry
Designer Dina White
Photo Editor Jim Franco
Photographer Daniela Stallinger
Publisher American Express Publishing
Issue September 1996
Category Reportage/Travel Story

■ 503
Publication Travel & Leisure
Design Director Pamela Berry
Designer Pamela Berry
Photo Editor Jim Franco
Photographer Kurt Markus
Publisher American Express Publishing
Issue September 1996
Category Reportage/Travel Story

PHOTOGRAPHY REPORTAGE & TRAVEL ■ MERIT

THE WORLD ACCORDING TO

Baedeker

Prized by collectors,

these slender

red guides recall a

vanished empire

by JAN MORRIS • photographed by HUGH KRETSCHMER

Multiple Personalities

Range Rovers

505

Publication The New York Times Magazine
Art Director Janet Froelich
Designer John Walker
Photo Editor Robert Bryan
Photographer Robert Trachtenberg
Publisher The New York Times
Issue September 1, 1996
Category Photo Illustration Spread

506

Publication W
Creative Director Dennis Freedman
Design Director Edward Leida
Art Director Kirby Rodriguez
Designers Edward Leida, Rosalba Sierra
Photographer Craig McDean
Publisher Fairchild Publications
Category Photo Illustration Spread

504

Publication Travel Holiday
Art Director Lou DiLorenzo
Designer Lou DiLorenzo
Photo Editor Bill Black
Photographer Hugh Kretschmer
Publisher Reader's Digest Association, Inc.
Issue February 1996
Category Photo Illustration Story

SHOPPING

SECONDHAND

The short list in acquisitive thinking, bargain hunting, sandal seeking, body hugging, low riding, metal smelting, bed making, screwdriving, wedding planning, kitsch coveting, green thumbing, and Fiestaware finding

SECONDHAND STORE

GARDEN STORE

RESTAURANT-SUPPLY STORE

LINENS

APPLIANCE STORE

CULTURE

The cultural elite of video viewing, catalogue scouring, private art dealing, 'zine reading, literati schmoozing, rarity collecting, CD browsing, movie reviving, Japanimation procuring, and quiet seeking

VIDEO STORE

ALTERNATIVE TO TOWER RECORDS

PHOTOGRAPHY CLASS

READINGS

ART-SUPPLY STORE

BEAUTY & HEALTH

The pick of the New York City pack for deft buffing, deep massaging, clean shaving, neat clipping, bright coloring, crisp highlighting, heavy contemplating, Zen inhaling, and luxe loofah-ing

DAY SPA

FACIAL

SHAVE

MEN'S FACIAL

A Prayer for The Dying

Keith Green was arrested for murder after helping his long-time lover, James Northcutt, kill himself. Sara Miles recounts their story and reports on the brewing debate surrounding AIDS-related assisted suicides.

Photograph by Adam Weiss

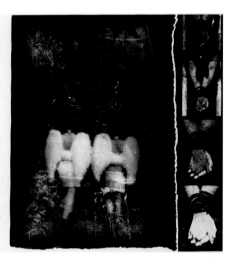

MURDER ON THE MOUNTAIN

The double slaying of lesbian hikers along the Appalachian Trail remains unsolved. Barry Yeoman investigates the tragic story of two women in love. Photo Illustration by Exum

The Silent Struggle

My husband's maddening restlessness, the rages that came out of nowhere, his inability to sit still, keep promises and stick to plans threatened our marriage. We did not understand how typical he was of someone with **attention deficit disorder.**

by Jane Bernstein Illustration: Nola Lopez

■ 507
Publication New York
Design Director Robert Newman
Art Director Deanna Lowe
Photo Editor Margery Goldberg
Photographer Butch Belair
Publisher K-III Publications
Issue April 15, 1996
Category Photo Illustration Story

■ 508
Publication Out
Art Director David O'Connor
Designer David O'Connor
Photo Editor Amy Steiner
Photographer Adam Weiss
Publisher Out Magazine
Issue July 1996
Category Photo Illustration Spread

■ 509
Publication Out
Art Director David O'Connor
Designer David O'Connor
Photo Editor Amy Steiner
Photographer Exum
Publisher Out Magazine
Issue November 1996
Category Photo Illustration Spread

■ 510
Publication Self
Design Director Richard Ferretti
Designer Eleftherios Kardamakis
Illustrator Nola Lopez
Photo Editor Suzanne Donaldson
Publisher Condé Nast Publications Inc.
Issue July 1996
Category Photo Illustration Spread

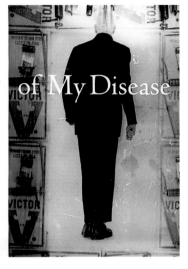

BY CHARLES P. PIERCE

In the Country of My Disease

The country's name is Alzheimer's: It may be my destiny to go there and live until I have forgotten all the things that made me a father and a son and a husband, until I forget how to swallow or how to breathe and the disease kills me, as it killed my father before me

men and eating disorders

Do you think bulimia and anorexia are just women's diseases? Think again.

by Karen Avenoso

BLOOD and MONEY

THE HEALTHY MALE

Can Aging Be Stopped?

BY DAN GREENBURG

■ 511
Publication GQ
Design Director John Korpics
Designer John Korpics
Photo Editor Karen Frank
Photographer Exum
Publisher Condé Nast Publications Inc.
Issue February 1996
Category Photo Illustration Story

■ 512
Publication Men's Journal
Art Director David Armario
Designer David Armario
Photo Editor Deborah Needleman
Photographer Guzman
Publisher Wenner Media
Issue February 1996
Category Photo Illustration Spread

■ 513
Publication New Woman
Creative Director Ann Kwong
Art Director Lisa Ilario
Designer Seema Christie
Photo Editor Lisa Ilario
Photographer Paul Sunday
Publisher K-III Publications
Issue May 1996
Category Photo Illustration Spread

■ 514
Publication Vibe
Art Director Lee Ellen Fanning
Designer Lee Ellen Fanning
Illustrator Alicia Exum
Photo Editor George Pitts
Publisher Time Inc.
Issue August 1996
Category Photo Illustration Story

ILLUSTRATION

RECORDINGS THE PLEASURE PRINCIPLE
BY DON McLEESE

★ ★ ★ ★
I FEEL ALRIGHT
Steve Earle
E-Squared/Warner Bros.

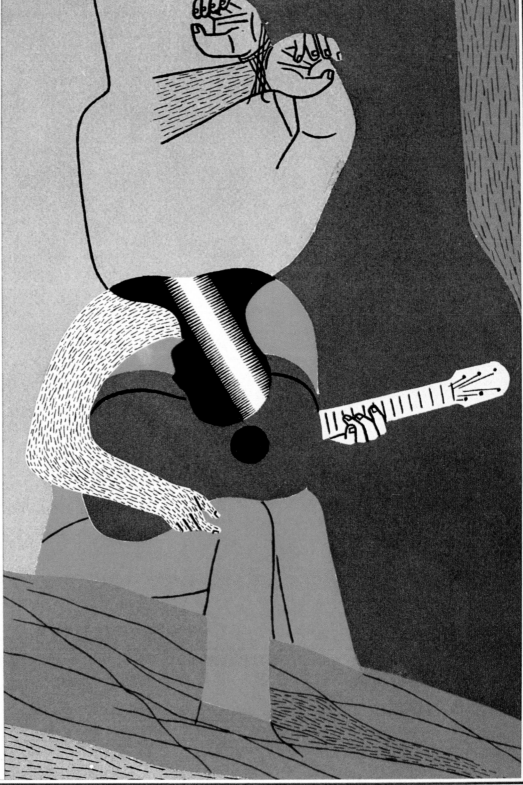

T SEEMS LIKE A COUPLE OF LIFE-times ago that Steve Earle appeared destined to become the Bruce Springsteen of country music. Introducing himself with 1986's *Guitar Town*, Earle arrived on a wave of "new traditionalism" that extended from the terse conservatism of Randy Travis to the hillbilly flash of Dwight Yoakam. While others in the class of '86 found popular acceptance more quickly, Earle showed the most potential. His Southern populism and unbridled rebelliousness offered a bridge between the hard twang of rural country music and the harder dynamics of rock, reinforcing the strengths of both camps rather than settling for a dilution more typical of the Eagles.

After continuing down the same road with 1987's *Exit 0*, an album almost as strong as *Guitar Town*, Earle took a metallic detour. Both *Copperhead Road* (1988) and *The Hard Way* (1991) buried some inspired material beneath too many guitars, undermining the country side of his music. As Earle began to attain greater notoriety for his drug use, divorces and tattoos than for his music, his once-promising career looked more like a highway wreck and was viewed with apprehension by those who slowed down to gape at the carnage. It was said that Earle couldn't even get arrested in Nashville –

ILLUSTRATION BY BRIAN CRONIN

ROLLING STONE, MARCH 7, 1996 · 47

515
Publication Rolling Stone
Creative Director Fred Woodward
Illustrator Brian Cronin
Publisher Wenner Media
Issue March 7, 1996
Category Single Page

Dr. Hunter S. Thompson

O N THE OCCASION OF THE
25th anniversary of the publication of *Fear and Loathing in Las Vegas*, an unfettered discussion on the values of the '60s, the addictive properties of professional journalism and the definition of *gonzo*

By P. J. O'Rourke

Illustrations by Ralph Steadman

64 · ROLLING STONE, NOVEMBER 28, 1996

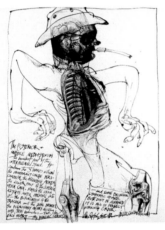

FEAR AND LOATHING IN LAS VEGAS was first published here in Rolling Stone 25 years ago. We, the times, the country and the world have changed. Dr. Hunter S. Thompson's book has not. It was then and it is now a perspicacious, seminal, nonpareil, virtuoso work, the kind of thing that sends you to the dictionary looking for a word that does it ...

"You know, acid will move your head around and your eyes, and whatever else you perceive things with. But bringing it back and putting it on the page was one of the hardest things I ever had to do in journalism."

FEAR AND LOATHING IN LAS VEGAS was first ...

FEAR AND LOATHING IN LAS VEGAS

A SAVAGE JOURNEY TO THE Heart of THE AMERICAN DREAM

Ralph STEADMAN

"Somehow there were 48 hours a day and 18 days in the week. But the suffering of going through 10 years of free-lance journalism. That sounds romantic now, right? But the desperation — teetering from one word to another."

NEW and RARE ... Two Weeks in LAS VEGAS ... a LIGHT-HEADED Feeling ... Drunk, HORNY and BROKE

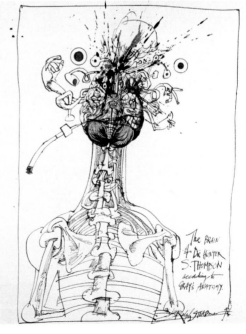

The BRAIN of Dr Hunter S. THOMPSON according to GRAY'S ANATOMY

Ralph STEADMAN

72 · ROLLING STONE, NOVEMBER 28, 1996

● 516
Publication Rolling Stone
Creative Director Fred Woodward
Designer Lee Bearson
Illustrator Ralph Steadman
Publisher Wenner Media
Issue November 28, 1996
Category Story

POWER 101

To paraphrase Tolstoy, happy mergers are all alike, but every unhappy merger is unhappy in its own way. You'll find plenty of both packed in our seventh annual Power Issue, with enough enigmatic characters and shocking plot twists to fill a Russian novel. Time Warner and Turner Broadcasting, Seagram and MCA, Disney and ABC, Westinghouse and CBS—we peek through the keyholes of Hollywood's biggest corporate marriages and tell you how their honeymoons are going. ■ Speaking of war and peace, you'll read about friction at Disney, between Michaels Eisner and Ovitz, as well as the escalating cable-TV battles between News Corp.'s Rupert Murdoch and Time Warner's Gerald Levin and Ted Turner. ■ We'll also deliver a Q&A with former Fox and Paramount honcho Barry Diller (a man who seems to personify power, even though he remains on the sidelines), take a look at power's next generation (featuring Eastwood's, Eisner's, and Murdoch's kids, plus others who are taking their birthrights very seriously), and serve up a special Power Diet (guaranteed to make you a lean, mean, Armani-suited machine). ■ Finally, there are reports on who's rising, who's falling, and who appears to have stalled—all of that in addition to the 101.5 most powerful people in entertainment. And get this: One of them isn't even out of diapers yet! Bet you never read that in Tolstoy.

ILLUSTRATION BY CSA DESIGN

ENTERTAINMENT WEEKLY **31**

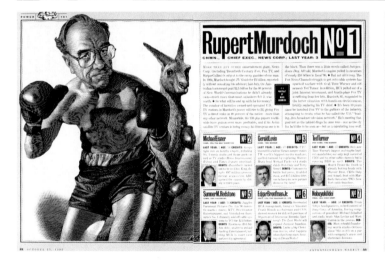

● 517

Publication Entertainment Weekly
Design Director John Korpics
Art Director Joe Kimberling
Designer Joe Kimberling
Illustrators CSA Design, Mark Summers, Mark Ulriksen, Greg Clarke
Publisher Time Inc.
Issue October 25, 1996
Category Story
■ **A Merit** Spread

Hollywood '37

Remember how Myer M. Myer, the pugnacious head of Pictograph, used to hire women to watch him lick fur coats? How status was having your own croquet-playing gorilla? In this satiric fable, BRUCE McCALL gets nostalgic for a time when the Googles Sisters baked pies every night for the crew and Hollywood was a *family*

Illustrations by BRUCE McCALL

Aeroboy, they called it. Hot meals delivered pronto, by low-flying planes based over in Burbank. Not pizza or such offal, either; but haute French. You kept the silk parachutes for tablecloths. Howard Hughes was behind it, and the man himself flew lots of meal runs; many will recall seeing him in his silver Northrop Omega, corkscrewing through Coldwater Canyon in that pinky L.A. dusk, heading for mogul Myer M. Myer's place and a dinner drop.

ILLUSTRATION SILVER ●

Rule Hudshaft made people do the hula or eat newspapers in auditions because he knew he could ...

The stars got   passes that let them run red lights after midnight.

● 518
Publication Vanity Fair
Design Director David Harris
Art Director Gregory Mastrianni
Illustrator Bruce McCall
Publisher Condé Nast Publications Inc.
Issue April 1996
Category Story

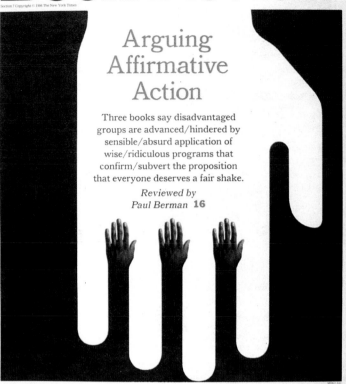

519
Publication The New York Times
Art Director Steven Heller
Illustrator Mirko Ilić
Publisher The New York Times
Studio Mirko Ili´c Corp.
Issue April 14, 1996
Category Single Page

520
Publication The New York Times
Art Director Steven Heller
Illustrator Steven Brodner
Publisher The New York Times
Issue May 5, 1996
Category Single Page

The New York Times

Book Review

December 29, 1996

Section 7 Copyright © 1996 The New York Times

A New Victorian Thriller

'Alias Grace,'
a novel by
Margaret Atwood,
reconsiders a
terrible crime of
1843 in the light of
current ideas and
modern fashions
of thought.
*Reviewed by
Francine Prose*
6

A. C. Grayling on
'Bertrand Russell:
The Spirit of
Solitude,' by
Ray Monk.
5

Joyce Carol Oates
reviews 'Just an
Ordinary Day,'
54 stories by
Shirley Jackson.
10

The New York Times

Book Review

April 28, 1996

Section 7 Copyright © 1996 The New York Times

It Wasn't Always Like This

A battered wife tries
to recall herself as she
used to be in Roddy
Doyle's new novel,
'The Woman Who
Walked Into Doors.'
*Reviewed by
Mary Gordon*
7

Reviews of books by Christopher Darden and Robert Shapiro **14-15**

The New York Times

Book Review

January 21, 1996
Section 7 Copyright © 1996 The New York Times

The Havoc in Yugoslavia

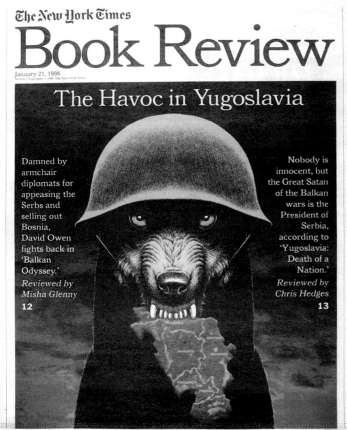

Damned by
armchair
diplomats for
appeasing the
Serbs and
selling out
Bosnia,
David Owen
fights back in
'Balkan
Odyssey.'
*Reviewed by
Misha Glenny*
12

Nobody is
innocent, but
the Great Satan
of the Balkan
wars is the
President of
Serbia,
according to
'Yugoslavia:
Death of a
Nation.'
*Reviewed by
Chris Hedges*
13

The New York Times

Book Review

August 4, 1996 $1.25
Copyright © 1996 The New York Times

A Russian In Spite of Himself

Richard Taruskin's
'Stravinsky and the
Russian Traditions'
reveals the debts the
composer suppressed.
*Reviewed by
Paul Griffiths* **10**

Brent Staples
on Michael Lind's
'Up From Conservatism' **5**

Jonathan Spence
on 'Science and Dissent
in Post-Mao China' **20**

■ 521
Publication The New York Times
Design Director Steve Heller
Illustrator Ray Bartkus
Publisher The New York Times
Issue December 29, 1996
Category Single Page

■ 522
Publication The New York Times
Art Director Steven Heller
Illustrator Mirko Ilić
Publisher The New York Times
Issue January 21, 1996
Category Single Page

■ 523
Publication The New York Times
Art Director Steven Heller
Illustrator Juliette Borda
Publisher The New York Times
Issue April 28, 1996
Category Single Page

■ 524
Publication The New York Times
Art Director Steven Heller
Illustrator C.F. Payne
Publisher The New York Times
Issue August 4, 1996
Category Single Page

ILLUSTRATION FEATURES ■ MERIT

GARRISON KEILLOR READS FOUR HUNDRED POEMS AND LIKES ONE

The Atlantic Monthly

FEBRUARY 1996

WHY AMERICANS HATE

THE
MEDIA

BY JAMES FALLOWS

$2.95 Can. $3.50

press

■ 525
Publication The Atlantic Monthly
Art Director Judy Garlan
Designer Judy Garlan
Illustrator Stephen Kroninger
Publisher The Atlantic Monthly
Issue February 1996
Category Story

CHOOSING BOOKS FOR KIDS: LESSONS THE VIRTUECRATS IGNORE

The Atlantic Monthly

JANUARY 1996

DO YOU KNOW THIS MAN?

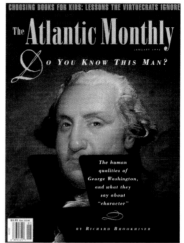

The human
qualities of
George Washington,
and what they
say about
"character"

BY RICHARD BROOKHISER

■ 526
Publication The Atlantic Monthly
Art Director Judy Garlan
Designer Judy Garlan
Illustrator C. F. Payne
Publisher The Atlantic Monthly
Issue January 1996
Category Story

A MAN ON HORSEBACK

If ever a man
did, George Washington
had "bearing," an attitude
of his body that helped
to make his fame.
He was also of strong
and daring temperament, which
lent energy to his purpose
but made his anger
terrible. And, to contain
and channel his high feeling,
he had a personal
moral code built on maxims
he had studied from youth.
An essay on character

BY RICHARD BROOKHISER

WHAT THE GENDER GAP IS REALLY ABOUT / ANGELS 'N' STUFF

The Atlantic Monthly

Recipe for a Depression

MIX
FALLING WAGES,
A PUSH FOR ZERO
INFLATION,
AND A BIPARTISAN
DRIVE TO ELIMINATE
THE BUDGET
DEFICIT.
SIMMER.

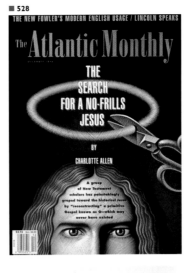

THE NEW FOWLER'S MODERN ENGLISH USAGE / LINCOLN SPEAKS

The Atlantic Monthly

THE
SEARCH
FOR A NO-FRILLS
JESUS

BY
CHARLOTTE ALLEN

A group
of New Testament
scholars has painstakingly
groped toward the historical Jesus
by "reconstructing" a primitive
Gospel known as Q—which may
never have existed

THE SEARCH FOR A NO-FRILLS JESUS

Q

by CHARLOTTE ALLEN

■ 528
Publication The Atlantic Monthly
Art Director Judy Garlan
Designer Judy Garlan
Illustrator Adam Niklewicz
Publisher The Atlantic Monthly
Issue December 1996
Category Story

■ 527
Publication The Atlantic Monthly
Art Director Judy Garlan
Designer Judy Garlan
Illustrator Brian Cronin
Publisher The Atlantic Monthly
Issue July 1996
Category Story

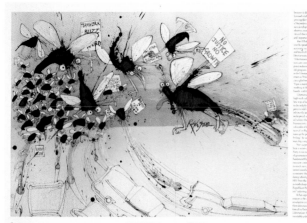

■ 529
Publication Fast Company
Art Director Patrick Mitchell
Designer Patrick Mitchell
Illustrator Ralph Steadman
Publisher Fast Company
Issue August/September 1996
Category Story

■ 530
Publication Fast Company
Art Director Patrick Mitchell
Designer Patrick Mitchell
Illustrator Barry Blitt
Publisher Fast Company
Issue April/May 1996
Category Spread

■ 531
Publication Garden Design
Creative Director Michael Grossman
Art Director Christin Gangi
Designer Toby Fox
Illustrator Anita Kunz
Publisher Meigher Communications
Issue April/May 1996
Category Spread

■ 532
Publication Health
Art Director Jane Palecek
Designer Jane Palecek
Illustrator Calef Brown
Publisher Time Inc.
Issue January/February 1996
Category Spread

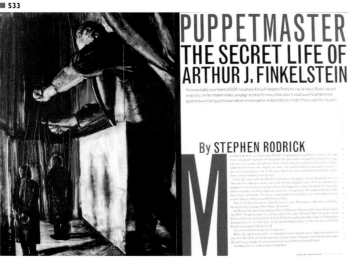

PUPPETMASTER
THE SECRET LIFE OF ARTHUR J. FINKELSTEIN

By STEPHEN RODRICK

Entertainers

Sanctified by Blood

The contents of Lincoln's pockets on the night he was assassinated show how ordinary objects can be transformed into national relics

By THOMAS MALLON

1996 THE Year That Was

Illustration by Christian Northeast

SOME LIKE IT HAUTE

THE Best & Worst 1996

Illustration by Christian Northeast

■ 533
Publication Boston Magazine
Art Director Gregory Klee
Designer Gregory Klee
Illustrator John Collier
Publisher Boston Magazine
Issue October 1996
Category Spread

■ 534
Publication Civilization
Art Director David Herbick
Designers David Herbick,
Maggie Gamboa
Illustrator Gary Kelley
Publisher L.O.C. Associates L.P.
Issue January/February 1996
Category Spread

■ 535
Publication Condé Nast Traveler
Design Director Robert Best
Art Director Carla Frank
Designer Carla Frank
Illustrator Maurice Vellekoop
Publisher Condé Nast Publications Inc.
Issue December 1996
Category Spread

■ 536
Publication Entertainment Weekly
Design Director John Korpics
Designer John Korpics
Illustrator Christian Northeast
Publisher Time Inc.
Issue December 27, 1996
Category Story

ILLUSTRATION FEATURES ■ MERIT

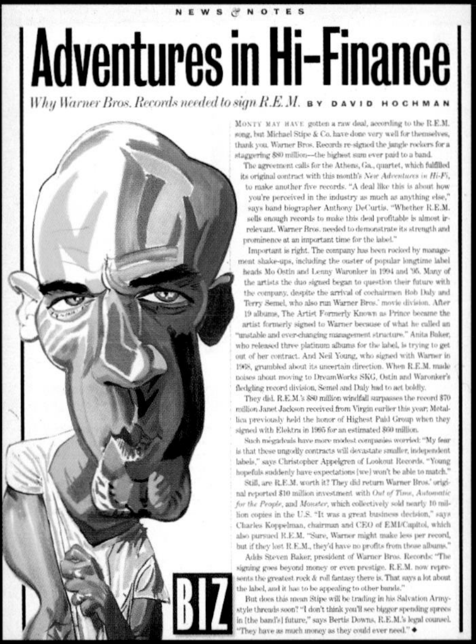

NEWS & NOTES

Adventures in Hi-Finance

Why Warner Bros. Records needed to sign R.E.M. BY DAVID HOCHMAN

MONTY MAY HAVE gotten a raw deal, according to the R.E.M. song, but Michael Stipe & Co. have done very well for themselves, thank you. Warner Bros. Records re-signed the jangle rockers for a staggering $80 million—the highest sum ever paid to a band.

The agreement calls for the Athens, Ga., quartet, which fulfilled its original contract with this month's *New Adventures in Hi-Fi*, to make another five records. "A deal like this is about how you're perceived in the industry as much as anything else," says band biographer Anthony DeCurtis. "Whether R.E.M. sells enough records to make this deal profitable is almost ir-relevant. Warner Bros. needed to demonstrate its strength and prominence at an important time for the label."

Important is right. The company has been rocked by manage-ment shake-ups, including the ouster of popular longtime label heads Mo Ostin and Lenny Waronker in 1994 and '95. Many of the artists the duo signed began to question their future with the company, despite the arrival of co-chairmen Bob Daly and Terry Semel, who also ran Warner Bros.' movie division. After 18 albums, The Artist Formerly Known as Prince became the artist formerly signed to Warner because of what he called an "unstable and ever-changing management structure." Anita Baker, who released three platinum albums for the label, is trying to get out of her contract. And Neil Young, who signed with Warner in 1968, grumbled about its uncertain direction. When R.E.M. made noises about moving to DreamWorks SKG, Ostin and Waronker's fledgling record division, Semel and Daly had to act boldly.

They did. R.E.M.'s $80 million windfall surpasses the record $70 million Janet Jackson received from Virgin earlier this year. Metal-lica previously held the honor of Highest Paid Band when they signed with Elektra in 1995 for an estimated $60 million.

Such megadeals have more modest companies worried. "My fear is that these ungodly contracts will devastate smaller, independent labels," says Christopher Appelgren of Lookout Records. "Young hopefuls suddenly have expectations [we] won't be able to match."

Still, are R.E.M. worth it? They did return Warner Bros.' origi-nal reported $10 million investment with *Out of Time*, *Automatic for the People*, and *Monster*, which collectively sold nearly 30 mil-lion copies in the U.S. "It was a great business decision," says Charles Koppelman, chairman and CEO of EMI/Capitol, which also pursued R.E.M. "Sure, Warner might make less per record, but if they lost R.E.M., they'd have no profits from those albums."

Adds Steven Baker, president of Warner Bros. Records: "The signing goes beyond money or even prestige. R.E.M. now repre-sents the greatest rock & roll fantasy there is. That says a lot about the label, and it has to be appealing to other bands."

But does this mean Stipe will be trading in his Salvation Army–style threads soon? "I don't think you'll see bigger spending sprees in [the band's] future," says Bertis Downs, R.E.M.'s legal counsel. "They have as much money as they could ever need." ◆

MUSIC

Come As You Were

On the nervously electric 'From the Muddy Banks of the Wishkah,' Nirvana manage to redeem the art of the live album—and leave a smokin' legacy to boot. BY TOM SINCLAIR

WORTHWHILE LIVE albums are as rare in rock & roll as enjoy-able drum solos. It may be that the form is inherently flawed—after all, attempting to transfer the magic of a great concert onto the frozen permanence of a CD is an iffy business at best (to one's yet fig-ured out how to capture the smoky, sweaty ambience of a rock club). Often, removed from the context of the venue where it was recorded, music that may have struck concertgoers as transcen-dent is revealed as wooden, lackluster, or just plain substandard.

While there have been some seminal live albums—like the Allman Brothers Band's *At Fillmore East*—too many don't measure up. There's also the per-ception (too often the reality) that such efforts are a way for an artist to turn a quick buck, to release a "new" album without working up fresh material.

In the case of FROM THE MUDDY BANKS OF THE WISHKAH (DGC), the record live recording to be released by Nirvana since its demise, these gripes are mitigated both by the band's historical importance and the void left by frontman Kurt Cobain's 1994 suicide. Wishkah (the title refers to the river that runs through Cobain's hometown, Aberdeen, Wash.) is the long-awaited electric sequel to Nir-vana's 1994 acoustic album, *MTV Unplugged in New York*. As selected by Nir-vana's surviving members, bassist Krist Novoselic and drummer Dave Grohl, along with Geffen A&R execs Mark Kates, *Wishkah*'s 16 songs (recorded in a variety of European and American venues between 1989 and 1994) present a vivid aural portrait of the unusual fury of Seattle's favorite grungemongers. Loud, abrasive, and yes, muddy, *Wishkah*

ILLUSTRATION BY ANDREA VENTURA

MUSIC

Counting Crows No. 2

A Counting Error

On 'Recovering the Satellites,' Counting Crows and gloomy frontman Adam Duritz again borrow liberally from Van Morrison and others, but return precious little. BY KEN TUCKER

ADAM DURITZ, lead singer for Counting Crows, is most intent on establishing his unhappiness over the culture of the band's second album, RECOVERING THE SATELLITES (Geffen). In song after song, he sounds depressed or re-morseful and grumpy about his condition: he takes on the persona of a murderer ("Murder of One") in metaphors for his condition: he take his lover off in "a lonely signal" and that he's "all messed up but that's nothing new" ("Monkey"), that he "can't find [his] way home" ("Chil-dren in Bloom"), that he's got insomnia

("I'm Not Sleeping"). In a rare flush of concern for a listener whose sympathy may be waning, he asks, "Won't you leave me alone?"—or, rather, moans repeatedly, "leave-leave-leave-leave-leave me alooonnne" ("Miller's Angels"). And, get-ting philosophical, Duritz allows as how he's got a "feeling that it's all a lot of oys-ters but no pearl" ("A Long December").

It ain't no Pearl Jam, either, Adam. The commercial success of the Crows' 1993 debut, *August and Everything Af-ter* (nearly 5 million sold) was tempered by frequent accusations that Duritz was doing a heavingly systematic Van Morri-son impersonation. On *Recovering the Satellites*, the singer alternates a persis-tent Van mania (honky scatting through jazz-lite melodies, arbitrary word repeti-tion of the "leave-leave-leave-leave" va-riety) with a shredded-vocal-cord attack that inescapably echoes Eddie Vedder. Indeed, no other current, moderately enjoyable, smash-hit band is so much a pastiche of its influences as is Counting Crows. Duritz, lead guitarist and newbie David Bryson, and their band mates are the momentary kings of post-

ILLUSTRATION BY DAVID HUGHES

NEWS & NOTES

101 Dalmatians
A WHO'S WHO
By Barry White

"Sky" • "Babe" • "Exxon" • "Lichtenstein" • "Gore" • "Steinbrenner" • "Chernobyl"

MONITOR

APPOINTED Former Fox En-tertainment Group chief **John Matoian**, 47, will take over as president of HBO Pictures, beginning Dec. 2. Ma-toian, who resigned from Fox last month, will replace Robert Cooper, who left to become president of Sony's Tri-Star Pictures in July. "The good news is HBO is not broken," says Matoian. "It's just a matter of moving forward."

ARRESTED Rap mogul **Marion "Suge" Knight**, 31, CEO and co-founder of Death Row Records, for fail-ing to show for a drug test as part of his probation, Oct. 22, in L.A. Knight, who was driving the car in which Tupac Shakur was fatally shot on Sept. 7, is on probation for a 1992 assault conviction.

EXITS Unchained by mortality, a showbiz legend **Bob Hope**, 93, is now a free agent. The comedian and NBC will end a 61-year relationship and part ways following the Nov. 23 broad-cast of *Laughing With the Presidents*, his 284th prime-time special. As he awaits offers, says his spokesman, Hope continues to play golf every day, even with impaired vision and hearing.

WEDDINGS Ex-Laker girl **Paula Abdul**, 34, can probably get all the pom-poms she wants since mar-rying sportswear manufacturer Brad Beckerman (age unavailable), Oct. 25, in Beverly Hills. It's Beckerman's first marriage and Abdul's second—she di-vorced actor Emilio Estevez in 1994.

SPLITS *The Nanny*'s **Fran Drescher** and her husband, Peter Marc Jacobson, both 38, are separating after 17 years of marriage; no reasons were given. The couple, who met at a Queens, N.Y., school when they were 15, currently have no plans to file for divorce, according to Drescher's pub-licist. They will continue to work togeth-er on the hit CBS show, where Jacob-son is an executive producer.

DEATHS Comedian **Morey Am-sterdam**, reported to be 87, of a heart attack, Oct. 27, in L.A. A veteran of vaudeville, radio, and TV, he was best known for his 1961–66 role as Buddy Sorrell, the quick-witted comedy writer on *CBS' The Dick Van Dyke Show*. "He was the human joke machine," says Mary Tyler Moore, his costar on the show. "You could name any subject and within two seconds he could make a joke. And a damn good joke, too."
—*Tom Sinclair and Anna Holmes*

ILLUSTRATION BY BARRY BLITT

NEWS & NOTES

Michael Prepares for Fatherhood
PART I THE ULTRASOUND
By Barry Blitt

MONITOR

DEALS In the Death Warmed Over Dept., **Brad Pitt**, 32, has been cast as the grim reaper in Uni-versal's *Meet Joe Black*, which is loose-ly based on *Death Takes a Holiday* (1934). The swoon-inducing actor will receive $17.5 million, his largest salary to date. Filming is set to begin April 30.

EXPECTING More Baldwins! **Stephen Baldwin**, 30, and his graphic-designer wife, Kennya, 30, are expecting a girl, whom they plan to name Hailey Rhode, in December. The couple have a daughter, Alaia, 3.

FIGHTS **George Clooney**'s "Stamp Out Stalkerazzi" cam-paign continues to draw supporters. Among the states who have joined his boycott of *Entertainment Tonight*—which is really a protest against the tactics of another Paramount show, *Hard Copy*—are **Whoopi Goldberg**, **Steven Spielberg**, **Madonna**, and, ac-cording to **Tom Cruise** and **Nicole Kidman**. "This [boycott] is a weapon, and it's something I want everyone to pay attention to," says Clooney. The shows won't comment.

RECOVERING As *Clueless*' **Cher** would have said, "My bad." Bruce Broxmeyer, 64, reportedly was treated at a hospital for minor injuries and released after being hit by a Ford Bronco driven by **Alicia Silverstone**, 20, in L.A., Oct. 29. Police did not cite the actress for a violation. Silverstone was unavailable for comment... **Don John-son**, 46, broke his ankle Oct. 25 after slipping on the perch of his San Francis-co home. The writers of his show, *Nash Bridges*, plan to incorporate the injury into future episodes... **Frank Sinatra**, 80, was admitted to L.A.'s Cedars-Sinai Medical Center, Nov. 1, with a pinched nerve. "Mr. Sinatra has requested that we not provide any additional informa-tion," says his spokeswoman.

DEATHS French director **Mar-cel Carné**, 90, of undisclosed caus-es, in Clamart, France. Carné was best known for *Les Enfants du Paradis* (1945), an intricate love story chosen as the best film ever made in a 1971 poll of French critics. Even though *Les En-fants* was shot under German supervi-sion, Carné created a thinly disguised allegory about the French Resistance during the Nazi occupation. —*Tom Sin-clair and Anna Holmes, with addition-al reporting by Geoff Williams*

MUSIC

'Don' of the Dead

The powerful legacy of troubled rapper Tupac Shakur deserves to be memorialized. But is the first set of his posthumous recordings more of a cash-in than a tribute? BY DAVID BROWNE

TUPAC SHAKUR died vio-lently, but is he resting in peace? Before his murder, the rapper left behind over 100 songs. Now, Death Row—a label not known for its discretion—has cob-bled together some of them for THE DON KILLUMI-NATI: THE 7 DAY THEORY (Death Row/Inter-scope), credited not to 2Pac but to an al-ter ego, Makaveli. In this regard, Death Row has done right by him: If Shakur were alive to hear this mess, he wouldn't want his name on it, either.

Posthumous records are old news in the music business, but *The Don Killu-minati* truly feels like a work in progress. The songs are riddled with re-peated, mumbling allusions to shoot-outs and Shakur's inevitable premature death ("Automatic gunfire makin' all my ene-mies run/Who should I call when I'm shot and bleeding"). But if Shakur had been planning an album playing off Machiavelli's theories on power, he nev-ther thought it through nor completed it. The songs have only fleeting references to "Makaveli" and occasional bits of Machiavellian advice ("Keep your ene-mies closer/Nigga, watch your homies"). The same can be said of the Christ im-agery: It extends no further than song titles like "Hail Mary" and the cover art, which depicts Shakur nailed to a cross.

Even the music feels unfinished. Dr. Dre and his posse licensed up Shakur's previous album, *All Eyez on Me*, but with Dre gone from Death Row, lesser-known producers were called in. The re-sults are plodding, amateurish gangsta rap. The album is top-heavy with cameos from second-rate rappers, and the depths of absurdity are reached on "Toss It Up," which grafts a vitriolic Shakur rap onto a standard new-jack strut. *The Don Killu-minati* isn't just a cash-in operation; it's

■ 537

Publication Entertainment Weekly
Design Director John Korpics
Art Director Michael Picon
Designer Michael Picon
Illustrator Phillip Burke
Publisher Time Inc.
Issue September 13, 1996

■ 539

Publication Entertainment Weekly
Design Director John Korpics
Art Director Julie Schrader
Designer Stacie Reistetter
Illustrator Andrea Ventura
Publisher Time Inc.
Issue October 4, 1996

■ 541

Publication Entertainment Weekly
Design Director John Korpics
Designer Julie Schrader
Illustrator David Hughes
Publisher Time Inc.
Issue October 25, 1996
Category Single Page

LEGACY
The Song of the Soused
BY TY BURR

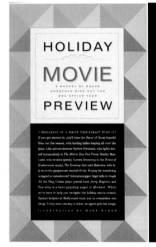

HOLIDAY
MOVIE
PREVIEW

[BOOK of the YEAR]

BOOKS 1

INTO THE WILD

edited by
Alexandra
Jacobs

[PROGRAM of the YEAR]

TV 1

NYPD BLUE

by Ken
Tucker

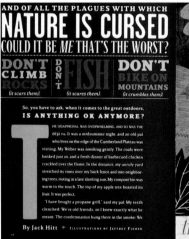

AND OF ALL THE PLAGUES WITH WHICH
NATURE IS CURSED
COULD IT BE ME THAT'S THE WORST?

DON'T
CLIMB
ROCKS
(it scars them).

DON'T
FISH
(it scares them).

DON'T
BIKE ON
MOUNTAINS
(it crumbles them).

So, you have to ask, when it comes to the great outdoors,
IS ANYTHING OK ANYMORE?

By Jack Hitt ✦ ILLUSTRATIONS BY JEFFREY FISHER

the evil one is cast from the garden

■ 543
Publication Entertainment Weekly
Design Director Robert Newman
Art Director Michael Picon
Designer Michael Picon
Illustrator Josh Gosfield
Publisher Time Inc.
Issue January 12, 1996
Category Spread

■ 544
Publication Entertainment Weekly
Design Director John Korpics
Art Director Rina Migliaccio
Designer Joe Kimberling
Illustrator Greg Clarke
Publisher Time Inc.
Issue November 22, 1996
Category Spread

■ 545
Publication Entertainment Weekly
Design Director John Korpics
Art Directors Rina Migliaccio, Joe Kimberling
Designer Rina Migliaccio
Illustrator Mark Ryden
Publisher Time Inc.
Issue November 22, 1996
Category Spread

■ 546
Publication Entertainment Weekly
Design Director John Korpics
Art Director Rina Migliaccio
Designer Rina Migliaccio
Illustrator Julian Allen
Publisher Time Inc.
Issue December 26, 1996
Category Spread

■ 547
Publication Entertainment Weekly
Design Director John Korpics
Art Director Rina Migliaccio
Designer Rina Migliaccio
Illustrator Gary Kelly
Publisher Time Inc.
Issue December 27, 1996
Category Spread

■ 548
Publication Outside
Creative Director Susan Casey
Art Director Dave Allen
Designer Dave Allen
Illustrator Jeffrey Fisher
Publisher Mariah Media
Issue December 1996
Category Story

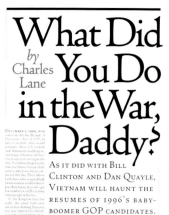

What Did You Do in the War, Daddy?

by Charles Lane

As it did with Bill Clinton and Dan Quayle, Vietnam will haunt the resumes of 1996's baby-boomer GOP candidates. Except one, who might be available for a draft ■

SIX MONTHS AFTER HIS OUSTER FROM THE SENATE, A DAZED, UNREPENTANT Bob Packwood IS STILL FEELING HIS WAY TOWARD BOTTOM

Groping

By Ruth Shalit

ILLUSTRATION BY DAVID HUGHES

OK, American audiences, *we can hear you—now shut up and let us enjoy the show*

Illustration by RALPH STEADMAN

Incontinent Cheering, Unwarranted Moshing, Excessive Whooping and Other Modern Nuisances

By David Kamp

Help for Your GUT Reactions

What doctors can now do for stomach and digestive problems

BY JOHN GROSSMANN

By NEAL KARLEN

Will testosterone make you more virile, more aggressive and hairier? One writer's search for (more) manhood

Illustration by EVERETT PECK

Jacked Like Me

RALPH REED: ANTICHRIST OR REVOLUTIONARY REFORMER?

As Pat Robertson's protégé, and Pat Buchanan's headache, the Christian Coalition boy wonder is shaking up the GOP. But what's his plan for lesbians and gay men? Gabriel Rotello investigates.

Ralph Reed bounds onto the stage at New York's 92nd Street Y like a loping schoolboy: sweet-looking, cherubic, appearing 20-something despite his 35 years. Journalists routinely describe him as "boyish," so it's surprising to hear such a deep, authoritative voice booming from such a cute little face. He's quite simply a dreamboat, somebody who would shine as a superstar on the lecture circuit.

But to wary lesbian and gay leaders, this dreamboat is one of the scariest nightmares in American politics. In his six years as executive director of the Christian Coalition, Ralph Reed has proved himself a genius at combining old-time religion with postmodern organizational techniques. His strategy has been so incredibly successful that his group now controls the Republican Party in a third of the states, has significant influence in another third, played a key role in the party's sweep of Congress in 1994, and was instrumental in securing this year's GOP nomination for Bob Dole.

Illustration by Ralph Steadman

■ 549
Publication GQ
Design Director John Korpics
Designer John Korpics
Illustrator Anita Kunz
Publisher Condé Nast Publications Inc.
Issue January 1996
Category Spread

■ 550
Publication GQ
Design Director John Korpics
Designer John Korpics
Illustrator Ralph Steadman
Publisher Condé Nast Publications Inc.
Issue February 1996
Category Spread

■ 551
Publication GQ
Design Director John Korpics
Designer Susan Dazzo
Illustrator Everett Peck
Publisher Condé Nast Publications Inc.
Issue April 1996
Category Spread

■ 552
Publication GQ
Design Director John Korpics
Designer John Korpics
Illustrator David Hughes
Publisher Condé Nast Publications Inc.
Issue April 1996
Category Spread

■ 553
Publication New Choices
Art Director Al Braverman
Designer Grace Alberto
Illustrator Brad Holland
Publisher R. D. Publications Co., Inc.
Issue February 1996
Category Spread

■ 554
Publication Out
Art Director David O'Connor
Designer David O'Connor
Illustrator Ralph Steadman
Publisher Out Magazine
Issue August 1996
Category Spread

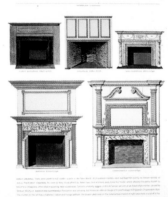

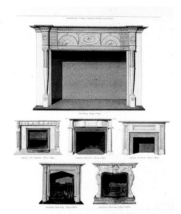

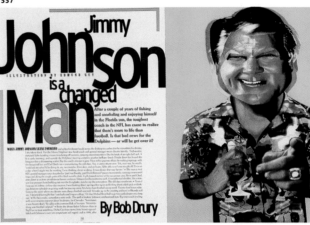

■ 555
Publication Martha Stewart Living
Creative Director Gael Towey
Design Director Eric Pike
Art Director Scot Schy
Designers Scot Schy, Celia Barbour
Illustrator Rodica Prado
Publisher Time Inc.
Issue October 1996
Category Story

■ 556
Publication Men's Journal
Art Director David Armario
Designer David Armario
Illustrator John Collier
Publisher Wenner Media
Issue March 1996
Category Spread

■ 558
Publication Men's Journal
Art Directors David Armario,
Designer David Armario, Tom Brown
Illustrator Ross McDonald
Publisher Wenner Media
Issue October 1996
Category Story

■ 557
Publication Men's Journal
Art Director David Armario
Designers Tom Brown, David Armario
Illustrator Edmund Guy
Publisher Wenner Media
Issue September 1996
Category Spread

THE SCREW-BALL SCHEME

New Jersey businessman Kenneth Byrnes says he was only trying to clean up the sex-for-hire escort business. Unfortunately, one of his partners bragged to undercover IRS agents that they were "running a national prostitution-money-laundering ring." BY DANIEL GREEN

[THE NEW YORK INTERVIEW]

Don't Call It a Comeback

Kiss, reunited, has launched the biggest rock show of the summer. But are inexplicably popular local galoots **Gene Simmons** and **Paul Stanley** actually… serious? Yes. BY CHRIS NORRIS

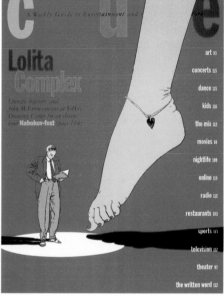

■ 559
Publication New York
Design Director Robert Newman
Designer Deanna Lowe
Illustrator Christian Northeast
Publisher K-III Publications
Issue July 22, 1996
Category Spread

■ 560
Publication New York
Design Director Robert Newman
Art Director Florian Bachleda
Designer Florian Bachleda
Illustrators Sue Coe, Gary Panter, Hungry Dog Studio, Kaz
Publisher K-III Publications
Issue July 29, 1996
Category Story

■ 561
Publication New York
Design Director Robert Newman
Art Director Syndi Becker
Illustrator Istvan Banyai
Publisher K-III Publications
Category Story

■ 562
Publication New York
Design Director Robert Newman
Art Director Florian Bachleda
Designer Pino Impastato
Illustrator Istvan Banyai
Publisher K-III Publications
Issue November 25, 1996
Category Single Page

■ 563

■ 566

■ 564

■ 567

■ 565

Publication The New Yorker
Designer Christine Curry
Illustrator Patrick D. Milbourne
Publisher Advance Publications
Issue August 12, 1996
Category Single Page

■ 567
Publication The New Yorker
Designer Christine Curry
Illustrator Gary Kelly
Publisher Advance Publications
Issue July 15, 1996
Category Single Page

■ 568

■ 563
Publication The New Yorker
Designer Christine Curry
Illustrator Lorenzo Mattotti
Publisher Advance Publications
Issue February 12, 1996
Category Single Page

■ 564
Publication The New Yorker
Designer Owen Phillips
Illustrator Susan Saas
Publisher Advance Publications
Issue February 26, 1996-March 4, 1996
Category Single Page

■ 565
Publication The New Yorker
Designer Christine Curry
Illustrator Phillip Burke
Publisher Advance Publications
Issue February 26, 1996-March 4, 1996
Category Single Page

■ 568
Publication Nickelodeon Magazine
Art Director Alexa Mulvihill
Designer Vanessa Johnson
Illustrator Melinda Beck
Publisher Nickelodeon Magazine Inc.
Issue May 1996
Category Single Page

227

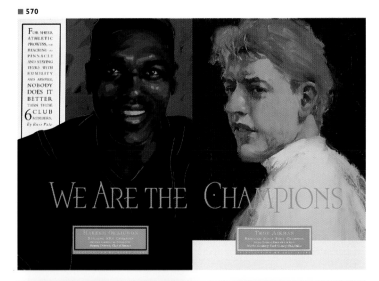

■ 569
Publication PC World
Art Directors Robert Kanes, Tim J. Luddy
Designer Tim J. Luddy
Illustrator Christian Northeast
Publisher PC World Communications
Issue November 1996
Category Story

■ 570
Publication Private Clubs
Design Director Steve Connatser
Designers Skip Liepke, Nancy Stahl
Illustrators Nancy Stahl, Skip Liepke
Publisher ACPI
Issue March/April 1996
Category Story

ILLUSTRATION FEATURES ■ MERIT

■ 571
Publication Premiere
Creative Director David Matt
Art Director Mariana Ochs
Illustrator Mark Ulriksen
Publisher
Hachette Filipacchi Magazines, Inc.
Issue Women in Hollywood 1996
Category Spread

■ 572
Publication Premiere
Art Director David Matt
Illustrator Matt Mahurin
Publisher
Hachette Filipacchi Magazines, Inc.
Issue April 1996
Category Spread

■ 573
Publication Playboy
Art Director Tom Staebler
Designer Len Willis
Illustrator Guy Billout
Publisher Playboy
Issue February 1, 1996
Category Spread

■ 574
Publication Swing
Creative Director Ellen Blissman
Designer Francesca Pacchini
Illustrators Mark Ulriksen,
Elizabeth Paul Avedon
Issue May 1996
Category Spread

■ 575
Publication Premiere
Art Director David Matt
Designer Sharon Cowen
Illustrator Jonathan Rosen
Publisher Hachette Filipacchi Magazines, Inc.
Issue April 1996
Category Single Page

■ 576
Publication Premiere
Art Director David Matt
Designer Sharon Cowen
Illustrator Blair Drawson
Publisher Hachette Filipacchi Magazines, Inc.
Issue October 1996
Category Single Page

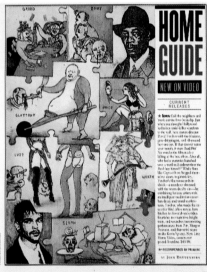

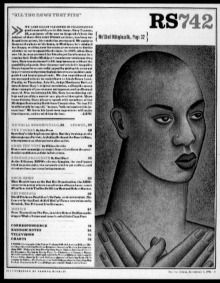

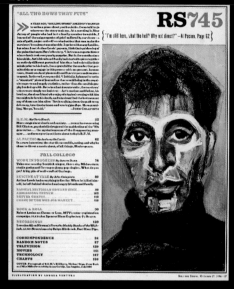

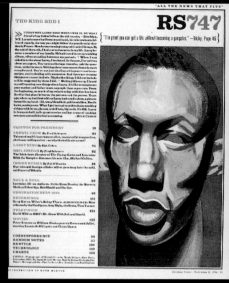

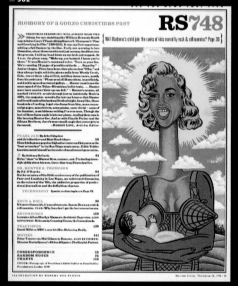

577
Publication Rolling Stone
Creative Director Fred Woodward
Illustrator Greg Clarke
Publisher Wenner Media
Issue June 13, 1996
Category Single Page

578
Publication Rolling Stone
Creative Director Fred Woodward
Illustrator Sandra Dionisi
Publisher Wenner Media
Issue September 5, 1996
Category Single Page

579
Publication Rolling Stone
Creative Director Fred Woodward
Illustrator Andrea Ventura
Publisher Wenner Media
Issue October 17, 1996
Category Single Page

580
Publication Rolling Stone
Creative Director Fred Woodward
Illustrator Steven Brodner
Publisher Wenner Media
Issue October 31, 1996
Category Single Page

581
Publication Rolling Stone
Creative Director Fred Woodward
Illustrator Ruth Marten
Publisher Wenner Media
Issue November 14, 1996
Category Single Page

582
Publication Rolling Stone
Creative Director Fred Woodward
Illustrator Hungry Dog Studio
Publisher Wenner Media
Issue November 28, 1996
Category Single Page

RECORDINGS
{ Marilyn Manson's rock alternative: Total escapism }
SHTICK OR TREAT?
BY LORRAINE ali

★★★☆
ANTICHRIST SUPERSTAR
Marilyn Manson
Nothing/Interscope

➤➤ THE RISE OF MARILYN MAN-
son marks the end of the
reign of punk realism in rock
& roll. This ill-behaved Florida-based
quintet, a visual and aural shake 'n' bake
of mutilation theatrics, Alice Cooper-
esque camp and metal-scraping-metal
tonality, is a volatile reaction to five years
of earnest, post-Nirvana rock. As ghoul-
ishly animated as the *Tales From the Crypt*
comic strip and gory enough for today's
discriminating ambulance chaser, Marilyn Manson offer total escapism as a
true alternative, complete with carefully
crafted gloom wear (no baggy shorts
allowed), a frontman who blatantly begs
to be in the spotlight and lyric imagery
rivaling that of the best slasher movies.
    And not only do the Mansons –
whose core members include the band's
male namesake vocalist and leader, guitarist Twiggy Ramirez and keyboard
player Madonna Wayne Gacy – look
post-mortem fabulous, they also rock.
The group's third and most accessible

ILLUSTRATION BY CHARLES BURNS · *ROLLING STONE, NOVEMBER 28, 1996 · 129*

FIGHTING BREAKS OUT ON THE WEST BANK; BENJAMIN NETANYAHU AND YASIR ARAFAT ENDORSE THE PEACE PROCESS.... MICHAEL J. FOX AND BILL COSBY RETURN TO TV.... THE FDA CONDITIONALLY APPROVES RU-486 ABORTION PILL.... U.S. BOMBS IRAQ TO PROTECT KURDS IN NORTHERN IRAQ.... BOB DOLE TUMBLES OFFSTAGE WHILE GIVING A SPEECH IN CHICO, CALIF.

Van Halen's Michael Anthony, and Alex and Eddie Van Halen with Roth (from left)

Crowds roared. A
reunited Van
Halen appeared with
David Lee Roth for
the first time in 10
years, at the MTV
Video Music Awards,
back in October,
news spread that the
schizophrenic band
was actually having
ex-Extreme singer
Gary Cherone. Roth
went back to Vegas.

Recently, it's been
easier to see Pearl
Jam in Congress than
in concert. Putting the
war against Ticket-
master aside, the band
kicked off its No Code
tour at Seattle's cozy
Showbox theater.
"Welcome to the
R.E.M. album-release
party," said Eddie
Vedder, "and the Pearl
Jam reunion tour."

Found: Eddie Vedder and Pearl Jam surface in Seattle.

When the short, eventful life of **TUPAC SHAKUR** came to an end in September –
he was gunned down in a drive-by shooting in Las Vegas – fans and critics alike groped
for the larger meaning. To some, the rapper's death was a simple case of frontier jus-
tice. Shakur chose the thug life, and now he had paid the price. Others saw Shakur as
a misunderstood artist caught up in the cycle of violence surrounding him. They held
him up as yet another symbol, and warning sign, of America's urban crisis. Even
though Shakur's death showed that sometimes the line between art and death can be a
flat one, it may be too early to say gangsta rap is finished: Shakur's posthumous LP,
the tossed-together *Don Killuminati*, is already platinum, and his Death Row label
mate Snoop Doggy Dogg's new album, *Tha Doggfather*, entered the charts at No. 1. On
the other hand, Death Row CEO "Suge" Knight is in jail, the label is being investigated
by the FBI, and many listeners are turning to the
softer sounds of the Fugees and the post-gangsta
Dr. Dre, the title of whose new single summarizes the
attitude of many OGs: "Been There, Done That."

❝ *"When I was in prison, I was wrapped up in all those deep
books. That Tolstoy crap. People shouldn't read that stuff."*
—MIKE TYSON, *who says that he now prefers comic books* ❞

We'd like to thank
Ms. Beck Han-
sen for *Odelay*, the Al-
bum of the Year. Hip-
hop beats, '70s flash,
bad clothes, post-
grunge/neofolkie/
hyphen-hyphen-hy-
phen. He's Bob Dylan
with a sampler, a
Beastie Boy with an
acoustic guitar. Soon
he'll be shaving, too.

Back outside the legendary Cain's Ballroom, in Tulsa, Okla.

BONNIE RAITT

"The most significant event for me this year was
participating in the rally to protect the Head-
waters forest, in a little town in Northern California called Carlotta. There were about
4,000 people there, and more than 900 of us
waited to get arrested. I got arrested, and my
dad, my brother and my husband did as well. It
was a very moving statement. We're not talking
about never cutting down trees again; we're talking
about a more-
responsible protection and preservation of the old-growth forests. Once
these trees are gone, that's it. They're not gonna be coming back."

78 · ROLLING STONE, DECEMBER 26, 1996–JANUARY 9, 1997   *Illustration by KAREN BARBOUR*

NATIONAL AFFAIRS BY WILLIAM GREIDER

DEA MAN TALKING

How Newt Gingrich went from being the life of the party to the GOP's pariah in two revolutionary years

ILLUSTRATION BY C.F. PAYNE

ILLUSTRATIONS BY ISTVAN BANYAI

deep in the heart of SIBERIA
BY P.J. O'ROURKE

ROLLING STONE, DECEMBER 9, 1996 · 37

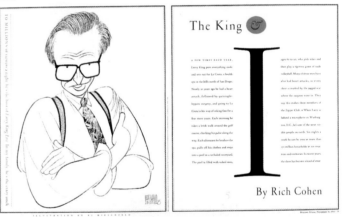

The King & I

A FEW TIMES EACH YEAR,
Larry King goes everything nods
and sees out for La Costa, a health
spa in the hills north of San Diego.
Nearly a year ago he had a heart
attack, followed by quintuple-
bypass surgery, and going to La
Costa is his way of asking fate for a
few more years. Each morning he
takes a brisk walk around the golf
course, checking his pulse along the
way. Each afternoon he heads to the
spa, pulls off his clothes and steps
into a pool as a secluded courtyard.
The pool is filled with naked men,

By Rich Cohen

ILLUSTRATION BY AL HIRSCHFELD *ROLLING STONE, NOVEMBER 14, 1996 · 77*

■ 583
Publication Rolling Stone
Creative Director Fred Woodward
Illustrator Charles Burns
Publisher Wenner Media
Issue November 28, 1996
Category Single Page

■ 584
Publication Rolling Stone
Creative Director Fred Woodward
Designer Karen Barbour
Illustrator Kevin Barbour
Publisher Wenner Media
Issue December 26, 1996-Jan. 9, 1997
Category Single Page

■ 585
Publication Rolling Stone
Creative Director Fred Woodward
Designer Lee Bearson
Illustrator C.F. Payne
Publisher Wenner Media
Issue October 3, 1996
Category Spread

■ 586
Publication Rolling Stone
Creative Director Fred Woodward
Designer Lee Bearson
Illustrator Istvan Banyai
Publisher Wenner Media
Issue November 14, 1996
Category Spread

■ 587
Publication Rolling Stone
Creative Director Fred Woodward
Designers Gail Anderson,
Fred Woodward
Illustrator Al Hirschfeld
Publisher Wenner Media
Issue November 14, 1996
Category Spread

ILLUSTRATION FEATURES ■ MERIT

HIGHLIGHTS OF THE
FELINE FANDANGO

BY DUNCAN CHRISTY

ILLUSTRATIONS BY RONALD SEARLE

THE COLOSSAL CATWALK

A New Leash On Life

When your favorite canine becomes a bête noire, trainer Brian Kilcommons knows how to retrieve the good dog within.

BY SALLIE DINKEL   ILLUSTRATIONS BY PIERRE LE-TAN

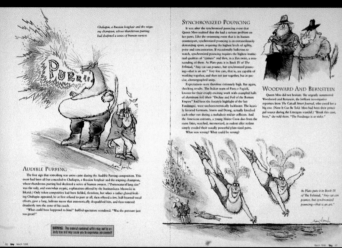

SYNCHRONIZED POUNCING

WOODWARD AND BERNSTEIN

AUDIBLE PURRING

A Sobering Tale

There is no station in life out of alcoholism's reach. But does the world of privilege create a climate for too much drinking? Does "having it all" lead to having all too much?

BY LANG PHIPPS   ILLUSTRATION BY EDUARD ERLIKH

MEDALING

CASE CLAWSED

THE BIG QUESTION

■ 589
Publication Town & Country
Creative Director Mary Shanahan
Art Director Margot Frankel
Designer Alice Kang
Illustrator Pierre Le-Tan
Publisher The Hearst Corporation-Magazines Division
Issue June 1996
Category Spread

■ 590
Publication Town & Country
Creative Director Mary Shanahan
Art Director Margot Frankel
Photographer Eduard Erlikh
Publisher The Hearst Corporation-Magazines Division
Issue December 1996
Category Spread

■ 588
Publication Sky
Art Director Chris Wilson
Designer Chris Wilson
Illustrator Ronald Searle
Publisher Pace Communications, Inc.
Client Delta Air Lines
Issue March 1996
Category Story

turn-ons

Researchers who study interpersonal
attraction and arousal
have discovered some very
surprising tantalizers.
By Colleen Durr Bates

real people's turn-ons

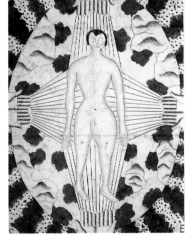

Ever thought about someone from the past
and — *hello* — they call? Visualized an event right
before it happened? Prayed for someone to get better . . . and they did?

PENICILLIN

prayer

spirituality in medicine
by liz brody

Through
quantum
physics
we are
coming
to the
realization
that what
we focus our
awareness
on we
influence

message
in the bottle

Is our culture to blame for the millions
of women on "happy pills"?

Sorry

By Liz Brody

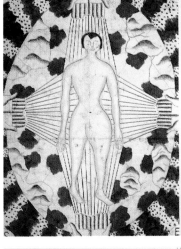

■ 591
Publication Shape
Creative Director Kathy Nenneker
Design Director Stephanie K. Birdsong
Art Director Yvonne Duran
Illustrator Maira Kalman
Publisher Weider Publications
Issue February 1996
Category Story

■ 592
Publication Shape
Creative Director Kathy Nenneker
Art Director Yvonne Duran
Illustrator Juliette Borda
Publisher Weider Publications
Issue November 1996
Category Spread

■ 593
Publication Shape
Creative Director Kathy Nenneker
Design Director Stephanie K. Birdsong
Art Director Yvonne Duran
Illustrator Philippe Weisbecker
Publisher Weider Publications
Issue June 1996
Category Story

■ 594
Publication
Los Angeles Times Magazine
Art Director Nancy Duckworth
Designer Steve Banks
Illustrator Greg Clarke
Issue May 12, 1996
Category Spread

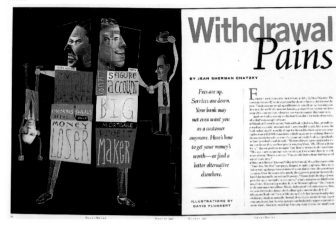

595
Publication Smart Money
Art Director Amy Rosenfeld
Designer Robin Terra
Illustrator David Plunkert
Publisher Dow Jones & Hearst Corp.
Issue August 1996
Category Story

596
Publication Smart Money
Art Director Amy Rosenfeld
Designers Robin Terra,
Amy Rosenfeld
Illustrator Jeffrey Fisher
Publisher Dow Jones & Hearst Corp.
Issue November 1996
Category Spread

597
Publication Smart Money
Art Director Amy Rosenfeld
Designers Robin Terra, Donna Agajanian
Illustrator Brian Cairns
Publisher Dow Jones & Hearst Corp.
Issue December 1996
Category Story

598
Publication Worth
Art Director Philip Bratter
Designer Jennifer Kapps
Illustrator Hanoch Piven
Publisher Capital Publishing
Issue June 1996
Category Spread

599
Publication Worth
Art Director Philip Bratter
Designer Philip Bratter
Illustrator Mark Ulriksen
Publisher Capital Publishing
Issue June 1996
Category Spread

■ 600
Publication This Old House
Design Director Matthew Drace
Art Director Timothy Jones
Illustrator Tom Christopher
Publisher Time Inc.
Issue July/August 1996
Category Single Page

■ 601
Publication Sports Illustrated
Design Director Steven Hoffman
Art Director Katharine Van Itallie
Illustrator Owen Smith
Publisher Time Inc.
Issue March 4, 1996
Category Spread

■ 602
Publication Sports Illustrated
Design Director Steven Hoffman
Illustrator Loren Long
Publisher Time Inc.
Issue July 15, 1996
Category Spread

■ 600

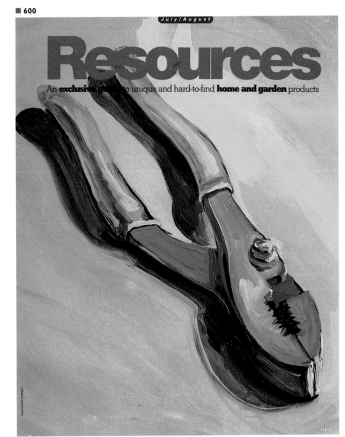

■ 601

■ 602

■ 603
Publication TIME
Art Director Arthur Hochstein
Designer Ken Smith
Illustrator Mark Fredrickson
Publisher Time Inc.
Issue February 5, 1996
Category Single Page

■ 604
Publication TIME
Art Director Arthur Hochstein
Designer Ken Smith
Illustrators David O'Keefe, Anita Kunz
Photographer Jay Conner
Publisher Time Inc.
Issue April 8, 1996
Category Single Page

■ 603

■ 604

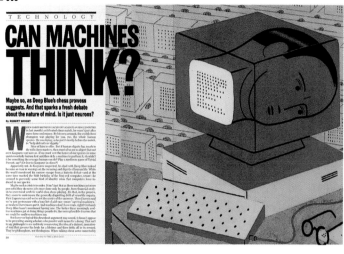

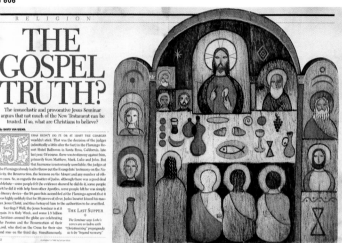

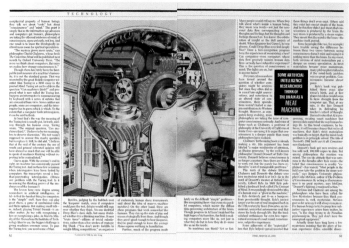

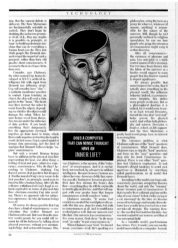

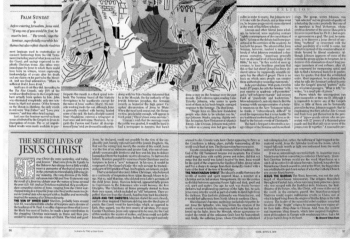

■ 605
Publication TIME
Art Director Arthur Hochstein
Designer Tom Miller
Illustrators Brian Cronin,
John Craig, Anita Kunz
Publisher Time Inc.
Issue March 25, 1996
Category Story

■ 606
Publication TIME
Art Director Arthur Hochstein
Designer Susan Langholz
Illustrators Stefano Vitale,
Joel Peter Johnson, Rafal Olbinski,
Brian Cronin, Sue Coe
Photographer Jay Conner
Publisher Time Inc.
Issue April 8, 1996
Category Story

■ 607

■ 608
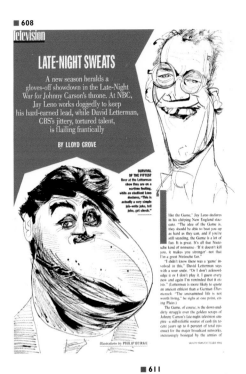

■ 609

■ 610

■ 611

■ 607
Publication Vanity Fair
Design Director David Harris
Designer Mimi Dutta
Illustrator Barry Blitt
Publisher Condé Nast Publications Inc.
Issue April 1996
Category Single Page

■ 608
Publication Vanity Fair
Design Director David Harris
Art Director Gregory Mastrianni
Designer Gregory Mastrianni
Illustrator Philip Burke
Publisher Condé Nast Publications Inc.
Issue October 1996
Category Single Page

■ 609
Publication Vanity Fair
Design Director David Harris
Designer Mimi Dutta
Illustrator Barry Blitt
Publisher Condé Nast Publications Inc.
Issue November 1996
Category Single Page

■ 610
Publication Vanity Fair
Design Director David Harris
Designer Gregory Mastrianni
Illustrator Robert Risko
Publisher Condé Nast Publications Inc.
Issue December 1996
Category Spread

■ 611
Publication Vanity Fair
Design Director David Harris
Art Director Gregory Mastrianni
Designers David Harris, Gregory Mastrianni
Illustrator Bruce McCall
Publisher Condé Nast Publications Inc.
Issue July 1996
Category Spread

It's NOT 'All in Your Head'

By Claire Conway

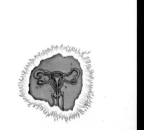

DEPENDENCE
DENIED

BY MAUREEN MCINANEY

PHOTO ILLUSTRATIONS BY POLLY BECKER

matchmaker, matchmaker make me a match

by rosanne spector

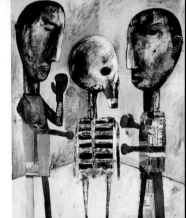

■ 612
Publication Stanford Medicine
Art Director David Armario
Designer David Armario
Illustrator Anita Kunz
Publisher Stanford Medicine
Issue Spring 1996
Category Story

■ 613
Publication Stanford Medicine
Art Director David Armario
Designer David Armario
Illustrator Jordan Isip
Publisher Stanford Medicine
Issue Summer 1996
Category Story
　■ A Spread

■ 614
Publication Stanford Medicine
Art Director David Armario
Designer David Armario
Illustrator Polly Becker
Publisher Stanford Medicine
Issue Fall 1996
Category Story

■ 615
Publication Stanford Medicine
Art Director David Armario
Designer David Armario
Illustrator Calef Brown
Publisher Stanford Medicine
Issue Fall 1996
Category Spread

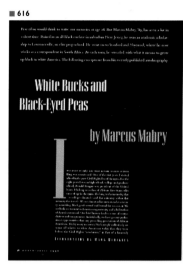

MoneyTalks

■ 616
Publication Stanford Magazine
Art Director Paul Carstensen
Designer Paul Carstensen
Illustrator Mark Ulriksen
Publisher
Stanford Alumni Association
Issue March/April 1996
Category Spread

■ 617
Publication Stanford Magazine
Art Director Paul Carstensen
Designer Paul Carstensen
Illustrator Henrik Drescher
Publisher
Stanford Alumni Association
Issue May/June 1996
Category Spread

■ 618
Publication
The Washington Post Magazine
Art Director Kelly Doe
Designer Kelly Doe
Illustrator Juliette Borda
Publisher The Washington Post Co.
Issue August 18, 1996
Category Spread

■ 619
Publication
The Washington Post Magazine
Art Director Kelly Doe
Designer Kelly Doe
Illustrator C.F. Payne
Publisher The Washington Post Co.
Issue January 21, 1996
Category Spread

■ 620
Publication
The Washington Post Magazine
Art Director Kelly Doe
Designer Sandy Schneider
Illustrator Brian Cairns
Publisher The Washington Post Co.
Issue January 21, 1996
Category Spread

■ 621
Publication
The Washington Post Magazine
Art Director Kelly Doe
Designer Kelly Doe
Illustrator Juliette Borda
Publisher The Washington Post Co.
Issue July 7, 1996
Category Spread

Stay on Their Backs

Getting a Ph.D. today means spending your 20's in graduate school, plunging into debt, writing a dissertation no one will read — and becoming more narrow and more bitter each step of the way.

How to Make a Ph.D. Matter BY LOUIS MENAND

If all Ph.D. programs were three-year programs, with no in-house and no dissertation — a getting a doctorate seems like getting a law degree — graduate education would secondarily occupy forms and efficiency.

The Drama Queens

Monroe, Garland, Callas . . . . They paid the price for living on the edge.

By Daniel Mendelsohn

The Girls Next Door

Debbie Reynolds, Doris Day, Mary Tyler Moore . . . Not the prettiest girls in the class, but the peppiest.

By Jennifer Baumgartner

Self-Fulfilling Prophets

Oprah, Madonna, Jane Fonda . . . The entrepreneurial zealots who preach by example.

By Barbara Grizzuti Harrison

622
Publication The New York Times Magazine
Art Director Janet Froelich
Designer Nancy Harris
Illustrator C.F. Payne
Publisher The New York Times

624
Publication The New York Times Magazine
Art Director Janet Froelich
Designer Joel Cuyler
Illustrator Billy Sullivan
Publisher The New York Times

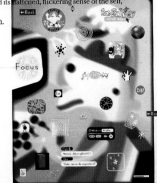

The Internet's Arrested Development

With its snarly notion of freedom, its ranting chats and its flattened, flickering sense of the self,
cyberspace is wallowing in its adolescence.
Therein lies its biggest problem – and a lot of the fun.

By Charles McGrath

Illustration by J. Otto Seibold

Because everyone must be free to speak what is on his or her mind, everyone is also presumed to have something worthwhile to say.
The Net is full of ranters standing on invisible soapboxes, and a great many exchanges essentially come down to:

Enough about you. Let's hear from me.

The hypertext philosophy ignores that at a certain level reading is not about freedom at all but about submission
– about stifling your own voice, stilling your mind and yielding fully to the designs (in every sense) of another.
Ultimately, reading is not a community activity.

Publication The New York Times Magazine
Art Director Janet Froelich
Designer Joel Cuyler
Illustrator J. Otto Seibold
Publisher The New York Times
Issue December 8, 1996
Category Spread

The Ultimate Approval Rating

by Arthur M. Schlesinger Jr.

The Schlesinger Poll

The Schlesinger Poll

Publication The New York Times Magazine
Art Director Janet Froelich
Designers Lisa Naftolin, Susan Dazzo
Illustrator Daniel Adel
Publisher The New York Times
Issue December 8, 1996
Category Story

STYLE

Show Time! A portfolio of images from the spring '96 collections.

We'd done grunge. We'd done the glamour revival. The clock was about to strike noon on the 90's — a decade that, by the time the clothes hit the stores, would be officially half over — and still no discernible style had emerged. There was no "look" that our children would grow up to dismiss as "so 90's," rolling their eyes; no unanimous silhouette like the hourglass shape that earmarked the 50's; no sartorial invention like the miniskirt or the bell-bottom pant, which set the 60's down in history. Fashion (we're reminded on a regular basis) is theater now; and as the curtain went up on spring 1996 — a round of shows that began in early October, in Milan, passed through Paris and drew to a close five weeks later, in New York — the 90's were still up for grabs, there for the taking by anyone with a vision strong enough to carry the next five years.

Drawings by Billy Sullivan

But perhaps strength of vision is not the problem. One after another, designers exercised their highly individual outlooks on the moment at hand. For those of us whose job it is to make sense of these proceedings, the hard part was finding any two designers who could agree on what the moment at hand ought to look like. Occasionally, there were intimations of a style beginning to emerge — one stripped of all decoration, with uncomplicated shapes rendered in unusual, often synthetic, fabrics, with (it must be said) a certain resemblance to the clothes of the 60's and 70's. But for every exponent of this new "minimalism," as it has been labeled, there was a dissenting voice, making a case for some other option — a case that not infrequently turned out to be persuasive.

This season, the fin-de-siècle retrospective impulse was rampant, as designers recapitulated the styles of our century, reprising each decade with impunity. So it seemed all the more remarkable when every now and again someone managed to rise above the past, with clothes that looked surprising and pertinent, consistent with the present tense in which our lives unfold. For those few visionaries: a round of applause. —HOLLY BRUBACH

Above: Backstage at JIL SANDER. Overleaf: An asymmetrical eyelet bias-cut evening gown, at JOHN GALLIANO, where the models moved among the spectators. Unlike in the theater, the audience in fashion stays the same for every performance, and it's the show that changes.

MILAN

Leading off the season, too. Front-left: Versace...

PARIS

Short Story Contest!

The Remedy

BY NICHOLSON BAKER

Two decades ago, The New York Times Magazine commissioned Donald Barthelme, a master of short prose, to write the beginning of a story that readers were invited to complete in 750 words or less, furnishing what Barthelme described as "the terrifying middle and the subtle, incomparably beautiful ending." The winning entry was published in a subsequent issue of the Magazine; Barthelme was the final judge. The prize was $250. Acknowledging inflation, the editors now offer $500 to complete a story begun by an equally eminent practitioner of the form; the other requirements remain the same.

IN A FLOODED CAVERN DEEP IN THE unmapped 12th socket of the Oppidural Cave System, several hundred feet below a Discovery Zone, where children ate birthday cake and leaped around screaming in cages filled with multicolored plastic balls that smelled faintly of throw-up, Shackleton Plunket, student of subterranean biota, discovered a new species of living thing. "Oh, look at them!" Shackleton whispered, although he was alone, as he slowly aimed his infrared "Puddle-peeker" this way and that in the chilly black water. "Look at those glorious cave oysters!"

They were smallish and mottled; their shells nipped in near the middle like fortune cookies. Cigarette-size feeding tubes glowed above their shadowy innards, beckoning to a mass of Turbinaria blodi, whose explosive self-patching aroma-bag was the subject of a hasty paper by Shackleton's supervisor, the unscrupulous Dr. Billy Bilbune, director of the once-prosperous Center for Cave Mapping. Shack carefully detached several oysteroids and brought them up to the surface to study by natural light, but they proved to be photosensitive, turning a cochineal red and dying in a matter of hours, embarrassed by the attention of a sun they had never known. Undeterred, Shackleton hauled up a few dozen more in opaque containers on a night when there was no moon. These he attempted to propagate in 18 steel sinks behind the blackened windows of an abandoned candy factory.

To Shackleton's surprise, the displaced creatures thrived in their new home, as long as he fed them a daily squirt of Oyster Choice — a solution of hydrogenated gull-waste and selected intestinal parasites — using a modified turkey baster. He was making good progress in documenting the life cycle of his charges, all in secret, planning to stun the world with a paper in Nature, when a small accident occurred one night. Kneeling on the floor to pick up his notebook, which he had dropped in his excitement while recording the weight gain of Ollie, one of the fastest-growing individuals in his colony, Shack caught the edge of his infra-goggles on the cord of the digital scale on which the elder oyster still rested. Ollie, lying open and defenseless, skittered off the pan of the table and landed, soft side down on Shackleton's head.

Shackleton's was a substantially bald head, and had been so since the age of 28, except for an old-growth fringe on the sides that he tamped down every morning with a solution of water and Mega Gel Extreme Hold by L'Oréal to keep it from sticking straight out and making him look insane. The damp, heavy impact of a cave oyster to his baldness did not repulse Shack; with a bow, he caused the misplaced creature to drop gently into his palm. That would have ended the episode, had Ollie not begun to foam distressingly around his third and fourth fessumarid hydroceles. It took an hour of steady rinsing and turkey-basting to put Ollie right. But the real surprise came the next morning, when Shackleton first looked in the mirror to shave and noticed, jutting from the top of his head, a luxuriant bivalve-shaped tuft of healthy adult hair.

Megan Sturm, Shack's fiancée (and a gifted cave-mapper herself), gave her betrothed a searching look when they met for lunch later that day at Vedge Out, a local salad bar. "You seem troubled," she said, taking his hand. "And why have you tied that odd-looking red kerchief around your head?"

THE RULES

1. Manuscripts must be mailed to:
Short Story Contest
The New York Times Magazine
229 West 43d Street
New York, N.Y. 10036

2. Manuscripts must be received before July 1, 1996.

3. Manuscripts should be no longer than 750 words, typed and double-spaced.

4. The contest is open to everyone except employees of The New York Times.

5. The prize is $500.

6. Contestants should include the following information with their entries:
Name
Address
City _____ State _____ Zip Code _____

7. Although every entry will be read, the editors regret that receipt of manuscripts cannot be acknowledged nor can manuscripts be returned.

8. The decision of the judge is final. Entries will become the property of The New York Times. The Times reserves the right not to award the prize if, in the opinion of the judge, there is no winning entry.

ILLUSTRATION BY MARK RYDEN

THE NEW YORK TIMES MAGAZINE / JUNE 2, 1996 41

▣ 629
Publication The New York Times Magazine
Art Director Janet Froelich
Designer Nancy Harris
Illustrator Billy Sullivan
Publisher The New York Times
Issue January 21, 1996
Category Story

▣ 630
Publication The New York Times Magazine
Art Director Janet Froelich
Designer Nancy Harris
Illustrator Mark Ryden
Publisher The New York Times
Issue June 2, 1996
Category Single Page

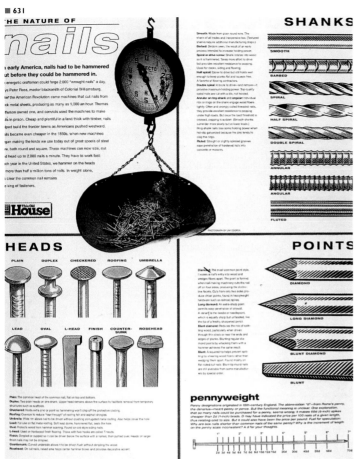

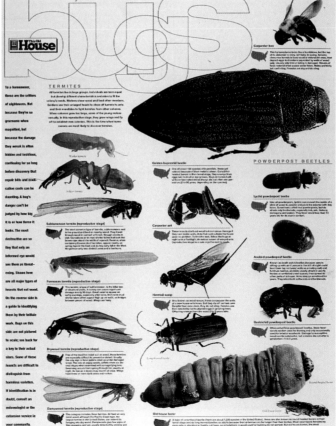

■ 631
Publication This Old House
Design Director Matthew Drace
Art Director Timothy Jones
Illustrator Clancy Gibson
Photographers Jim Cooper, Spencer Jones
Publisher Time Inc.
Issue January/February 1996
Category Information Graphics

■ 632
Publication This Old House
Design Director Matthew Drace
Photographer Darrin Haddad
Publisher Time Inc.
Issue May/June 1996
Category Information Graphics

■ 633

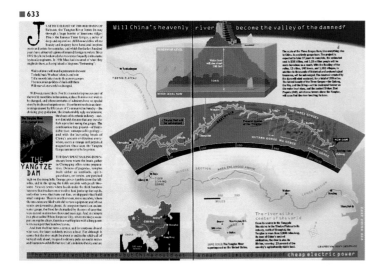

Will China's heavenly river become the valley of the dammed?

■ 634

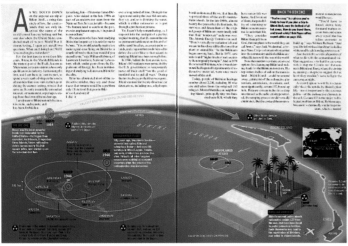

■ 635

THE GARDEN DESIGN KITCHEN GARDEN

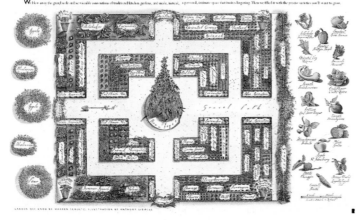

■ 636

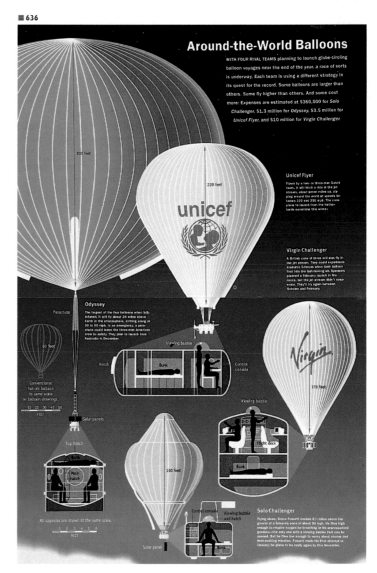

Around-the-World Balloons

WITH FOUR RIVAL TEAMS planning to launch globe-circling balloon voyages near the end of the year, a race of sorts is underway. Each team is using a different strategy in its quest for the record. Some balloons are larger than others. Some fly higher than others. And some cost more: Expenses are estimated at $360,000 for *Solo Challenger*, $1.3 million for *Odyssey*, $3.5 million for *Unicef Flyer*, and $10 million for *Virgin Challenger*.

■ 636
Publication Popular Science
Design Director Christopher Garcia
Illustrator John Grimwade
Publisher Times Mirror Magazines
Issue May 1996
Category Information Graphics

■ 633
Publication Condé Nast Traveler
Design Director Robert Best
Illustrator John Grimwade
Publisher Condé Nast Publications Inc.
Issue May 1996
Category Information Graphics

■ 634
Publication Condé Nast Traveler
Design Director Robert Best
Art Director Carla Frank
Designer Robert Best
Illustrator John Grimwade
Publisher Condé Nast Publications Inc.
Issue December 1996
Category Information Graphics

■ 635
Publication Garden Design
Creative Director Michael Grossman
Art Director Carla Frank
Designer Carla Frank
Illustrator Anthony Sidwell
Publisher Meigher Communications
Issue February/March 1996
Category Information Graphics

SPOT ILLUSTRATION

■ 636
Publication Condé Nast Traveler
Illustrator Ross MacDonald
Title Cross-Country Road Trip
Art Director Carla Frank
Publisher Condé Nast Publications Inc.
Issue September 1996
Category Color Single

■ 637
Publication Entertainment Weekly
Illustrator Susan R. Saas
Title Dalmation
Art Director Stacie Reistetter
Publisher Time Inc.
Issue November 15, 1996
Category Color Single

■ 638
Publication Entertainment Weekly
Illustrator Jonathan Carlson
Title Action
Art Director Rina Migliaccio
Publisher Time Inc.
Issue August 1996
Category Color Single

■ 639
Publication Entertainment Weekly
Illustrator Robert de Michiell
Title Stephen King
Art Director Keith Campbell
Publisher Time Inc.
Issue September 27, 1996
Category Color Single

■ 640
Publication Entertainment Weekly
Illustrator Drew Friedman
Title Rocking the Votes
Art Director Julie Schrader
Publisher Time Inc.
Issue October 18, 1996
Category Color Series

■ 641
Publication Los Angeles Magazine
Illustrator Drew Friedman
Title From Hitler to Hollywood
Art Director Holly Caporale
Issue May 1997
Category Black & White Series

■ 642
Publication The New Yorker
Illustrator Drew Friedman
Title Nut's to the Nut
Art Directors Chris Curry, Nick Parker
Publisher Condé Nast Publications Inc.
Issue April 22, 1996
Category Color Single

■ 643
Publication Infoworld
Illustrator Carolyn Fisher
Title Info Toons
Art Director Brian Duval
Issue Various
Category Color Series

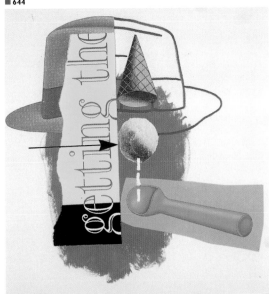

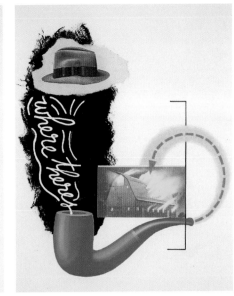

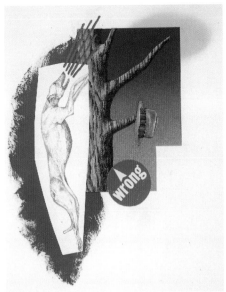

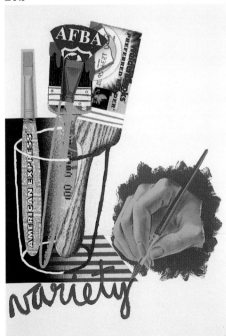

■ 644
Publication Infoworld
Illustrator Gene Greif
Title Notes from the Field/Various
Art Director Lisa Sergi
Issue January 6, 1997
Category Color Series

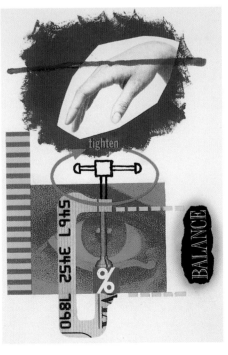

■ 645
Publication Smart Money
Illustrator Gene Greif
Title Credit Check-Best & Worst of the Credit Cards
Art Director Amy Rosenfeld
Publisher Dow Jones & Hearst Corp.
Issue March 3, 1997
Category Color Series

ILLUSTRATION SPOTS ■

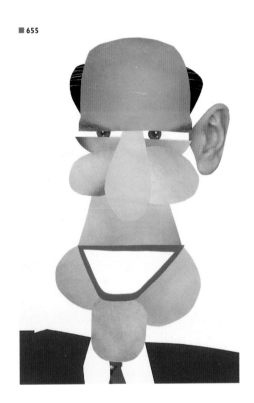

■ 650
Publication New York
Illustrator KAZ
Title Don't Call it a Comeback
Design Director Robert Newman
Art Director Florian Bachleda
Publisher K-III Publications
Issue May 1996
Category Color Series

■ 651
Publication New York
Illustrator Istvan Banyai
Title Chuck the Vote
Design Director Robert Newman
Art Director Andrea Dunham
Publisher K-III Publications
Issue November 4, 1996
Category Color Single

■ 652
Publication New York
Illustrator Hungry Dog Studio/Bob & Val Tillery
Title Don't Call it a Comeback
Design Director Robert Newman
Art Director Florian Bachleda
Publisher K-III Publications
Issue May 1996
Category Color Series

■ 653
Publication New York
Illustrator Hungry Dog Studio/Bob & Val Tillery
Title Tax Cutups
Design Director Robert Newman
Art Director Deanna Lowe
Publisher K-III Publications
Issue June 10, 1996
Category Color Single

■ 654
Publication New York
Illustrator Stephen Kroninger
Title The Lesson of Mission; Impossible and Twister
Design Director Robert Newman
Art Director Deanna Lowe
Publisher K-III Publications
Issue June 24-July 1, 1996
Category Color Single

■ 655
Publication New York
Illustrator Stephen Kroninger
Title Michael Milken Just Wants to Be Loved
Design Director Robert Newman
Art Director Robert Newman
Publisher K-III Publications
Issue May 1996
Category Color Single

■ 656
Publication Kiplinger's Personal Finance
Illustrator Gary Baseman
Title The Wild, Wild Web
Art Director Cynthia L. Currie
Issue November 1996
Category Color Single

■ 658
Publication Saveur
Illustrator Michael Bartalos
Title Bebos Cooks
Creative Director Michael Grossman
Art Directors Jill Armus, Toby Fox
Publisher Meigher Communications
Issue July/August 1996
Category Color Single

■ 657
Publication Saveur
Illustrator Calef Brown
Title Tut's Tipple
Creative Director Michael Grossman
Art Director Jill Armus
Publisher Meigher Communications
Issue January/February 1996
Category Color Single

■ 659
Publication Saveur
Illustrator Edwin Fotheringham
Title Covert Pelemeni
Creative Director Michael Grossman
Art Directors Jill Armus, Toby Fox
Publisher Meigher Communications
Issue May/June 1996
Category Color Single

■ 660
Publication Saveur
Illustrator Kathy Osbom
Title Food With a Title
Creative Director Michael Grossman
Art Directors Jill Armus, Toby Fox
Publisher Meigher Communications
Issue July/August 1996
Category Color Single

■ 661

■ 662

■ 663

■ 664

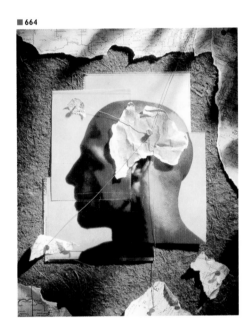

■ 665

■ 666

■ 661
Publication Shape
Illustrator Juliette Borda
Title Night Owl Workouts
Art Director Lisa Hatfield-Leconte
Publisher Weider Publications
Issue August 1996
Category Color Single

■ 662
Publication Shape
Illustrator Jennifer Jessee
Title The Power of Faith
Art Director Chrystal Falciovi
Publisher Weider Publications
Issue September 1996
Category Color Single

■ 663
Publication Worldbusiness
Illustrator Anthony Freda
Title Strike One
Art Director Ina Saltz
Issue July 1996
Category Color Single

■ 664
Publication Worldbusiness
Illustrator Clay McBride
Title Bouncing Back
Art Directors Ina Saltz, Donald Partyka
Issue November 1996
Category Color Single

■ 665
Publication Worldbusiness
Illustrator Pol Turgeon
Title Auto Biz
Art Director Ina Saltz
Issue May/June1996
Category Color Single

■ 666
Publication U of T
Illustrator A.G. Duffy
Title Portrait of the Artist As a Lowbrow
Art Director Sara Tyson
Issue Spring 1996
Category Color Single

253

■ 667
Publication The Atlantic Monthly
Illustrator Jeffrey Fisher
Title A War That Never Ends
Art Directors Judy Garlan, Robin Gilmore-Barnes
Publisher The Atlantic Monthly
Issue March 1997
Category Color Single

■ 670
Publication The Atlantic Monthly
Illustrator Greg Clarke
Title Word Improvisation
Art Directors Judy Garlan, Betsy Urrico
Issue November 1996
Category Color Single

■ 668
Publication The Atlantic Monthly
Illustrator Peter Horvath
Title From Willow Temple
Art Directors Judy Garlan, Robin Gilmore-Barnes
Publisher The Atlantic Monthly
Issue October 1996
Category Color Single

■ 669
Publication The Atlantic Monthly
Illustrator Caty Bartholomew
Title Welding With Children
Art Directors Judy Garlan, Betsy Urrico
Publisher The Atlantic Monthly
Issue March 1997
Category Color Single

■ 671
Publication The Atlantic Monthly
Illustrator Brian Cronin
Title The Capitalist Threat
Art Director Judy Garlan
Publisher The Atlantic Monthly
Issue February 1997
Category Color Single

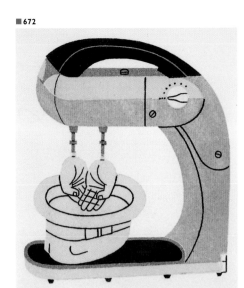

■672
Publication The Atlantic Monthly
Illustrator Brian Cronin
Title Recipe for Depression
Art Director Judy Garlan
Publisher The Atlantic Monthly
Issue July 1996
Category Color Single

■673
Publication The Atlantic Monthly
Illustrator Brian Cronin
Title Recipe for Depression
Art Director Judy Garlan
Publisher The Atlantic Monthly
Issue July 1996
Category Color Series

■674
Publication Time
Illustrator Brian Cronin
Title The Gospel Truth-Palm Sunday
Art Directors Arthur Hochstein,
Susan Langholz
Publisher Time Inc.
Issue April 8, 1996
Category Color Series

■675
Publication Time
Illustrator Rafal Oblinski
Title The Gospel Truth-The Resurrection
Art Directors Arthur Hochstein,
Susan Langholz
Publisher Time Inc.
Issue April 8, 1996
Category Color Series

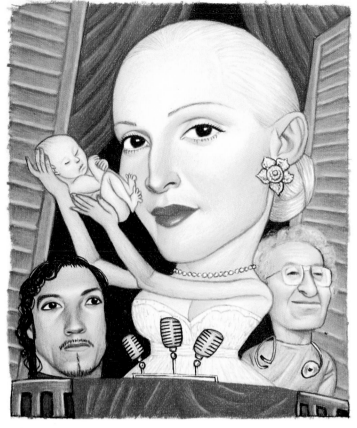

■ 676

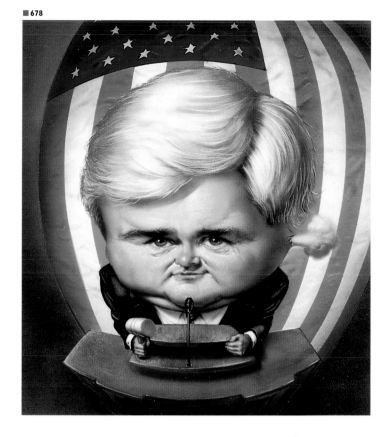

■ 678

■ 677

■ 679

678
Publication Time
Illustrator
Mark Fredrickson
Title Newt Gingrich
Art Directors
Arthur Hochstein,
Kenneth B. Smith
Publisher Time Inc.
Issue January 20, 1997
Category Color Single

679
Publication Time
Illustrator
Christian Clayton
Title Orwellian Assault
Art Directors
Arthur Hochstein,
Steve Conley
Publisher Time Inc.
Issue December 9, 1996
Category Color Single

■ 680

680
Publication Time
Illustrator
James R. Bennett
Title Roberto Alomar-
Pavlovian Response
Art Directors
Arthur Hochstein,
Joseph Aslaender
Publisher Time Inc.
Issue October 1996
Category Color Single

676
Publication Time
Illustrator Glynis Sweeny
Title (MOM) Madonna
Art Directors Arthur Hochstein,
Kenneth B. Smith
Publisher Time Inc.
Issue October 28, 1996
Category Color Single

677
Publication Time
Illustrator Anita Kunz
Title Madonna & Child
Art Directors Arthur Hochstein,
Kenneth B. Smith
Publisher Time Inc.
Issue April 29, 1996
Category Color Single

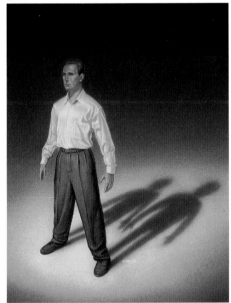

681
Publication Time-Asian Edition
Illustrator Cathie Bleck
Title Where the Weaker Sex is Stronger
Art Director Arthur Hochstein, Vicki Nightingale
Publisher Time Inc.
Issue October 1996
Category Color Single

684
Publication Time
Illustrator Frances Jetter
Title A Desecration of the Truth
Art Director Arthur Hochstein, Steve Conley
Publisher Time Inc.
Issue October 14, 1996
Category Color Single

682
Publication Time
Illustrator Tim O'Brien
Title Cloning
Art Directors Arthur Hochstein, Joe Zeff
Publisher Time Inc.
Issue March 10, 1997
Category Color Single

683
Publication Time
Illustrator C. F. Payne
Title Bill Clinton As FDR
Art Directors Arthur Hochstein, Kenneth B. Smith
Publisher Time Inc.
Issue January 27, 1997
Category Color Single

685
Publication Philadelphia
Illustrator Frances Jetter
Title Playing with Fire
Art Director Frank Baseman
Publisher Metrocorp
Issue January 1997
Category Color Single

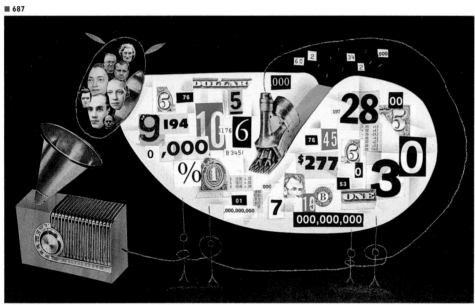

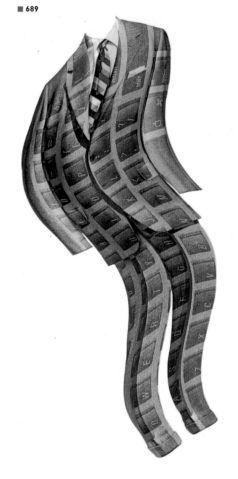

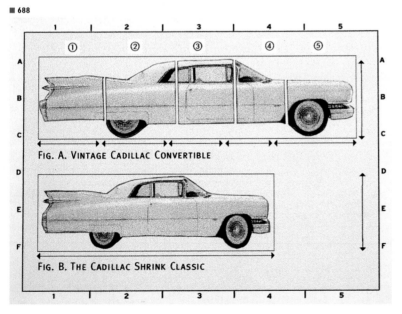

Fig. A. Vintage Cadillac Convertible

Fig. B. The Cadillac Shrink Classic

■ 686
Publication Bloomberg Personal
Illustrator Sean Kelly
Title The Risk Quiz
Art Director Don Morris
Publisher Blommberg LP
Issue November/December 1996
Category Color Single

■ 687
Publication Bloomberg Personal
Illustrator David Plunkert
Title Sec Sleuths
Art Director Carol Macrini
Publisher Bloomberg L.P.
Issue March 20, 1997
Category Color Single

■ 688
Publication New York Times Magazine
Illustrator Mara Kurtz
Title Pink Cadillacs
Art Director Lisa Naftolin
Publisher The New York Times
Issue January 26, 1997 1996
Category Color Single

■ 689
Publication Men's Fashion of the Times
Illustrator Margaret Riegel
Title Digital Dressing
Art Director Michael Valenti
Publisher The New York Times
Issue March 24, 1996
Category Black & White Single

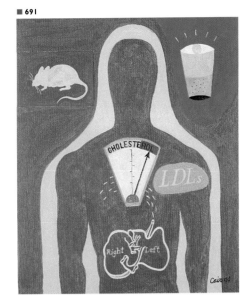

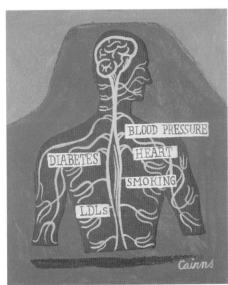

■ 690
Publication Family Circle
Mary Higgins Clark Mystery
Illustrator Julia Gran
Title The Games Afoot
Art Director Diane Lamphron
Issue May 1996
Category Black & White Series

■ 691
Publication Men's Journal
Illustrator Brian Cairns
Title The New Cholesterol Cutters
Art Director Tom Brown
Publisher Wenner Media
Issue March 14, 1997
Category Color Series

■ 692
Publication Harper's
Illustrator Janet Wooley
Art Director Angela Riechers
Issue May 1996
Category Color Series

■ 693

■ 694

Best Critical/Biographical Book
Savage Art: A Biography of Jim Thompson
by Robert Polito

Best Fact Crime
Circumstantial Evidence by Pete Earley

Best Motion Picture Screenplay
The Usual Suspects
by Christopher McQuarrie

Best Original Paperback
Tarnished Blue by William Heffernan

Best First Novel by an
American Author
Tight Shot by Kevin Allman

Best Novel
Come to Grief by Dick Francis

■ 695

■ 696

DOUG STEVENS - INSIGHT

■ 693
Publication Worth
Illustrator Kamil Vonjar
Title Self Service
Art Director Philip Bratter
Publisher Capital Publishing
Issue March 20, 1997
Category Color Single

■ 694
Publication American Way
Illustrator Johanna Goodman
Title Oscar Wilde
Art Director David Moreno
Publisher
American Airlines Inflight Media
Issue November 1996
Category Color Single

■ 695
Publication
American Health for Women
Illustrator Alison Seiffer
Title Shrink & Tell: Is Your
Confidentiality Being Compromised?
Art Director Syndi Becker
Issue December 1996
Category Color Single

■ 696
Publication Insight
Illustrator Doug Stevens
Title Mystery Writers
Art Director Sharon Roy Finch
Issue May 27, 1996
Category Color Single

STUDENT COMPETITION

★697
Designer Lara Weber
Award B.W. Honeycutt Award
Title C Magazine
School Georgia State University
Instructor Jeff McGinnis

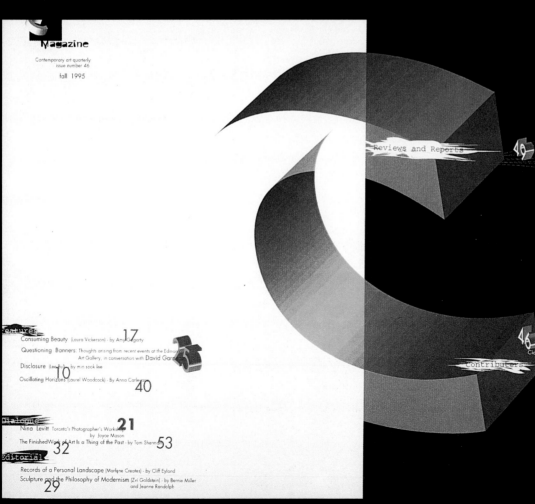

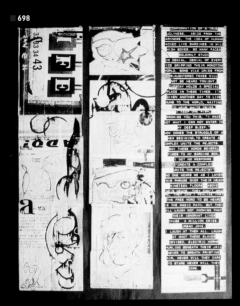

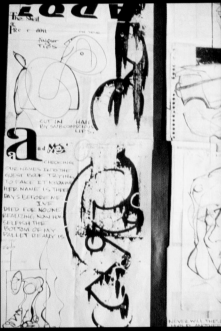

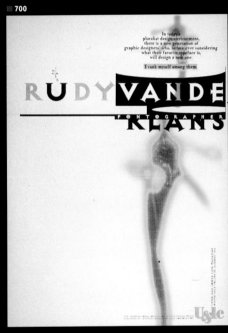

■ 698

Designer Yarrow Earth Hock
Award Excellence
Title An Original Poem
School School of Visual Arts, New York City
Instructor David Carson

■ 699

Designer Felicia Utomo
Award Excellence
Title Urban Outfitters
School Academy of Art Collge
Instructor Julia Brown

■ 700

Designer Surasak Luengthaviboon
Award Excellence
Title U&lc
School Svannah College of Art & Design
Instructor Amy Kern

■ 701

Designer Julia Michry
Title Roberto Edwards Painted Bodies
School School of Visual Arts, New York City
Instructor Carin Goldberg

■ 702

Designer Kai Leong Chu
Title Picture
School School of Visual Arts, New York City
Instructor Carin Goldberg

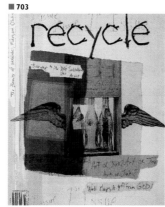

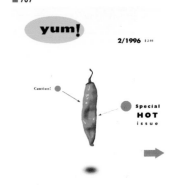

703
Designer Edith L. Guiterrez
Title recycle
School Fashion Institue of Technology, New York City
Instructor Susan Cotler-Block

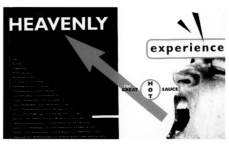

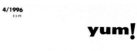

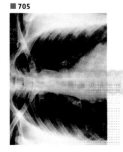

704
Designer Angela Valle
Title Rodman
School School of Visual Arts, New York City
Instructor Terry Koppel

705
Designer Cheng Kwee Teo
Title Nothing Short of Everything
School Ringling School of Art & Design,
Instructor Toby Thompson

706
Designer Jennie J. Chang
Title Asian Culture
School School of Visual Arts, New York City
Instructor Henrietta Condak

707
Designer Mieko Kojima
Title Yum
School School of Visual Arts, New York City
Instructor Christopher Austopchuk

INDEX

INDEX PHOTOGRAPHY ■

■ PUBLISHING COMPANIES

■ CLIENTS

■ STUDIOS

■
This book was set in Gill Sans.
Designed by Eric Gill in 1928, it was modeled on Edward Johnston's 1918
alphabet for the London Transport Railway.

STUDIOS INDEX